Jan Krämer

Bundling Telecommunications Services: Competitive Strategies for Converging Markets

Studies on eOrganisation and Market Engineering   10
Universität Karlsruhe (TH)

Herausgeber:

Prof. Dr. Christof Weinhardt
Prof. Dr. Thomas Dreier
Prof. Dr. Rudi Studer

Bundling Telecommunications Services:

Competitive Strategies for Converging Markets

by
Jan Krämer

universitätsverlag karlsruhe

Dissertation, Universität Karlsruhe (TH),
Fakultät für Wirtschaftswissenschaften, 2007
u. d. T. „Service Bundling and Quality Competition on Converging
Communications Markets : A Game-Theoretic Analysis"
Tag der mündlichen Prüfung: 13. Dezember 2007
Referenten: Prof. Dr. S. Berninghaus, Prof. Dr. C. Weinhardt

Impressum

Universitätsverlag Karlsruhe
c/o Universitätsbibliothek
Straße am Forum 2
D-76131 Karlsruhe
www.uvka.de

Universitätsverlag Karlsruhe 2009
Print on Demand

ISSN: 1862-8893
ISBN: 978-3-86644-377-8

To my parents.
And especially to Anne.

Acknowledgements

Foremost I would like to jointly thank Prof. Dr. Siegfried Berninghaus and Prof. Dr. Christof Weinhardt for supervising this thesis and supporting me in all my scientific endeavors. I am also indebted to Prof. Dr. Karl-Martin Ehrhart for his availability and constructive comments throughout all stages of my dissertation and for volunteering to serve on my board of examiners. Prof. Dr. Jan Kowalski has been so kind to chair the board of examiners.

Moreover, I would also like to acknowledge the support of all professors and students of the DFG Graduiertenkolleg Information Management and Market Engineering (IME) at the Universität Karlsruhe (TH), which I have been honored to be a student of. The IME has considerably widened my academic viewpoint and enabled me to approach this thesis with an interdisciplinary spirit.

I am also very grateful for the excellent working atmosphere at the Institute for Economic Theory and Operations Research (WiOR), especially due to my fellow colleagues at the chair for economics VWL3. In particular, I would like to thank Ralf Löschel, who has not only been my room mate and most constructive critic within the last years, but has also become a dear friend.

Furthermore, I would like to express my thankfulness for the unconditional support and love of my parents, Margarete and Dr. Karl Krämer. They have always encouraged me to pursue my dreams and fostered everything I did. I owe them more than I could ever express in writing.

Last but not least this thesis would not have been possible without the constant encouragement, comic relief, helpful insights and caring love provided by my partner Anne. Throughout the years of my studies she has always stood aside me and supported me at all circumstances. Next to my parents, she is the most important pillar of my life.

Contents

Introduction

The communications industry is one of the key drivers of economic growth (Röller and Waverman 2001) and has recently, following the liberalization of the sector in the late twentieth century, undergone a tremendous transformation. In particular, *digital convergence* is at present a key factor in the developments underlying electronic communications (OECD 2006). The notion of digital convergence has its origins in the early 1980s when Pool (1983) predicted a "convergence of modes" which would eventually integrate every communications service into one grand system. In fact, Latzer (1997) divides the convergence phenomenon into two distinct phases. In the first phase, beginning in the 1960s, telecommunications and data communications started to converge. This phase of convergence has subsequently been labeled as *telematics* (Nora and Minc 1980). The second phase, which Latzer calls *mediamatics*, was characterized by convergence of telematics with mass media and begun in the early 1990s. Today, the term digital convergence is widely used and therefore eludes precise definition. The authors of the most comprehensive overviews on the topic, such as Baldwin, McVoy, and Steinfield (1996) and Yoffie (1997), follow the original notion expressed by Pool, however, and envision the emergence of an integrated broadband network. For the course of this thesis, I will also follow this notion and adopt a definition put forward by the European Commission (COM 1997).

Definition (Digital Convergence). *Digital Convergence refers to the the ability of different network platforms to carry essentially similar kinds of services.*

Digital Convergence can take place at different levels. Damjanovic (2002), for example, differentiates between technological, regulatory and economic convergence. While there is a significant body of literature concerned with technological and regulatory convergence, Bauer (2007) points out that economic "literature fails to embed convergence in a broader economic theory of networks and service provision". Furthermore, he concludes that "convergence unfolds in ways that are more complicated and with effects that are more multilayered than commonly recognized".

It is the aim of this thesis to fill into this hiatus of economic literature. More precisely, I consider the competition between integrated network operators, such as telephone and cable network incumbents. Digital convergence has led to a platform competition between these two network operators, i.e. between the services provided by them. In most leading OECD countries today, former telecommunication monopolists offer not only Internet and telephony services over their network, but also digital TV (Ortiz Jr. 2006). On the contrary, regional cable network monopolists, have also invested in network digitization in order to augment their traditional TV broadcasting service by a telephony and Internet service themselves. Maldoom et al. (2005, p.80) affirm that consumers view the services delivered over different platforms as close substitutes. While each network provider has a strategic advantage on his home market, both firms compete head-to-head on the converged markets for market share and profits.[1] I argue that digital convergence has created a prisoners' dilemma which forced the network operators into entering each others markets: Each firm found it profitable to capture a share of the competitor's market and hence no one could commit not to do so. Consequently, both firms entered each other's markets and ceteris paribus end up with lower overall profits. I refer to this market structure as a *reciprocal duopoly* because monopolies have transformed into duopolies through reciprocal entry. The peculiar feature of the reciprocal duopoly is that each firm originates from a home market where it is considered to have some strategic advantage over its competitor.

As the convergence of communications markets is inevitable today, Bauer (2007) notes that the literature on the topic "emphasizes the centripetal forces leading towards a more integrated communications sector, but tends to ignore the forces that contribute to divergence and differentiation within the sector". Indeed, the economic literature recognizes that the increase of competition has led to a decay of profit margins in the sector. However, only very few authors, like Bauer, conclude that "combinations of high sunk costs and low profit opportunities are not stable and will necessitate adjustments by the service providers." Also Maldoom et al. (2005,

---

[1]In this respect Germany currently constitutes and exception among the leading OECD countries (cf. OECD 2007b and Section 1.3). Due to historic legacies, the incumbent telephone network operator, Deutsche Telekom AG, has had a significant head start in the provision of its broadband delivery technology (DSL). However, the German cable network operators are currently investing over one billion Euros in the upgrade of their infrastructure and gain market share at an ever growing pace (Kabelverband 2006). In their newest press release, the cable companies affirm that within the last year the number of cable broadband subscriptions tripled, while the number of voice telephony subscriptions (over the cable infrastructure) even quintupled (Kabelverband 2007). By these figures, together with historical evidence from other comparable countries, we can conclude that also in Germany cable and telephony incumbents will eventually become symmetric competitors.

p.51) write that in the light of digital convergence "non-price product differentiation is likely to become increasingly important". While these authors provide a rather qualitative analysis, I approach the topic with a formal game-theoretic model in this thesis. In particular, the interplay of two possible sources of differentiation is considered: *service bundling* and *quality competition.*

Communications firms often sell their services in a bundle only, although it would be technically possible to offer each service separately. For example, if a customer wants to use the cable company's telephony service, he will also have to sign up for a TV contract - the firm's home product. Likewise, telephony incumbents make the provision of their digital TV service conditional upon the purchase of their telephony service. This business strategy, by which communications firms are supposed to achieve some differentiation of their service portfolio over competitors has become known under the buzz word *Multiple Play.*[2] Especially *Triple Play* receives increased attention in the literature, from an economic (e.g. Picot, Bereczky, and Freyberg 2007) as well as from a regulatory perspective (e.g. Bundesnetzagentur 2006). Therein, bundling is attributed with a central accomplishment (or concern): Its ability to differentiate facilities-based competitors, which are able to provide the whole range of communications services because they have their own infrastructure, from access-based competitors, which rely on foreign infrastructure and can therefore only provide one or two services at most. However, while bundling may help the integrated multi-service providers to differentiate themselves from the single-service providers, it does not differentiate them among each other. By offering Triple Play packages in order to evade the ruinous competition in the voice telephony segment, cable and telephone network incumbents create a joint duopoly market in which they compete for bundles. Current empirical evidence confirms that the firms' bundles are very similar to each other and therefore regarded as close substitutes by consumers. Consequently, given firms compete in prices, the classical Bertrand argument predicts a price war with near competitive outcomes even for this (reciprocal) duopoly setting.

Hence, the integrated network operators must find another means of service differentiation. I suggest that such differentiation will take place along the quality dimension. Communications services are not a homogeneous good and can e.g. differ in terms of reliability, customer

---

[2]The term *Multiple Play* subsumes a variety of different service bundles, which may range from *Double Play*, e.g. the bundle of voice and data services to *Triple Play*, which includes voice, data and video services. Today, one can also observe an increasing trend to *Quadruple Play* which amends the Triple Play package by mobile services. The latter term, however – albeit used by firms' marketing departments worldwide – is not completely coherent, because it does not add another service variety but merely locational flexibility to the package.

service, transfer speeds, video quality or content. In such vertically differentiated markets, a standard result in the theoretical Industrial Organization literature states that the firm providing the service of higher quality will also earn the greater profits. Therefore, in the absence of cross-market effects, each of the facilities-based competitors will exploit its home market advantage by establishing itself as the high-quality provider in its home market. Thus, when firms offer their services separately, each firm will be the high-quality provider in its home market and the low-quality provider in its secondary market.

Moreover, I will show that in mature vertically differentiated markets, service bundling can have an additional powerful effect, quite distinct from those previously known. In particular, my main result is that Triple Play, i.e. tie of a firm's home service with some (or all) of its secondary services, creates a cross-market interdependency which serves as a market leverage device through which one firm may carry its home market advantage over to the secondary market. This is achieved through a quality-differentiation effect which emerges as firms seek to soften price competition by specializing on providing either the high- or low quality service in *both* markets, thereby leaving the high-end provider better and the low-end competitor worse off than under separate pricing. I will show that such *quality leverage* is feasible for a very generic type of cost function, assuming that the costs of service quality stem from fixed costs mainly.[3]

The remainder of this thesis follows the Market Engineering process methodology as described in Section 2.3 and is structured as follows.

In Chapter 1 the technological and legal foundations underlying the digital convergence phenomenon are laid out. More specifically, Section 1.1 provides the reader with background information on communications protocols and current network architectures enabling the convergence process. In Section 1.2, I survey the regulatory developments in the European Union empowering integrated network operators to engage in reciprocal market entry. Finally, Section 1.3 analyses the current state of competition in the European, and especially German, broadband market.

Next, Chapter 2 discusses the economic peculiarities of communications markets and relates the present framework with previous ones in which the digital convergence phenomenon has been explicitly addressed.

---

[3]This seems to be a natural assumption in the context of network industries, where scale economics are rather prominent since each additional customer induces near zero marginal costs, whereas (fixed) costs of e.g. network maintenance are very high (cf. Section 2.1).

Chapter 3 constitutes the heart of this thesis and presents the base framework. My model is distinct to others in the sense that it provides an integrated analysis of bundling and vertically differentiated markets in a reciprocal duopoly market. I employ a three-stage game, where firms decide whether to price their services separately or in a bundle first, then determine their optimal service qualities and finally compete in prices. I can show that bundle pricing is an an equilibrium strategy for both firms, even without prior commitments, and that it can facilitate quality leverage.

In Chapter 4, I extend the base model in several ways, for example, by considering (unilateral) mixed bundling, economies of scope or correlated consumer preferences. I can show that the main implications of my model are robust.

Chapter 5 considers the welfare effects imposed by quality leverage through bundle pricing. In oligopoly settings, bundling has traditionally been attributed to have highly ambiguous welfare consequences, where consumers' and even producers' surplus may rise or fall. In my model, for symmetric firms the net effect on both producers' and consumers' surplus is nonnegative, such that bundle pricing leads to an increase (or constancy) of overall welfare.

Finally, Chapter 6 presents policy implications with respect to price regulation, discusses my findings in the light of current empirical evidence from the European communications markets and comments on possible future developments of competition in this industry.

Chapter 1

The Anatomy of Digital Convergence: Technological and Legal Background

1.1 Technological Background

In order to understand the economic consequences of digital convergence, it is indispensable to have at least a basic understanding of its technological underpinning. To make this work self-contained within the Market Engineering framework, I will therefore introduce some of the most fundamental technological concepts and definitions regarding the provision of telecommunications and media services. Readers already familiar with the matter may therefore skip this section and return only if necessary. If not otherwise noted, the following content is adapted from the books of Stallings (2007), Maldoom et al. (2005) and Baldwin, McVoy, and Steinfield (1996).

1.1.1 Foundations of Communication

Information, Data, Signal, Communication

The most basic communications scenario is constituted by the exchange of *information* from a sender to a receiver. Information is encoded into *data*, i.e. logical entities which are able to convey meaning. *Signals* are electric or electromagnetic representations of data which may be propagated from the receiver to the sender along a suitable medium (signaling). Finally, *communication* is the process of *transmitting* data (or information) between sender and receiver by the propagation and processing of signals.

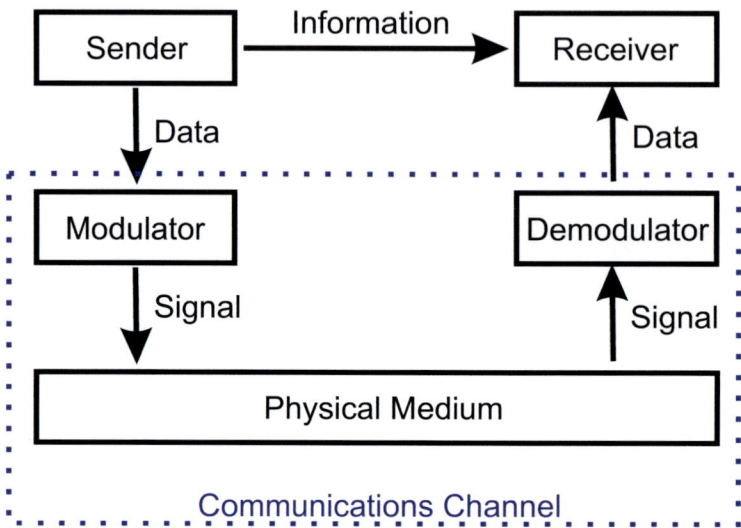

Figure 1.1: *Basic Communications Scenario*

Modulation and Transmission

Data transmission requires a physical medium, such as the air or a wire, which propagates the signals. However, first data has to be transformed into a signal through a modulator. A microphone, for example, converts audio data into a small electrical signal which is in direct proportion to the strength of the sound wave hitting it. Conversely, on the receiver side, signals have to be demodulated back into data (cf. Figure 1.1). In the example this can be achieved by a loudspeaker, which transforms the electrical signal back into a sound wave.

More technically, *modulation* refers to the modification of a carrier signal, which is a pure wave of electromagnetic radiation send over the medium, in any way suitable to represent data. There are many forms of modulation, such as amplitude modulation (AM), frequency modulation (FM) or phase modulation (PM).[1] The simplest form of modulation, however, is just to switch the carrier signal on and off, as used by early telegraph systems utilizing the Morse code to encode and decode the data.

---

[1]For more detailed information the reader is referred to Stallings (2007).

Digital and Analog

Generally, the terms *analog* and *digital* are used to distinguish between continuous and discrete values of parameters, respectively. For example, all forms of modulation described above are analog because the carrier signal being modified is time-continuous. Analog modulation is fairly easy if the input data is also analog (as the sound wave in the example above), because then the carrier has just to be modulated in proportion to the strength of the input data. However, analog modulation can also be used to represent *digital data* like text, for example. The most prominent example here is the modem (modulator, demodulator) which sends digital data over the public voice telephony network by converting it to analog signals. More recently, also digital modulation systems have evolved which are in a sense a regression to the early analog modulation forms where the carrier is simply turned on and off. A digital signal is a sequence of discrete, discontinuous voltage pulses; each pulse being a signal element. In the simplest case, there is a one-to-one correspondence between bits and signal elements. In this case the *data rate* (measured in bits per second, bps) corresponds to the *modulation rate* (expressed in baud), which is the rate at which the signal level is changed. In practice, however, other encoding schemes are used in order to make the transmission more reliable, such that data rate and modulation rate must not coincide.

Data Rate, Bandwidth and Channel Capacity

The maximum rate at which data can be transmitted over a given communications channel under certain conditions is referred to as the *channel capacity*. If the communications path was perfect, one could achieve an unlimited data rate. However, real communications channels are constraint by *bandwidth* and noise. The bandwidth of a channel is defined as the maximum modulation rate achievable if the channel was noise free.[2]

According to Nyquist, the data rate which can be supported by a medium with B Hz bandwidth is $2B$ bps. The voice channel of the public telephone system, for example, has roughly a bandwidth of 3100 Hz. Then, the capacity of the channel is $C = 2B = 6200$ bps. This formula holds only if each signal element represents only one bit. In real modems, for example, more than two signal levels are used such that each signal element can represent more than one bit.

---

[2]Another definition of bandwidth is the difference between the highest and the lowest frequency which can be send over the medium. Although this definition relates more to analog modulation, bandwidth is therefore measured in Hertz (Hz).

When M is the number of discrete signal or voltage levels, the Nyquist formula becomes

$$C = 2B \, \log_2 \, M.$$

Thus, data rate can be increased by increasing the number of signal elements, M. In practice, however noise and other impairments of the communications channel will constitute an upper limit to M.

Moreover, the Shannon-Hartly Capacity Formula gives further insights into the relationship between channel capacity and noise. In particular, the signal-to-noise ratio (SNR) is usually taken as the ratio of the power in a signal to the power contained in the noise at the receiver (measures in decibels). Thus, a higher SNR means a higher signal quality and therefore fewer transmission errors. The Shannon-Hartly Capacity Formula then states that the maximum channel capacity depends on bandwidth and SNR:

$$C = B \, \log_2(1 + \text{SNR}).$$

In summary, what is important to understand is that both formulas express a basic linear relationship between bandwidth (being a physical characteristic of the transmission medium) and data rate. Consequently, the only practically viable way to boost the performance of a communications channel (in terms of data rate) is to increase bandwidth.

Transmission over Wires

As I have noted earlier, in principle signals can use a wired or unwired (i.e. air) transmission medium. I will focus on the presentation of wired transmission media here, because they have generally higher bandwidths and are thus capable of conveying the extremely high data rates necessary in the future. Although the data rates achieved over the wireless medium have constantly increased in the past, they will never be able to replace or outperform wired technologies. Today, three wired technologies are most commonly used for data transmission: twisted pair, coaxial cable, and optical fiber.

Twisted Pair consists of two insulated copper wires arranged in a regular spiral pattern to cancel out electromagnetic interference from external sources and crosstalk from neighboring wires. One wire pair acts as a single communications link. Usually, a number of these pairs are bundled together into one cable. Twisted pair installations were originally designed to support voice traffic using analog modulation. However, today twisted-pair is used for both, digital and analog transmission. Using analog modulation an *amplifier* is required every 5-6 km to refresh the signal and improve the SNR. For digital modulation *repeaters* are required every 2-3 km. On long distances, twisted pair can achieve a bandwidth of about 1 MHz under analog modulation and data rates of a few Mbps under digital modulation. For very short distances, data rates of up to 1 Gbps are possible. Compared to other wired technologies (i.e. coaxial cable or optical fiber) twisted pair is the least expensive, but also limited in bandwidth, distance and data rate. Most critically, twisted pair cables are very susceptible to interference and noise, especially at higher frequencies. However, because of its early application in the telephone system (cf. Section 1.1.2), twisted pair is still by far the most common transmission medium for both analog and digital signaling.

Coaxial Cable also consists of two conductors like twisted pair. Thereby a hollow outer cylindrical conductor surrounds a single inner wire conductor. This concentric, shielded architecture makes coaxial cable much less susceptible to interference than twisted pair and can therefore be used over longer distances and at wider frequency bands. For long distance transmission of analog (digital) signals, amplifiers (repeaters) are needed every 1-9 km depending on the frequency (data rate) used. The bandwidth is at about 500 Mhz and thus about 500 times higher than that of twisted pair. Coaxial cable has traditionally been an important part of the long distance telephone network, but is today most common as a means of distributing TV signals to individual homes (cf. Section 1.1.2).

Optical Fiber is a thin, flexible medium capable of carrying an optical ray. Optical fiber also has cylindrical shape and consists of three concentric sections. The innermost section is called the core and consists of very thin strands (fibers) made of glass or plastic. Each fiber is surrounded by the cladding, a glass or plastic coating with different optical properties acting as a reflector. The outermost layer is the jacket, whose sole purpose is to protect its content from environmental influences. Optical fibers have been a breakthrough in transmission media and are mainly used for digital modulation. They transmit a signal encoded beam of light by means of total internal reflection. Optical fiber outperforms twisted pair and coaxial cable by far in all relevant characteristics: Its bandwidth is immense, amounting to hundreds of Gbps over long distances. Moreover, optical fiber is considerably smaller and lighter, has much lower attenuation and is not affected by external electromagnetic fields. Thus, repeaters must only be spaced at about 40km intervals. Optical fiber is becoming increasingly important for long-distance communications links and is due to its high data rate capabilities recently also being deployed in local networks (see next Sections). Optical fiber certainly is the transmission medium of the future as digital convergence drives up the (bandwidth) demand for all types of information (i.e. data, voice and video).

1.1.2 Communications Network Architectures

In order to be able to understand the economics of communications networks later, it is necessary to introduce their basic architecture. In this section, I will focus on the stylized presentation of the two most important and independent communications systems connecting to many households in industrialized countries today: The Public Switched Telephone Network (PSTN) and the Cable-TV Network also known as Community Antenna Television (CATV).

The Public Switched Telephone Network (PSTN)

Until today most telephone networks use a star architecture (Figure 1.2) with twisted pair cables running from each *terminal node* (end user) to the *local exchange* (also called local switch or central office). One cable pair, called the *local line*, is required for each phone line and the connection between the local exchange and the terminal node consisting of the local line and a line card (located at the local exchange) is referred to as the *local loop*. Furthermore, the local exchange contains the switching equipment to route calls to and from the end-users served by it and stores all data associated with the local loop, such as billing data and the type of service. The network spanned by a single local exchange to all end-users connected to it is called the *customer access network*. On the contrary, the *long distance network* connects the different local exchanges (possibly in other countries) through a number of other exchanges called *trunk exchanges*. Lines within the long distance network are therefore also called *trunk lines*. Today, most trunk lines are made of optical fiber. Exchanges are hierarchically organized, which is due to historical legacies. In the late 19th century, when telephones were first introduced, people would buy a pair of phones and run a wire between them. Soon, cities were enmeshed in telephone cables running in all directions. Hence, early phone companies built local exchanges such that customers could run their wires to a single location and let operators connect them with other phones via a manually operated switching system. At first, customers could only connect with other customers at the switch, but soon, trunk lines were established between

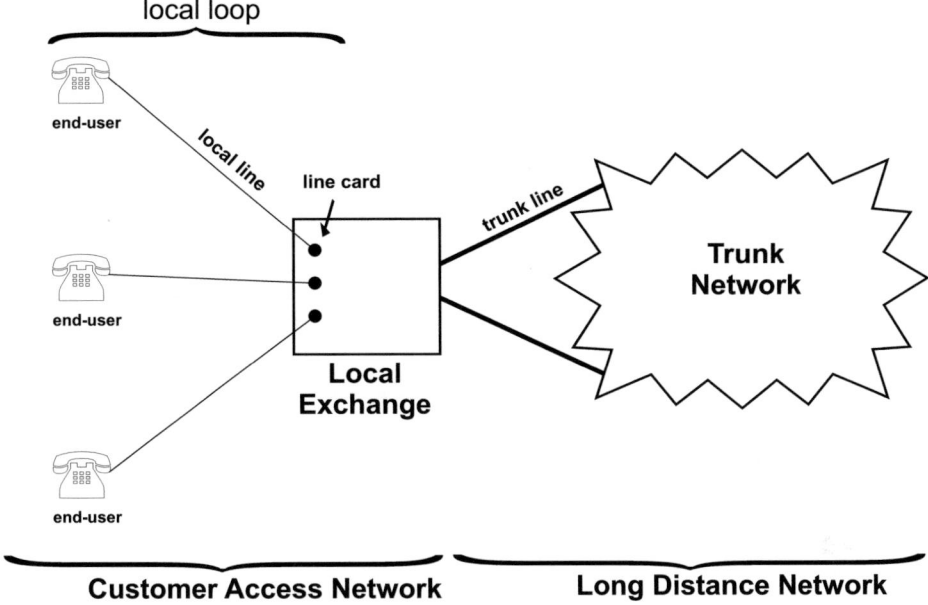

Figure 1.2: *Stylized Architecture of the Public Switched Telephone Network*

phone companies and everybody could call everybody else in the same local area. This grew into the hierarchy of switches that eventually extended to outlying areas and other cities. The telephone system now uses digital signaling except in the local loop. The local loop still uses analog transmission methods for voice calls. In the local switch the analog signals are then digitized and conveyed over the trunk lines to other (local or trunk) exchanges.

The Cable TV Network (CATV)

Whereas the telephone network was build for one-to-one (bidirectional) communication, the architecture of the cable-network was designed as a one-to-many (unidirectional) communications system. This was reasonable because at the time of deployment, in the 1980s, its sole purpose was to broadcast analog TV signals to the homes. Therefore, the cable network is organized in a tree and branch structure where a single thick coaxial cable, the *trunk*, originates from the headend (similar to the local exchange of the PSTN) and is routed through each neighborhood (Figure 1.3). At each neighborhood a tree structure unfolds which is subdivided into *A- and B-lines* responsible for transporting the signal within the neighborhood, *C-lines* serving

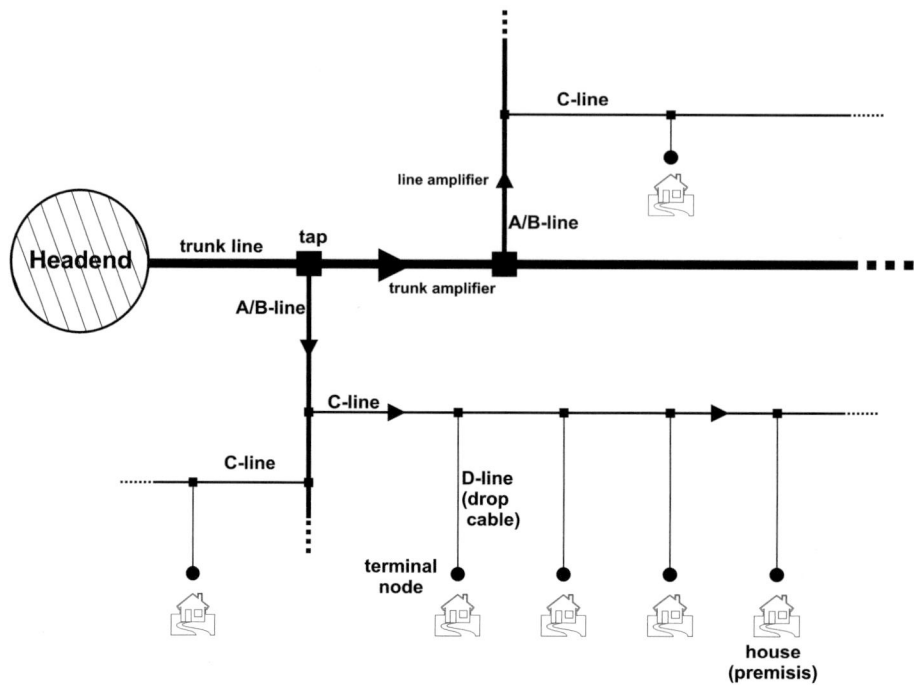

Figure 1.3: *Stylized Architecture of the CATV Network*

individual streets and *D-lines* connecting individual premises (terminal nodes). Thus, D-lines, also called the *drop cable*, may be considered as the local line. No end-user is served directly from the trunk. Each node of the resulting tree is called a *tap*. As signals travel down the coaxial cable tree structure, they lose strength and must be amplified (especially at the taps). In analogy to the PSTN, the whole network cascading from the headend to the individual homes shall be called the *customer access network*.[3]

Since the 1990s (in Europe mainly since 2000) the CATV customer access network has been largely upgraded to allow for bidirectional traffic (i.e. *downstream* from the headend and *upstream* to the headend), which is necessary to offer such services as the Internet or voice telephony. Upstream and downstream signals can be distinguished by using a different frequency spectrum for each direction. The coaxial cable per se is bidirectional already, but amplifiers had to be renewed, such that they would route upstream and downstream signals in opposite directions. Pure coaxial-cable bidirectional systems are very difficult to maintain because over-the-air signals use similar frequencies than the upstream signals and can thus easily leak into

---

[3]In Germany, this part of the network is referred to as network level 3. In fact, there also exists a network level 4 which denotes the wiring on the individual premises behind the terminal node.

the cable network and cause interference. Reliability has thus always been an issue of the early bidirectional cable networks. Reliability was dramatically increased, however, when fiber optic cables were used to replace the old coaxial trunk lines (and even some of the A- and B-lines). At the point where the optical fiber terminates, the so called *fiber node*, photodetectors are installed to convert the light energy back into electrical energy used for the coaxial lines. Each fiber node usually serves 1500 - 6000 households. Because the signals send through optical fiber cannot interfere with the electromagnetic over-the-air signals and because the remaining amplifier cascade within the tree structure is much shorter, both reliability and bandwidth are increased in this hybrid fiber coaxial cable network (HFC). Moreover, each fiber node can be programmed with different content, thus allowing for video on demand. However, in the CATV network no user has a dedicated local loop because many users share the cascading coaxial lines (which are constraint in bandwidth) on the way eventually up to the fiber node. Thus, also in the HFC network performance still depends crucially on how many users are concurrently connected.

1.1.3   Network Transparency and the IP Protocol

Both, the PSTN and the CATV network have traditionally been *line switched networks*, meaning that signals use a dedicated communications channel for the transmission. Until today most voice calls over the PSTN are still line switched with the switching systems being installed at the different exchanges. Line switching has been intended for voice telephony and is very reliable with respect to this task. However, it has many disadvantages if used for data communications. First, line switching is very inefficient and inflexible in terms of network utilization, because it reserves an exclusive end-to-end communications channel for each transmission. Often users request short high-volume data bursts and remain idle for a while thereafter. With line switching, extended demand for bandwidth can only be accommodated by reserving multiple lines. During the idle time, however, the excess bandwidth cannot be utilized by other users. Second, line switching is not very robust to line or switch failures along the dedicated communications path. If failures occur, the connection will inevitably be lost. *Packet switching* is an alternative switching technology that has been invented in the 1960s alongside with computer communications networks. Under packet switching, data is split up into small *packets* containing a *header* and the digital data to be send.[4] The header contains information about the source and the destination of the data packet, as well as error correction information. Each packet is

---

[4]Thus, packet switching requires the use of digital data. Analog data, such as voice, must be digitized first before it can be send packet switched (as in Voice over IP).

then autonomously routed through the network where switches are now called *routers*. Each router keeps a list of its neighboring routers and the shortest paths connecting to them. When a data packet arrives, the router reads its destination address and decides to which neighboring router it will be passed on. Network reliability is increased, because there is no dedicated route through the network which all packets have to take. If failures occur, packets are simply rerouted. Also network utilization is increased because the small packets can be well distributed over the network, such that network resources may be allocated more evenly. On the contrary, packet switching cannot guarantee bandwidth to any one user (as in line switching), because there is no real control of the data flow in the network. This shortcoming concerning the provision of *quality of service (QoS)* has been improved by current research, but remains an issue, however (OECD 2007a).

The just described process of packet routing is handled by the *IP protocol* which constitutes a logical overlay network, independent of the physical network, and is responsible for signal transmission. In very general terms, one can distinguish three different hierarchical layers or tasks involved in any communications process, which are depicted by Figure 1.4.[5]

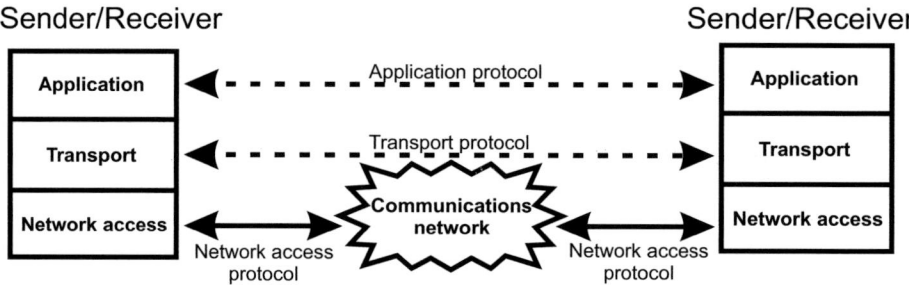

Figure 1.4: *Simplified Communications Protocol Architecture (Stallings 2007)*

The *network access layer*, which is the lowest layer, is concerned with the exchange of data between a sender and receiver in the sense specified earlier (cf. Figure 1.1). For example, the network access layer is in charge of the modulation and demodulation of data or recognition of transmission errors and therefore specific to the network architecture and physical medium used. Consequently, the layers above the network access layer must not be concerned with the specifics of the physical network and can provide network transparent higher level functionality. The IP protocol is located within the *transport layer* which is responsible for data routing

---

[5]Usually the protocol stack involves five (Internet Protocol Stack) or seven layers (ISO/OSI Protocol Stack). However, in the present context three layers are sufficient for an understanding.

through possibly heterogeneous network architectures and reliable data exchange. The transport layer ensures that the data finds its way from the sender to the receiver, but is not concerned as to what type of data (e.g. voice, video or text) it is carrying. This is the functionality provided by the highest layer, the *application layer*. What makes the IP protocol so unique, however, is that it is a universal protocol which is used for all packet switched communication scenarios. Whereas other protocols above and below the IP protocol may vary with the specific communications task, the IP protocol is always employed because, essentially, it provides *physical network transparency*. In the light of digital convergence, this functionality has become crucial because it allows to carry all sorts of data simultaneously and to physically different network architectures. Next to the Internet, recent prominent applications running over IP are *Voice over IP (VoIP)*, a voice telephony service, and *IP Television (IPTV)*, an interactive TV broadcasting service (cf. Ortiz Jr. 2006).

1.1.4 Broadband Delivery Technologies

Today the term *broadband* is simply used as an abbreviation for high-speed always-on data connections (Maldoom et al. 2005). Broadband is generally associated with the packet-switched digital data, as opposed to (dial-up) narrowband connections which are analog and line-switched and therefore tie up an end-users phone line during connection. Although today the two dominating network architectures, PSTN and CATV, employ both analog and digital services (in different segments of their frequency spectrum), only digital (broadband) services will prevail in the future (COM 2005). The definition of broadband itself is deliberately kept network neutral because it can be offered over a variety of network architectures. The different network architectures employ different technologies, however, in order to deliver broadband access to the homes and businesses. In particular, the two technologies employed over the PSTN and the CATV network shall be discussed in more detail. These are also the most prevalent technologies because they make use of already existing infrastructure.

DSL

Digital Subscriber Line (DSL) is the predominant broadband technology in most European countries because it uses the PSTN as the underlying network platform. The broadband connection is established between a modem at the user end and a DSL access multiplexer (DSLAM) at the local exchange over the existing twisted pair local line. The broadband traffic is send at considerably higher frequencies than those used by the regular narrowband voice traffic. Both signals are separated by a line splitter, which allows for the simultaneous use of the line-switched phone line and the packet-switched broadband connection. However, since the twisted pair cables are very susceptible to inference at higher frequencies, DSL can generally only be offered for those homes with relatively short local lines. The local loop of homes in rural areas are usually too long in order to provide reliable broadband access over DSL. Different versions of DSL are currently deployed:

Asymmetric DSL (ADSL) is the most common version. It provides much higher downstream (up to 8 Mbps) than upstream (up to 1 Mbps) data rates which resembles the requirements of standard Internet users.

Very high-speed DSL (VDSL) achieves much higher bandwidths than standard ADSL (up to 52 Mbps downstream and 16 Mbps upstream) due to the use of fiber optics. Optical fiber is run close to the neighborhoods in order to shorten the remaining distance over the copper twisted pair lines. Because VDSL requires deployment of new (optical fiber) infrastructure, it is relatively costly and most suited for densely populated areas.

In summary, the biggest advantage of DSL is its reuse of the ubiquitously existing twisted pair wiring. It is a very mature technology and equipment is available at relatively low cost. On the contrary, the inferior physical properties of the twisted pair lines also considerably limit the bandwidth achievable over DSL. Actual data rates are extremely contingent upon the length of the local line: While the maximum acceptable line length is at about 5,5 km for ADSL it is at about 1,2 km for VDSL.

Cable Broadband

Cable broadband uses the HFC infrastructure whose deployment varies widely across Europe. However, since the coaxial local lines are superior to the twisted pair cables used in the PSTN, cable broadband is generally able to offer higher bandwidths than DSL. Again, line splitters are used to distinguish between analog (i.e. television broadcasting) and digital services and to allow for the simultaneous use of data, television and voice traffic. Contrary to DSL, in cable networks voice traffic is usually packet-switched (Voice over IP) and not line-switched. As discussed earlier, the main drawback of cable broadband is that the users connected to the same fiber node share bandwidth. At peak times bandwidth may be reduced for some users. Because of this and other technical difficulties related to the tree and branch architecture of the initially unidirectional cable network, cable broadband service providers are still struggling with the reliability and quality of their service, especially their voice telephony service.

Other Broadband Technologies

For completeness, some of the less common broadband technologies should be mentioned as well.

Power Line Communications (PLC) uses the existing electricity distribution system to transmit data. Although the ubiquity of power lines seems to offer an interesting alternative to DSL, PLC remains to have some significant technical and regulatory obstacles questioning its commercial success. First, bandwidth is rather limited (up to 200 Mbps) taking into account that it must be shared by many users. Moreover, power lines were not designed to carry data and thus high frequencies. The amount of energy radiated by power lines is significant and interferes with radio signals.

Satellite Broadband The main advantage of satellite broadband is its availability even for remote areas. However, currently downstream bandwidth is very limited (up to 2 Mbps) and the upstream connection has to be established via a dial-up connection over the phone line.[6] Therefore satellite broadband is and will remain a niche service.

Other Wireless Technologies The remaining wireless technologies like UMTS or WiMax also have one common drawback: their limitation in bandwidth. Wired technologies generally allow for higher bandwidth and as the demand for bandwidth is steadily increasing with its availability, wireless technologies will always lag behind and remain either complementary (as in the case of UMTS) or niche services, as for example WiMax.

Fiber-to-the-home (FTTH) ,finally, is a very promising alternative to the dominating broadband delivery technologies DSL and cable. In principle, it is similar to the cable network

---

[6]Although most recently two-way satellite broadband services are offered. These require expensive equipment on the side of the end-user, however.

architecture but consists of optical fiber links only. It is thus capable of much higher bandwidths. Its main obstacle, however, is the requirement for large new deployments of fiber, even up to the individual premises, which is therefore currently only reasonable where cable ducts are available. Nevertheless, FTTH seems to be the broadband technology of the future.

1.1.5 Organization of the Communications Industry

Having introduced the technological fundamentals of communications networks, it remains to identify some rather organizational characteristics of the communication industry. The *business model* of firms active in this industry can be roughly differentiated into (de Bijl and Peitz 2002):

Network Operators: Firms building, maintaining and operating their own communications infrastructure

Service Providers: Firms offering communications services, such as voice telephony, Internet or TV, over existing communications infrastructure

Resellers: Firms engaging merely in resale (including marketing and billing) of foreign communications services.

However, often firms are *integrated*, i.e. both network operators and service providers of a communications service. This gives them the opportunity to control every step in the value chain of the final retail communications service and thus allows for maximal control of the service characteristics. This is particularly important because different services have different requirements of the physical characteristics of the network. VoIP, for example, requires relatively low latency (the time a data packet needs from the sender to the receiver), but can run at modest bandwidth. TV broadcasting, on the contrary, requires high bandwidth but is not as demanding in terms of latency. Other services again, such as video telephony, necessitate both, high bandwidth and low latency.

Consequently, pure service providers are technologically bound to the capabilities of the foreign infrastructure. This limits the scope of (quality) characteristics under their control. Yet service providers can decide which services and service variants they want to offer in principle. Finally, resellers have virtually no control over the type and quality of services they are selling, but may only control price and billing options.

Today, regulatory intervention (see Section 1.2) has blurred these organizational bound-aries, however. In short, in order to achieve competition in the local access network, which constitutes a natural monopoly due to the high sunk costs involved in deploying new wiring to individual homes, the regulator forced the incumbent PSTN operators to allow new entrants in the telecommunications market access to the local loop. In particular, three forms of access to the local loop are feasible:

Local Loop Unbundling (LLU) refers to the case where an alternative network provider takes over technical control at both ends of the local loop. This includes also the installation and provision of own equipment, such as the DSLAM and the DSL modem. If the alternative network provider also owns a trunk network, providing connectivity form the local exchange onwards, LLU provides him with the same amount of control over the physical network as the incumbent PSTN operator.[7]

Line Sharing of unbundled local loops is often employed if the alternative provider wants to offer a broadband service only. The line is then shared in the narrowband voice telephony frequency spectrum, remaining at the incumbent PSTN operator, and the broadband frequency spectrum leased to the alternative provider. Although with this form of access the alternative provider does not have control over the whole frequency spectrum of the local line, it has full control over the broadband service, including the provision of own equipment.[8]

Bitstream Access is a less common form of access to the local loop. Here the alternative provider may only access the IP layer of the broadband service and thus has no control over the technical infrastructure.[9]

In the remainder of this text, I will focus on *platform or facilities-based competition*, i.e. competition of vertically integrated service providers owning their own infrastructure, because only this type of competition allows for unconstrained choices of all relevant service character-

---

[7]From July 1, 2007 the Bundesnetzagentur approved access prices of 36.19€ and up to 20.93€ (set up and cessation fee, respectively) and 10.65€ (monthly fee) for the access of a single twisted pair local loop. In Germany, LLU access is offered since 1998.

[8]As of July 1, 2007, fees for line sharing in Germany are at 60.82€ (set up fee) and 1.91€ per month. Line sharing must be offered in every Member State of the EU since January 1, 2001 by regulatory order No. 2887/2000.

[9]Bitstream access will soon be offered in Germany. It was imposed by regulatory order in September 2006.

istics. More precisely, I will consider the *inter-modal* competition between PSTN and CATV network operators offering substitutive broadband services over different platforms.

1.2 European Regulation and Legal Background

The communications sector has been regulated ever since its existence. At first, regulation has been justified by arguing that the provision of communications services was as an official duty which should not be left to private firms. Part of this reasoning has been that the telecommunications sector was viewed as a natural monopoly due to the large economies of scale and high amounts of sunk costs needed to install the necessary infrastructure. The cost function of communications firms is usually U-shaped with respect to the number of subscribers: First scale economies drive down unit costs while it becomes increasingly expensive to connect subscribers in remote areas to the communications network. In order to guarantee nationwide access to communications at affordable and identical prices, i.e. to prevent firms' *cream skimming* the market, legislators worldwide thought that only a State owned monopolist could provide such service. Due to technological developments (cf. Section 1.1) and subsequent changes in the cost and demand structure of the telecommunications sector, today almost all telecommunications markets are privatized (the monopolistic firm has been transferred from State to private ownership) and liberalized (opened for competition). However, the legal history of countries worldwide differs greatly. Since many English publications have already presented a thorough picture of the developments in the precursing North American and British communications markets, I will focus on the presentation of the developments in the remaining European countries, following the regulatory regime issued by the European Commission (EC).[10] The present section has been largely adapted from Larouche (2000), Koenig, Loetz, and Neumann (2004) and Säcker (2006), if not noted differently.

1.2.1 Liberalization of Communications Services

With the Green Paper on the Development of the Common Market for Telecommunications Services and Equipment (COM 1987) the European Union (EU) started to think about a change in regulation of the telecommunications sector for the first time. Back then, almost all Member States employed a State owned monopoly to control infrastructure and services of their network

---

[10]See Thatcher (2001) for a discussion on the closeness of interaction between the EC and national governments.

industries, including telecommunications, mail and public transport.[11] The main reasons why the EC put the telecommunications sector on topic just now are spelled out in the introduction of the Green Paper and to a large extend even remain valid today. In particular, the afore mentioned technological developments (including convergence) and increasing demand for telecommunications services boosted the economic and social importance of the communications sector. Moreover, other countries, foremost the USA, have shown that at least partial liberalization of the telecommunications market could well work and thereby increased the political pressure on the EU in changing the regulatory framework to support the development of state-of-the-art communications infrastructure. Among others, the main aims of the 1987 Green Paper thus included the gradual liberalization and harmonization of the telecommunications markets within the EU. More precisely, the Green Paper identifies the following goals:[12]

a) Member States must preserve network integrity in any event, and may therefore leave telecommunications infrastructure under monopoly

b) Amongst services, only public voice telephony may be left under monopoly

c) All other services must be liberalized

d) An Open Network Provision (ONP) framework must be put in place to regulate the relationship between monopoly infrastructure providers and competitive service providers

e) Community-wide interoperability must be achieved through harmonized standards

f) Terminal equipment must be liberalized

g) Regulatory and operational functions of the Public Telephone Operators (PTOs) must be separated

h) Competition law must be applied to PTOs and new service providers

The 1987 Green Paper has been a milestone in European telecommunications legislature and each of its goals has subsequently been transformed into Community Law. In particular four key conceptual distinctions have been made: i) regulatory and operational functions, ii) reserved and

---

[11]The only exception was constituted by the United Kingdom. See Laffont and Tirole (2000, Section 1.3.2.1) for a comprehensive overview.

[12]Listing taken from Larouche (2000).

non-reserved services, iii) access and interconnection and iv) services and infrastructure. For the purpose of this paper, only the latter distinction deserves special attention.

The Green Paper has made a distinction between the *telecommunications network infrastructure* and the *telecommunications services* running on that infrastructure.[13] Thus, the Green Paper calls only for a liberalization of the service sector, an does not yet induce platform competition in the sense defined before. Consequently, in 1990, Directive 90/388 ruled that the network infrastructure could remain in the hands of the State own monopolist, while services–with the exception of voice telephony (for the public)–were opened to competition (goals a-c). This exception has been issued on the legal basis of Article 86(2) because at the time it was believed that the sufficient provision of voice telephony could be at risk if left to the market. Moreover, voice telephony was by far the largest and most profitable service and has been used by the publicly run PTOs to cross-subsidize other possibly loss-making services. Opening the market to hastily might have endangered the provision of other services, such as the postal service for example. However, realizing that the competition in the service sector relies upon the access to monopolized infrastructure, a regulatory framework (ONP) is needed to ensure that the monopoly cannot negatively affect the competitive part (goal d). To this extend, Directive 90/387 was enacted in 1990 on the basis of Article 95.

Harmonization of telecommunication standards and equipment (goals e and f) was tackled by EU Directive 88/301 of 1988, which completely opened the terminal equipment market for competition on the basis of Article 86(3), and EU Directive 91/263 of 1991, which provided a framework for the mutual recognition of terminal equipment throughout the Community. Finally, the separation of regulatory and operational functions of the PTOs (goal g) has been undertaken in Directive 88/301 and Article 7 of Directive 90/388, while goal h was addressed in the 1991 Guidelines.

In 1992, the Commission issued a review (COM 1992) and started a consultation process in order to determine further steps in the liberalization of the telecommunications sector. Subsequent to that consultation the Commission presented an ambitious timetable (COM 1993), including the liberalization of the cable TV network for the provision of liberalized services

---

[13]Although the distinction between the terms 'infrastructure' and 'service' is intuitively clear, a precise definition, as e.g. implemented by EU Directives 90/387 (Article 2) and 90/388 (Article 1) remains very difficult. As I have argued before, due to LLU, line sharing or bitstream access, the boundary between facilities-based competition and access-based competition has become very fuzzy. However, later I consider facilities-based competition only, such that there is no need to further elaborate on the issue.

until 1996 and the full liberalization of telecommunications services (i.e. the liberalization of public voice telephony) until January 1, 1998. The Council, however only agreed to the latter and laid off any decisions concerning the competition of network infrastructures to the upcoming 1994 Green Paper (COM 1994) on the liberalization of telecommunications infrastructure and cable television networks.

1.2.2 Liberalization of Communications Infrastructure

While the 1987 Green Paper has been the starting point for the liberalization of communications services, the 1994 Green Paper marks the beginning of the liberalization of communications infrastructure. More precisely, in the 1994 Green Paper the new regulatory concept of *alternative infrastructure* was introduced which referred to the provision of infrastructure for liberalized communications services. The provision of liberalized infrastructure is so important because of the bottleneck constituted by the local loop. Suppliers of telecommunications services have to lease lines from the infrastructure monopolist, which in turn also competes in the service sector. This remedy could especially be overcome by the cable TV network, which provides another means of wired access to individual homes. Recall, however, that at the time the liberalized services did not include public voice telephony, thus the aim of the 1994 Green Paper has merely been to allow for platform competition with alternative services. Nevertheless, following the consultation process of the 1994 Green Paper (COM 1995), the Council agreed to align the full liberalization of the alternative infrastructures with the timeline of the liberalization of public voice telephony as scheduled for January 1, 1998. For the transitional period from 1996 to 1998 two Directives addressed the alternative infrastructure constituted by the mobile and the cable TV networks:

Directive 95/51 explicitly recognizes the CATV networks as communications networks and obliges the Member States to "abolish all restrictions on the supply of transmission capacity by cable TV networks and allow the use of cable networks for the provision of telecommunications services, other than voice telephony." Moreover, Member States were obliged to allow for interconnection of the cable and other communications networks and mandated to non-discriminatory behavior and transparent accounting. In particular, in Member States where both the PSTN and the CATV network were operated by the same firm (e.g. in Germany), "the separation of financial accounts as concerns the provision of each network and its activity as provider of telecommunications services" had to be ensured.

Similarly, by Directive 96/2 the terrestrial mobile telephony infrastructure market has been fully liberalized. Interestingly, by this directive voice telephony was liberalized on the mobile market as early as 1996, because the definition of public voice telephony in Directive 90/388 did not include telephony services over the mobile communications infrastructure.

Eventually, Directive 96/19 marked the final step to full liberalization of the communications market.[14] In Article 2(1) the Member States were bound to revoke all exclusive rights for the operation and provision of communications infrastructure and services. However, as the build of telecommunications infrastructure involves large investments and high risks,[15] the market dominance of the former monopolistic PTOs remained a regulatory challenge in the years after 1998. Most PTOs have been privatized and released as a vertically integrated firm (i.e. owning infrastructure and providing services) into competition. While long distance (trunk) networks were build up relatively fast by new entrants, especially the local loop remained a central point of concern. To this extend, Regulation No. 2887/2000 was issued in December 2000 to grant access to the local loop e.g. by local loop unbundling (LLU), line sharing or at least bitstream access.[16] Although these measures improved the competition in voice telephony services, broadband competition would still not really pick up. The key driver of broadband competition was seen in promoting inter-modal competition between the PSTN and the CATV network.[17] The, in principle, higher bandwidths achievable over the CATV network were also thought to animate quality competition and not just price competition. Only such vertically integrated firms can control the whole spectrum of technologies necessary to deliver proper services to the customer, including investments into the infrastructure necessary to improve quality of service. Unfortunately, in the Member States both fixed-wired infrastructures (i.e cable and telecommunications networks) were mostly owned by the same operator, which, of course, had no interest in cannibalizing itself through self-inflicted platform competition. Recognizing this short-coming, the EC issued a second cable Directive in 1999 (Directive 99/64). This directive was especially addressed to those network operators which were "dominant in the provision of public telecommunications networks and public voice telephony services and which have established their cable TV networks under special or exclusive rights". These operators were

---

[14]Although some special rights and obligations remained for the operators of public networks and providers of public voice telephony services to ensure minimum quality and service standards.

[15]Compare Section 2.1.1.

[16]Recall these concepts form the previous section.

[17]Indeed, in an empirical study Distaso, Lupi, and Manenti (2006) confirm that only platform competition can assure effective competition and broadband uptake.

henceforth not only obliged to keep separate financial accounts for each network platform (as demanded by Directive 95/51), but to operate their cable TV network in a separate legal entity.

1.2.3   Regulatory Convergence

With the fall of legal barriers and separation of legal entities, competition–and especially inter-modal platform competition–within the communications and particularly broadband market of the Member States really started to pick up momentum. Integrated cable network operators were struggling for market share and quickly sought to upgrade the old coaxial-only cable networks to bidirectional HFC networks in order to offer new digital broadband services. CATV network operators really lived up to the capabilities put forward by digital convergence in offering a *Triple Play* service, including voice telephony, TV broadcasting and data communications. Of course, the incumbent telecommunications network operators did not stand behind for long and also quickly implemented digital services such as IPTV into their service portfolio. Hence, platform competition brought a rich bouquet of digital services to the market.

Realizing the possibility of such development, the Green Paper on the Convergence of the Telecommunications, Media and Information Technology Sectors (COM 1997) addressed some of the legal problems implied by this process. Most prominently, much of the regulatory framework had thus far differentiated between one-to-one (unicast) communication (as historically present in the PSTN) and one-to-many (multicast) communication (as originally intended by the CATV network). Through digital convergence, however, the distinction between both communications forms and thus network infrastructures steadily vanished (Schultheiß 2004; Damjanovic 2002). Today one-to-one and one-to-many communication may be offered on the basis of IP and thus on both network architectures. Moreover, also new forms of communications such as many-to-many[18] or many-to-one-to-many[19] communication emerged. A contemporary definition of communication must thus be able to comprise all of these different means of communications and cannot be bound to a specific network architecture. The results of the consultation on the 1997 Green Paper (COM 1999) also pointed into this direction and favored an horizontal approach which refers to the "homogeneous treatment of all transport network infrastructure and associated services, irrespective of the types of services carried".

This view of *regulatory convergence* is expressed in the new regulatory framework, which

---

[18]Call-in-conferences, for instance.

[19]E.g. chat rooms or Internet forums.

encompasses the Framework Directive 2002/21 and four further directives concerned with issues of *access* (Directive 2002/19), *authorization* (Directive 2002/20), *universal service* (Directive 2002/22) and *privacy* (Directive 2002/58).[20] The regulatory framework became effective on April 24, 2002 and had to be incorporated into national law by all Member States within one year time. The framework was complemented by Directive 2002/77, which addresses the competition in the markets for electronic communications networks and service and thereby replaces the previously mentioned directives 90/388, 94/46, 95/51, 96/2, 96/19 and 99/64. In Germany, the directives have been implemented into the new German Telecommunications Law (TKG), which was enacted on June 26, 2004.[21]

The new regulatory framework promotes not only competition and consumer surplus, but also emphasizes *technological neutrality*. Stimulated by the convergence phenomenon, this latter concept has been pursued with great intensity by the European Commission (Säcker 2006, p.45). To this extend, the terms *electronic communications network* and *electronic communications service* are newly defined in Article 2(a) and replace the previously used terms 'telecommunications service' and 'telecommunications network'. In this way, an unbiased view of all systems which are "concerned with the conveyance of signals by wire, radio, optical or other electromagnetic means (i.e. fixed, wireless, cable television, satellite networks)" has been achieved (Directive 2002/77). Consequently, all imaginable current and future communications networks as well as the services supplied thereon fall under the present regulatory framework and must thus be treated equally.

1.3   The German Fixed-Line Communications Market

Before discussing the economic dimension of digital convergence on the fixed-line communications market in the subsequent chapters, it is helpful to survey the current state of competition and the developments that have led to it. I chose Germany as a proxy for the European Communications Market because the incumbent PSTN operator, Deutsche Telekom (DT), is the largest facilities-based provider of communications services and infrastructure in Europe, and much of the European legislature seems to have been tailored for the German market. Today, the German

---

[20]The former four directives were adopted on March 7, 2002, while Directive 2002/58/EC was adopted later on July 7, 2002.

[21]Previously, the European Commission had filed a suit against Germany and some other Member States on the basis of Art. 226 EC Treaty, because the directives had not been implemented within respite.

communications market alone is attributed to have a total market volume of 76 billion Euros (Freyberg 2007). Moreover, the potential for platform competition is very large in Germany, because about 86% of the households have the choice between cable broadband and DSL.

The era until 2002: In the late 1980s the communications monopoly of DT was manifested in the German Constitution, giving it only little incentive to invest more into its network than was demanded to provide sufficient and reliable service. As a consequence, DT's service quality was very low at the time: Following Waverman and Sirel (1997), the exchanges' digital switching level was the lowest in the west, while calling prices where among the highest. In fact, DT was misused as a cash cow paying 10 per cent of its revenue as a government tax as well as a 4 per cent special reunification tax and a 6 per cent tax to cross subsidize the losses of the Post Office, which was also under State control.

In the 1980s the German government also approved the deployment of the CATV network.[22] Cable TV revolutionized the quality and reliability of TV broadcasting, which had been terrestrial and restricted to three channels before. Thus, until the mid 1990s roll-out was rapid, and until the end of 2002 about 22.3 million German households had cable TV subscriptions, while the CATV network passes about 86 per cent of all homes (Maldoom et al. 2005). By these figures, the German CATV market is the second largest behind the USA (Digitalfernsehen.de 2007). However, during the first roll-out phase only few cable licenses were granted to providers other than DT.[23] Thus, until DT was forced to sell its CATV network, it operated about 90 per cent of the existing cable infrastructure (Cawley 1997).

Consequently, when DT started to offer its DSL broadband service in April of 1999, it had little incentive to upgrade its CATV infrastructure to HFC in order to be able to offer broadband over cable as well. In fact, DT aggressively pushed DSL take up through very low initial subscription charges, which had to be raised later, because they were deemed by the regulator to foreclose the market.[24] Furthermore DT's DSL roll-out also benefited from technical and regulatory circumstances, such as on average relatively short local lines (1.5 km - 2 km) allowing DSL at rather modest investments and the absence of bitstream access obligations, which would have allowed entrants to free-ride on DT's infrastructure roll-out. Hence, by the end of 2002, 98 per cent of broadband subscribers in Germany had DSL over DT infrastructure.

---

[22]Initial deployments started in 1984, following a proposition by the "Kommission für den Ausbau des technischen Kommunikationssystems".

[23]VEBA, for example, applied successfully for a cable license in Berlin.

[24]This and the following data of this paragraph are taken from (Maldoom et al. 2005).

However, the overall broadband penetration rate was at 4.1 per cent rather low in Germany, giving it a middle rank in the EU (OECD 2007b).

Platform competition from 2003: The reason for relatively low broadband penetration can be mainly explained by the absence of platform competition through cable broadband. DSL had a considerable head start, because it would take another four years after DSL had first been offered, before cable broadband would become available all over the country by 2003:

In the advent of second EU cable directive, DT divested its cable infrastructure into the newly found Kabel Deutschland GmbH (KDG) during the late 1990s. The KDG was subdivided into nine regional organizations which were supposed to be sold individually to investors. First, the cable infrastructure in North Rhine-Westphalia (NRW) was sold in February 2000 to the American investor Callahan, who subsequently also bought the regional network of Baden-Wuerttemberg (BW). The respective cable operator were named ish (NRW) and Kabel BW. Hesse's CATV network was sold to a group of investors under the leadership of A. Gary Klesch and operated by a company called iesy.[25] The remaining six regional organizations were sold to a group of investors comprising Apax Partners, Providence Equity Partners and Goldman Sachs Capital Partners in 2003 to form the new Kabel Deutschland Group. The sale of this largest part of the fomer DT cable infrastructure has been considerably delayed by an objection of the German Federal Cartel Office (Bundeskartellamt) to a previous offer of the Liberty Media Group. Investors had been so reluctant in purchasing German CATV infrastructure because of its peculiar ownership structure. More specifically, DT had only sold its network level 3 infrastructure, i.e. the customer access network from the headend to the terminal node located at each premises. Network level 4 infrastructure (i.e. the wiring on the premises to the individual households) was in largely distributed private ownership, making it very difficult to coordinate the necessary infrastructure upgrades (Marcus and Stamm 2006). Although all regional operators quickly began upgrading their infrastructure to two-way HFC networks, DT has had enough time to build a large installed based of DSL broadband subscriptions. Cable broadband subscriptions just recently seem to gain momentum. Figure 1.5 (OECD 2007b) shows that Cable and DSL broadband compete head-to-head especially in those countries where effective platform competition has been in place for some time (e.g. Denmark, Netherlands, Korea, Switzerland, Canada or United States). In Germany, however, the aforementioned regulatory barriers, the reluctance in cable broadband provision and DSL's head-start have led to

---

[25]Iesy and ish were combined under the brand of Unitymedia in May 2007.

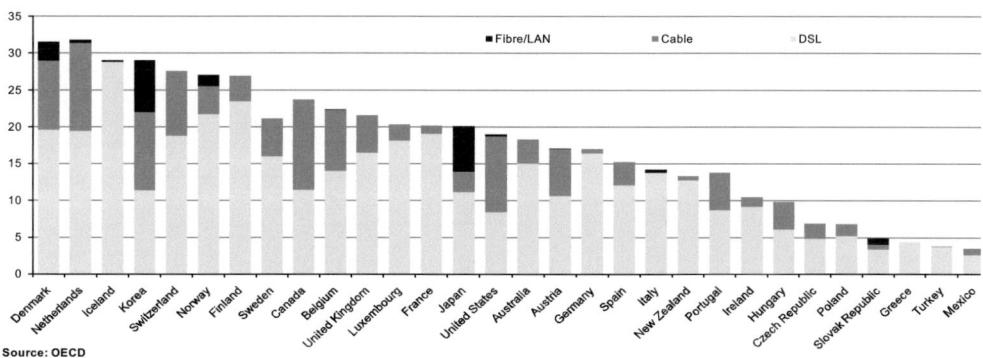

Figure 1.5: *OECD Broadband Subscribers per 100 Inhabitants, by Technology, Dec. 2006*

an overwhelming DSL predominance. Furthermore, the figure shows that although broadband penetration has significantly increased in Germany within the past four years (from 4.1 per cent in 2002 to 17.1 per cent in 2006), Germany is still at a medium rank EU or OECD wide. However, Table 1.1 shows that the potential for platform competition (without virgin build) is among the highest in Europe, as over 80 per cent of the homes having access to broadband have the choice of technology.[26] As the market matures, we can therefore expect a similar pattern as in other leading OECD countries where the market is split up more or less evenly among DSL- and cable-broadband subscribers.

While the convergence of voice, video and data, on the one hand, may signal more competition in individual markets for each of these services, there are, on the other hand, only very few firms which can provide all of these services bundled together. In particular incumbent PSTN and CATV operators seek to differentiate themselves from other access-based firms by offering a *Triple Play* bundle comprising these three essential services. CATV operators can most naturally offer a bundle of a TV-subscription, Internet and voice telephony service: TV-broadcasting has been the CATV firms' home product. Not only the physical network is perfectly suited for this task, but also existing contracts with content providers give the cable companies a head start with respect to this service. In addition, the new HFC infrastructure allows for the provision of broadband services such as Internet and VoIP.[27] Therefore, today all of the aforementioned regional cable companies in Germany offer various Triple Play service bundles. On the other

---

[26]As Maldoom et al. point out, actual company data is very limited for this domain: Nevertheless, British Telecom suspects that 50.9 % of its DSL lines are in areas also covered by cable, whereas Comcast, the leading cable network operator in the US, estimates that DSL services are availabe to 77% of the households it passes.

[27]Reliability, especially of the voice telephony service remains an issue in the CATV network, however, as they depend on the packet switched IP protocol which cannot give performance guarantees like line-switched networks

	DSL coverage (% of lines)	Cable homes passed (% households)	Fiber homes passed (%households)	Upper bound on overlap
Austria	77%	53%	-	53%
Belgium	95%	100%	-	95%
Denmark	95%	77%	-	77%
France	86%	51%	-	51%
Germany	90%	86%	-	86%
Ireland	50%	88%	-	50%
Italy	68%	11%	6%	17%
Luxembourg	89%	100%	-	89%
Netherlands	85%	94%	-	85%
Portugal	61%	93%	-	61%
Spain	89%	38%	-	38%
Sweden	75%	65%	7%	72%
UK	63%	62%	-	62%
US	62%	97%	-	62%

Table 1.1: *Potential Platform Competition in Selected EU States and the US by end 2002 (Maldoom et al. 2005)*

hand, Deutsche Telekom also offers a Triple Play bundle under the brand name of "T-Home".[28] As a classical PSTN operator, DT has a strategic advantage in the voice telephony and Internet service markets, but struggles in providing competitive content for its TV broadcasting service.[29] Moreover, due to the more limited bandwidth of the PSTN, DT is also experiencing technical problems with its IPTV service. Thus, either one of the vertically integrated platform operators seems to have some strategic advantage in providing its home service.

Offering Triple Play bundles as a differentiation strategy may lead to a reduction of competition in the communications sector as a whole. However, when firms compete in prices, the classical Bertrand argument yields that two firms may be enough to achieve near competitive outcomes. Thus, although Triple Play may be sufficient to differentiate the facilities-based

---

[28] At the time of writing, the Triple Pay packages are called "Entertain". See http://www.t-home.de

[29] Whereas customers may access over 200 channels over the CATV network (depending on their regional provider), DT currently provides their customers with just over 100 channels.

from the access-based operators, it will not protect the facilities-based operators from (potentially harsh) competition in the market for bundles. The point I would like to make in this paper is that firms may find a way out of this dilemma by adding another dimension to competition, namely *quality*.[30] I will show that incumbent firms seek to offer bundles of different qualities in equilibrium in order to mitigate competition. Before I proceed to the discussion of the formal game theoretic model, I will point out the economically most important facets of the communications industry in the next chapter.

---

[30]I use the term quality very generically and will refine its notion in Section 2.1.9.

Chapter 2

The Economics of Digital Convergence

Having established a sufficient legal and technological understanding of digital convergence, this chapter seeks to provide the reader with some rather general insights into the economics of the communications industry, and converging communications markets in particular. However, in several points I break with conventional wisdom, e.g. by proposing that communications services are not a homogeneous good. This chapter is also meant as a tie between the physical world of communications, comprising many small and individual facets which make up the complex whole, and the abstract world of economics, where the most prominent features of these complex markets are extracted in an effort to explain large parts of the economic activity observed. In the second part of the chapter the related literature concerned with multi-market, multi-product competition in general and digital convergence in particular is surveyed and contrasted with my framework. The chapter concludes with a detailed exposition of the structure of this thesis within the Market Engineering methodology.

2.1 Communications Markets Characteristics

The communications markets exhibit some very peculiar economic features deserving special attention. In following, I present a list of those which seem to be most outstanding in the present context and will discuss the rationale, applicability and relevance of each in turn.

2.1.1 Sunk Costs

Communications network operators distinguish between Capital Expenditures (CapEx) and Operational Expenditures (OpEx). Generally, CapEx are the costs associated with setting up a communications system, while OpEx are the costs of running the system (Verbrugge et al. 2005). Thus, CapEx are constituted by the purchase of fixed network infrastructure (e.g. optical fiber, IP routers), land and buildings, software (e.g. network management systems) or license fees (e.g. frequency spectrum licenses). In network industries, CapEx have traditionally been associated with large *sunk costs*, due to the tremendous initial investment necessary to build up sufficient infrastructure. These investments are typically sunk because they cannot be recovered should the firm leave the market and are dedicated to the particular use. Take the German 3G spectrum auction for example. The licenses acquired by MobilCom and Quam were never used and there has been an ongoing legal struggle on whether these firms are allowed to sell or give back their licenses (Bundesnetzagentur 2007). In any case, it is inevitable that neither firm is able to recoup its initial expenses. More traditionally, also the deployment of new cable requires large amounts of manual labor for digging and trenching that cannot be recovered later on.

The existence of high sunk costs, which are often coupled with economies of scale (cf. Section 2.1.2), give rise to a *natural monopoly*, because it would be (socially) inefficient to make two such sunk investments concurrently. The rationale that network industries constitute a natural monopoly has persisted in the minds of regulators (and economists) for many decades. Consequently, the communications sector has almost exclusively been operated and owned by the State until the late twentieth century (cf. Section 1.2). However, since then, rapid technological advancements have successively reduced the importance of sunk costs: Today it is more economical to deploy long distance networks (e.g. due to the rise of fiber optics[1]) and infrastructure becomes obsolete at a much higher rate, requiring constant reinvestment. While this argumentation is largely true for the trunk networks, it is not valid for the customer access networks (Vogelsang 2003). Here the natural monopoly prevails, because it is prohibitively expensive to deploy new infrastructure to each individual premises. Therefore, both DSL and cable broadband technologies reuse the local loop, although its wiring is inferior with respect to fiber. Likewise operators have been very reluctant with the roll-out of FTTH, especially in sparsely populated areas.[2]

---

[1]Recall that fiber optics are able to carry oder of magnitudes more data while necessitating significantly less repeaters.

[2]In Korea or Japan, for example, where FTTH is already available at large (see Figure 1.5), cities are densely

Finally, Sutton (1991) has shown that market structure relies upon whether sunk costs are endogenous or exogenous. Exogenous sunk costs are those which cannot be influenced by competitors and are outside a business's control. They usually comprise the purchase of production factors and production facilities. On the contrary, endogenous sunk costs of entry may be influenced by the firm or its competitors. Sutton himself refers to advertisement as a key endogenous sunk cost of market entry, because the amount a firm needs to spend on effective advertisement depends on the competitors' advertisements efforts. The distinction between endogenous and exogenous sunk costs may also be artificially created by regulatory circumstances. For instance, consider the case where licenses are an essential production factor (e.g. spectrum or broadcasting licenses). If these licenses are sold in an auction, they constitute an example of endogenous sunk costs since the final price to be paid is determined by the other firms' bids. However, if the licenses were to be given away at a predetermined price, the acquisition of the same production factor constitutes exogenous sunk costs. Moreover, sometimes the transition between exogenous and endogenous sunk costs can be blurred, as in the UK 3G spectrum auction, for example, where some licenses were reserved for newcomers, such that only some of the firms had influence on their final price.

2.1.2 Fixed Costs and Economies of Scale and Scope

The OpEx of communications network operators are mainly constituted by fixed costs. According to Verbrugge et al. (2005) these costs comprise:[3]

- *Continuous Infrastructure Costs* include rental payments for equipment space, leasing of equipment, energy costs for cooling and power, but also right-of-ways, e.g. to run cables or fiber over someone else's property. These costs occur, even if the network was error-free.

- *Maintenance Costs* are those costs associated with maintaining and operating a network under potential failures. In particular, they include costs of monitoring the network and its services in order to enable stock management, software management, security man-

---

populated and people frequently live in apartment buildings, such that a single premises connected with fiber can provide access for hundreds of customers.

[3]I mention only those OpEx costs specific to communications network operators. Of course there are other OpEx which accrue in every firm and may thus be summarized as (administrative) *overhead costs*.

agement, change management and preventive replacement of possibly faulty components. Changes in equipment may also fall under this category.

- *Reparation Costs* occur if a failure has occurred and contain all costs associated with the actions taken to repair the failure, such as technicians traveling to the place of failure, diagnosis and analysis of the failure, the actual fixing of the failure and verification that the problem has been corrected.

- *Operational Network Planning Costs* include costs of the ongoing network planning activity like day-to-day planning, re-optimization and upgrade planning.

- *Marketing Costs* are those costs associated with the ongoing marketing and promotion activities of the communications firm, especially those with promoting its service and providing price information.[4]

- *Service Provisioning Costs* arise with providing a predefined service to the end customer. These costs are mainly constituted by providing appropriate content (according to the service), but also comprise costs associated with the order entrance and switching the customer onto the network as well as costs of service cessation.

- *Billing and Accounting Costs* accrue by sending bills to the customers and making sure they pay, but also include costs of collecting user information, such as service usage and costs per customer.

With the exception of billing and accounting costs, OpEx are not directly related to an individual customer. Furthermore, billing and accounting costs comprise only a negligible fraction of the total OpEx, especially when bills are send out electronically. Also the digital switching technology has decreased the marginal costs per call to zero. Thus, one can justify to make the simplification that the marginal cost of serving an additional customer are negligible, while almost all remaining costs fall on fixed costs.[5] Certainly, the existence of high fixed costs (while variable costs tend to zero) implies strong economies of scale. For network industries in particular, economies of scale may stem from *economies of density* and *economies of size*

---

[4]These costs are distinguished from the sunk costs of marketing associated with market entry. As I have argued above, the latter fall under CapEx because they accrue only once when the new firm enters a market or sets up a new service or infrastructure.

[5]This assumption is common for the present industry. See de Bijl and Peitz (2002), Laffont and Tirole (2000), or Economides and Lehr (1995) among others.

(Keeler 1974).[6] Economies of density refer to those economies of scale which result from increased traffic volume along existing network paths. In the PSTN, for example, advances in technology have made it possible to increase the bandwidth of the local line and thereby enabled the provision of additional services. Similarly, new digital compressing techniques allow for more effective utilization of existing bandwidth. These examples exhibit economies of density, because one can increase the traffic (and thus revenue) of the existing network with only little modification. On the other hand, economies of size refer to a broader notion of scale economies, because they also incorporate adjustments of the physical network. Deploying optical fiber, for example, multiplies the traffic capabilities of the network by magnitudes, but does not incur a proportional increase in costs.[7] This means that a larger network is likely to have lower unit costs than a smaller one, which in turn hampers entry by new competitors, since they would need to capture a large share of the market in order to be competitive (cf. Section 2.1.3).

Moreover, in the above listing of cost types one can distinguish between network related costs, and service related costs (Machuca et al. 2007). A communications firm can run several services on its network without necessarily implying an increase of the network related costs. Thus, the communications industry exhibits large *economies of scope*, because only few of the OpEx cost types will experience a significant increase with the introduction of a new service.

2.1.3   Barriers to Entry

The presence of large scale and scope economies along with significant sunk costs of market entry promotes the existence of high entry barriers to (facilities-based) competition in the communications market. Any competitor willing to compete in the market faces the risk of enormous irreversible investments, while superadditivity of costs require for a large market share. In order to acquire sufficient demand, the entrant is likely to price below the incumbent, which diminishes profits and therefore makes it difficult to recover the sunk costs.

In particular the local loop remains to constitute an *essential facility* (Haucap, Heimeshoff, and Uhde 2006). Essential facilities are parts of resistant natural monopolies, access to which is necessary to compete in the specific market. Of course, the owner of an essential facility or bottleneck would like to prevent or at least hinder access by potential competitors, which in turn

---

[6]Actually Keeler determined these cost types by looking at the railroad industry.

[7]Although fiber optic cables are costlier than coaxial or twisted pair cables, they are also very robust and therefore cheaper in maintenance.

warrants regulation (Areeda 1990). In the case of the communications industry, the regulator has therefore demanded the incumbent PSTN operator to grant access to its local loop in the form of LLU, line-sharing or bitstream-access.[8] In this paper I focus on facilities-based competition by incumbent PSTN and CATV operators, each of which control their own customer access network. Hence the problem of access to essential facilities does not arise. In fact, in the light of digital convergence the same arguments of irreversibility and superadditivity which constitute insurmountable entry barriers should have prevented the simultaneous existence of two independent communications networks in the first place. However, at the time of construction, the analog nature of signal transmission justified the coexistence of these networks because the present technology allowed only one service at a time. Each network served a distinct market. Through digital convergence these formerly disjoint markets have converged, bringing about the possibility of inter-modal platform-competition. Following this argumentation of the local loop as a resistant natural monopoly, it seems reasonable to acknowledge the existence of a reciprocal duopoly market in the facilities-based fixed-wire communications industry.

2.1.4 Flatrate Pricing

For a long time we could observe *non-linear pricing* on the fixed-line communications market. Non-linear pricing refers to those pricing schemes where the unit price depends on the total quantity demanded. Typically non-linear pricing is achieved through *two-part tariffs*, where customers pay a fixed (subscription) fee and a variable fee depending on the marginal costs and demand elasticity of the good requested. In his seminal paper, Oi (1971) showed that a monopolistic firm can fully capture consumers' surplus by employing a two part tariff. Thereby, the fixed subscription fee covers the firm's fixed costs, while the variable fee is set at marginal costs. Without the fixed fee, the monopoly would price above marginal costs, resulting in a dead weight loss. Oligopolistic firms, on the other hand, generally cannot extract the full consumer surplus and should set the variable fee at the "perceived" marginal costs, as Laffont, Rey, and Tirole (1997, 1998a) point out.

Today, ongoing digitization and resulting cost efficiencies have lead to another form of non-linear pricing, the so-called *flatrate pricing* (OECD 2007c, Chapter 7). Flatrate pricing

---

[8]For CATV network operators such regulation does not exist at present, but is vividly discussed. Brunell (2005) provides a comprehensive list of the various arguments in this discussion. See also Hausman, Sidak, and Singer (2001) on the topic.

is a degenerate two-part tariff, where the variable fee is set to zero. This type of pricing has become reasonable for communications services because metering a consumer's usage is relatively costly compared to the marginal costs created by this usage. This form of pricing is particularly common if there exist excess capacities in the network. The roll-out of fiber along with the rise of digital compression and transmission techniques, for example, has created excess capacities especially in the long-distance networks. Of course, if capacity is not scarce, marginal costs and thus prices will eventually drop to zero. Thus the best a firm can do is to recover its fixed costs by setting its flatrate tariff accordingly.[9]

2.1.5 Network Effects and Compatibility

One speaks of *network effects* whenever the value of a product depends on how many other people are using the same or *compatible* products (Katz and Shapiro 1985; Farrell and Saloner 1985). Let us briefly consider the implications for the fixed-line communications markets. As a point of departure, suppose communications networks, i.e. the services provided over them, were incompatible, such that users connected to the PSTN (or CATV network) could only communicate with other users connected to the PSTN (CATV network). In this case, consumers would most probably prefer the larger network because it would allow them to communicate with more people, which in turn raises their benefit from subscribing to this particular network. In this vein, networks experience *increasing returns to scale* and much of the early literature on network effects has therefore been concerned with early adoption and lock-in (e.g. Arthur 1989).

This simple view is flawed in two respects, however. First, people generally value more how many people they regularly communicate with are connected to the network, rather than how many subscribers the network has in total. The emergence of a global network effect then depends crucially on the microstructure and embedding of the local networks into the larger network (see e.g. Durlauf 1993) Second, today all communications networks are interconnected and compatible:

Compatibility has been achieved through digital convergence (or more precisely the Internet

---

[9]In the mobile telephony market, non-degenerate two-part tariffs are still very common, because capacity is more limited and marginal costs (due to mobile termination prices) are higher. Very recently, however, many operators have begun to offer flatrate tariffs for on-net and landline calls. Therefore, as the capacities of the mobile network increase, we can also expect a general tendency towards flatrate pricing in this market.

Protocol) which unified heterogeneous network architectures by allowing for network transparent service provision. In particular, this means that voice, data and video services are therefore not exclusive to any network. Furthermore, compatibility between services provided over different architectures does not seem to be a relevant problem today. Subscribers of the CATV network can most naturally call people which are connected to the PSTN and vice versa. Also, given the same technical quality of the connection, consumers should not care about whether they are connected to the Internet via DSL or cable broadband; or if they receive their TV signal via a coaxial or twisted pair cable. Consumers may therefore *Mix and Match* (Matutes and Regibeau 1988; Economides 1989; Einhorn 1992) services from different providers.[10]

Interconnectedness of networks belonging to different firms immediately raises the question of cost sharing. On the one hand, firms wish to connect their network in order to increase the network effect and thereby consumers' willingness-to-pay. On the contrary, firms must agree to connect through or terminate calls on their network which were originated on the competitors network. If capacity is limited, and especially if networks are very asymmetric in size, this can lead to increased costs on the terminating network while the benefit (in form of subscription or connection fees) is received by the originating network provider. Therefore, firms usually charge a *termination price* for each call that terminates on their network, but was originated from a different network (*off-net call*). For *on-net calls*, costs and benefits fall upon the same provider, of course, such that no such extra charge is necessary. If both networks are fairly equal in size, or if capacity is not limited, one could argue that the additional costs accruing by foreign traffic balance each other out, or are even negligible. While this argumentation seems to hold for the fixed-line telecommunications market, it is rather not valid for mobile communications. This is also why we can frequently observe flatrate offers for on-net or mobile-to-fixed-line calls, but generally not for off-net mobile calls.[11] Theoretical considerations have shown that both firms can individually gain from charging different on- and off-net prices, because they evoke *tariff-mediated network externalities* (Laffont, Rey, and Tirole 1998b): While network interconnection eliminates network effects, discriminatory pricing of on- and off-net calls is able to artificially restore these network externalities.[12] Still, the existence of tariff-mediated network

---

[10]I will elaborate more on the findings of the Mix-and-Match literature in Section 4.2.

[11]At the time of writing, among the four big mobile network operators (T-Mobile, Vodafone, E-Plus and O2) only O2 has just begun to offer a genuine off-net mobile-to-mobile flatrate for the consumer segment.

[12]Other important papers in this strand of the literature, such as Laffont, Rey, and Tirole (1997, 1998a) or Economides, Lopomo, and Woroch (1996), are more concerned with the effects of termination based pricing on collusive agreements and welfare.

externalities hinges upon the fact that customers pay per call (or minute). Consequently, under a flatrate pricing scheme, network effects vanish.

2.1.6 Switching Costs

Consumer switching costs arise because consumers make investments specific to the service or product they have bought. Klemperer (1995) notes that such costs may stem from a *physical investment*, either for equipment or due to transaction costs of switching suppliers. A consumer wishing to switch from DSL to cable broadband, for example, will need to replace his DSL router by a cable modem. Also, very likely there might be a charge from the providers in either canceling the old or setting up the new service.

Furthermore, switching costs may also be constituted through *informational investment* costs in finding out how to use and configure a product/service or due to quality uncertainties of competing services. Again, consider a consumer wishing to switch from DSL to cable. Once his new service is up and running he has to re-configure his router and other equipment from the factory defaults to the settings which fit his needs best. This might involve reading of manuals as well as tedious trial-and-error processes. Switching the voice telephony service may also result in a different telephone number. The efforts necessary to inform friends and relatives of the new number also cause switching costs related to informational investment.

Next, switching costs can also be *artificially created* by firms, especially by means of contracts. Communications firms typically try to lock-in their customers for a period of time by offering them one- or two-year subscriptions. In this way, a consumer wishing to change his service just now will need to pay both services for some time and might therefore be reluctant to switching in the first place.

Finally, also *psychological* attachment to the current service might lead to perceived switching costs. Klemperer argues that the mere fact of using a service or product can change a consumer's relative utility for it and thereby create a preference for the current service. For example, a consumer might want to stick with a certain provider only because he has subscribed with this provider before and made good experience, although other providers have objectively better offers.

In recent years considerable efforts have been undertaken to lessen switching costs in the communications industry:[13] These efforts include free set-up charges and equipment for new customers, plug-and-play equipment configuration or telephone number portability between providers. Moreover, it is important to understand, that switching costs arise only *after* a consumer has subscribed to some service. Thus, consumer switching costs give firms only market power over those customers who want to repeatedly purchase a service. If consumers have not subscribed to any service yet, switching costs cannot account for competitive advantages.[14] On the contrary, *shopping costs* denote those costs related to buying services from different suppliers (Klemperer 1992). In traditional markets, shopping costs are relevant because products of different suppliers might not be compatible or simply because of the transaction costs involved in visiting many stores. In the communications industry, shopping costs seem to be less pronounced. As I have mentioned before, services are generally compatible and set-up fees often exempted. Also, due to the digital nature of the product, transaction costs of purchasing from different providers are rather low. It is often argued that consumers prefer to receive one bill for all their communications services. While this argument is questionable in itself (Pernet 2007, p.25), taken alone it is certainly not decisive in the presence of heterogeneous service offerings.[15] Besides, price discounts for bundles seem to be a much better explanation of why consumers prefer to buy all of their services from one provider.[16] All in all, it is therefore doubtful whether shopping costs are of relevance in the present context.

2.1.7 Home Markets

The PSTN was designed to provide voice telephony; likewise cable networks were originally deployed to provide video programming. At the time of erection, each of these networks provided a distinct service - and only this service. Thus, each network was fine-tuned for its *home service*, and the providers gained technical and market expertise in running and marketing it. In short, there is reason to believe that prior incumbency in a service market gives firms a strategic advantage over its competitors, should they seek to enter its *home market*. The precise nature of this advantage can be manifold:

---

[13]Compare Neumann (1999).

[14]In what follows, I will consider a one-shot game of platform competition and therefore neglect any switching costs.

[15]Compare Subsection 2.1.9 for more on product differentiation.

[16]See Subsection 2.1.8 for more on bundling & tying.

- *Installed Base:* Incumbents may have an installed base of customers, which would experience switching costs if choosing a different provider.

- *Market Expertise:* Incumbents have greater market expertise and can therefore "read" their home market better. This may include marketing efforts, customer appeal or recognition of future trends.

- *Technological Know How:* Incumbents have better technological know how. Their technology is generally more mature and tailored to the provision of their home service. Technicians have experience with various sorts of failures and thus malfunctions can be repaired more quickly and cheaper (cf. Subsection 2.1.2).

- *Existing Market Relationships:* In their home market, incumbents are likely to have existing and better relationships with other vertically distinct firms (such as equipment manufactures or content providers) or horizontally related competitors (e.g. operating in geographically distinct markets). A telephony service provider wishing to enter the video service market, for example, needs to make new contract arrangements with content providers first. Conversely, the telephony service provider may be able to negotiate better off-net termination prices with foreign telcos.

- *Psychological Adherence:* Finally, existence of (possibly sunk) investments in physical assets together with the mere fact that a firm used to be the incumbent in a particular market may lead to psychological adherence to the home market: As a consequence, the firm (or better its employees and management) is not willing to give up market share and/or reputation in its home market (see e.g. O'Reilly and Chatman 1986). This incitement may renew the firms' spirit and can well lead to a superiority above competitors.

2.1.8 Bundling & Tying

After communications services and infrastructure have been liberalized, there has been a general tendency to package services into a *bundle* (Bauer 2007; Welfens 2006). Each of the vertically integrated PSTN and CATV network operators, for example, have recently started to offer so called Triple Play packages, comprising a video, data and voice telephony service (cf. Section 1.3). Of course, naively one can suspect that these bundle pricing strategies are cost side driven since there exist high economies of scale and scope in the production of network products (cf. e.g. Chae 1992; Bakos and Brynjolfsson 1999). However, there is also a large strand of literature which studies the more interesting strategic and demand-side effects of bundling. In particular, bundling might serve as a price discrimination or product differentiation device, mitigate competition, deter entry or even leverage market power from one market to another. I will survey this literature in great detail in Chapter 3. At this point, I will therefore only clarify the definition of different forms of bundling.[17]

Pure Bundling refers to a pricing strategy where two services, say A and B, are only sold together (at some fixed proportion). Neither A nor B is available for individual purchase.

Mixed Bundling denotes a pricing strategy where A and B are sold individually *and* in a bundle. The A-B package is generally offered at a discount over the sum of the individual prices of A and B. Of course, mixed bundling is a generalized form of pure bundling, because firms can always choose to set the individual prices arbitrarily high and thereby establish a de-facto pure bundle pricing regime.

Tying is used ambiguously in literature, but generally refers to a firm's practice of making the purchase of good B conditional upon the purchase of good A. In a static tie, or *unilateral mixed bundle* (Bundesnetzagentur 2005), a consumer may buy A alone, or the combination of A and B, but not B alone. In a dynamic tie, consumers must buy one unit of B together with at least one unit of A. Thus, consumers may purchase bundles of $A - B, 2A - B, 3A - B,...$ and so on.

One can generally assume that consumers desire only one communications service of each type. There would be no added value in having two voice telephony or data services, for example. Thus, in what follows, I will assume that no consumer ever purchases more than one unit of any service type. Therefore, in the present context dynamic tying is not relevant and pure bundling always refers to the $A - B$ package.

Integrated network operators frequently employ unilateral mixed bundling. Consumers have the choice of a basic subscription to the firms' home service, or a Multiple Play package, including the home service and additional services. An IPTV subscription of DT, for example, requires a basic telephony subscription with DT. Likewise the voice telephony and data service of all German cable operators require at least a basic TV broadcasting subscription. The point is that firms do not offer their additional services individually. In the subsequent chapters I will

---

[17]The definitions follow Nalebuff (2003) if not noted otherwise.

explore why and how such bundle pricing strategies might be profitable under facilities-based competition.

2.1.9 Product Differentiation

Communications services are not a homogeneous good[18] and may be either horizontally or vertically differentiated, or both.

Under *horizontal service differentiation* consumers have different biases towards particular services. These biases can be constituted through various means, such as switching costs or marketing efforts. Consider switching costs, for example. If a consumer has already subscribed to DT's voice telephony service, he might likely also subscribe to its DSL broadband subscription, because this involves the least amount of time and costs. However, another consumer which has previously assigned to the cable companies TV service may apply the same type of rationale and choose cable broadband instead. Hence, given identical service offerings, switching costs induce some degree of ex-post heterogeneity upon firms' services, once consumers have previously purchased from that particular firm. Therefore market power through switching costs translates directly into (previous) market share. Also marketing efforts may have evoked a different service awareness and reception in different consumers, although these services are in principle identical. Or a consumer may subscribe to a service because his neighbor or friend has recommended this service to him. The crucial feature about horizontal service differentiation is that consumers do not agree upon a ranking of services in terms of better or worse: Each consumer has his own (unique) perception of the ideal service characteristics. While horizontal service differentiation is well suited to study markets with asymmetries, it adds little to the analysis of symmetric markets.[19] Moreover, horizontal differences often stem from exogenous influences, such as historic events or physical location, and may only be indirectly influenced by firms' efforts, such as marketing. Communications services have little prestigious (or image) value, however, and thus horizontal service differentiation can only insufficiently explain why and how symmetric markets compete. Here, each firm's efforts to change the horizontal characteristic to its favor is prone to canceling each other out.

Vertical service differentiation, on the contrary, assumes that consumers share a common

---

[18] Although some authors claim the difference. See e.g. Lommerud and Sorgard (2003).

[19] Usually these asymmetries are deduced from the incumbent vs. entrant relationship under intra-modal (or access-based) competition. See. e.g. de Bijl and Peitz (2002) or Wang and Wen (1998).

understanding of the desirable service characteristics. These characteristics are usually comprised into one single parameter, called *service quality*. The difference to horizontal service differentiation is that at equal prices *all* consumers prefer services with higher quality over services with lower quality. Service quality is a very generic term in this context and stands as a proxy for various service characteristics. Moreover, these characteristics may also vary across services.

For example, §32 of the German Telecommunications Customer Protection Ordinance (Telekommunikations-Kundenschutzverordnung: TKV) prescribes the following quality measures which must be collected by all network operators and dominant providers:

- Time until first provision of network access

- Failures per customer access line per year

- Failure repair response time

- Frequency of failed connections

- Time for connection

- Switched services response time

- Information services response time

- Share of functioning public phones

- Precision of billing

While these quality measures are published annually by the German Federal Network Agency (Bundesnetzagentur), they are by far not the only one relevant quality characteristics. Further possible measures of voice telephony services could be, but are not limited to:

- Speech quality

- Number of calling countries included in flatrate subscription

- Support availability

- Value added services availability

In addition, data communications services could differentiate in:

- Bandwidth

- Quality of hardware provided

- Quality of software provided

Finally, video broadcasting services can be distinguished by:

- Video/sound quality

- Content quantity/availability

- Content diversity[20]

- Content quality[21]

The richness of quality measure shows that communications services are indeed far from being a homogeneous good. In fact, the aim of this paper is to show that *quality competition*, i.e. competition in the quality dimension, is a key mode of competition in convergent communications markets.[22]

2.2 Digital Convergence and Competition

2.2.1 Reciprocal Duopoly and the Prisoners' Dilemma

Established Entry vs. De-Novo Entry

Among the many characteristics of the communications industry, regulators are most concerned with the existence of resistant natural monopolies in essential facilities, such as the customer

---

[20]Under analog broadcasting, providers (especially CATV operators) were forced to distribute an assortment of prescribed (public) channels bouquets (*Must-Carry-Rule*); in some States so much that there was little room for individual packaging of content. With the latest amendment of §52 of the Interstate Broadcasting Agreement (Rundfunkstaatsvertrag) enacted on March 1, 2007, only one third of the digital broadcasts fall under the Must-Carry-Rule, allowing for sufficient differentiation.

[21]§11(4) of the Interstate Broadcasting Agreement even demands the German Public Content Providers (ARD, ZDF and Deutschlandradio) to biannually publish a report about the quality and quantity of their content.

[22]It shall be annotated that in context of another network industry (namely the railroad industry) Braeutigam, Daughety, and Turnquist (1984) even find that the extend of scale economies and service quality are highly related.

access network, which prevents entry and thereby effective competition. In the course of this text some of the regulatory measures (e.g. LLU, line-sharing or bitstream access) seeking to dismantle entry barriers have already been discussed. However, all of these measures, like most of the economic literature on entry, implicitly assume *de-novo entry*, i.e. entry by firms without any history in this (geographically distinct) or a related market.[23] The traditional rationale then implies that the new entrant first needs to make high (possibly sunk) initial investments in order to acquire the necessary assets to compete in this new market. If these initial investments seem unrecoverable to the new firm, for example due to scale economies, we speak of a natural monopoly.

However, often potential entrants are not start-ups, but established firms having a related home market (Andrews 1949; Brunner 1961). In fact, for *established entry* Bain (1956)'s classical arguments certifying high entry barriers, may be reversed for established firms. Yip (1982), for example, argues that economies of scale may even facilitate entry by established firms who probably have realized sufficient size already in their home market. Likewise, established firms may already have relations with vertically related firms, or have an established brand and can exploit their own customer base. Moreover, Cairns and Mahabir (1988) assure that firms in related industries find it more attractive to enter due to their own sunk costs, forcing them to utilize the excess capacity in their home market. This view, of course, implies that the opportunity costs of entry are zero, i.e. no profits are foregone in the home market by entering the secondary market. This is particularly true whenever a firm may exploit its (intangible) assets with public good character, such as know how, consumer goodwill and management skills in the new market (Teece 1982). Generally, if physical and intangible capital is rather firm- than product specific, such that it can be easily transfered from one product market to another, established firms may be able to move fast and at large scale into markets with high entry barriers (van Wegberg and van Witteloostuijn 1992; van Wegberg 1995). Therefore, it is not surprising that the empirical evidence for entry by established firms is overwhelming.[24]

---

[23]Sutton (1991, 1998) calls this the "symmetry principle", meaning that all firms are equally likely to enter a market, irrespective of their background.

[24]See van Wegberg and van Witteloostuijn (1991, Section 3) and the references therein for a comprehensive overview.

Reciprocal Entry

In the communications industry we observe precisely the same situation: Facilities-based entry into the PSTN's local loop seems infeasible to a de-novo entrant, but CATV network operators have their own customer access network with excess capacity, exhibiting large scale and scope economies and a installed base of customers. Thus, with digital convergence and the fall of legal barriers, the cable companies' entry into the voice telephony and data service market–the PSTN incumbent's home market–was indispensable. However, ceteris paribus the incumbent's profits are reduced after entry. Therefore, even if the incumbent did not find it profitable to enter the CATV firms' home market before, entry might change the incumbents equilibrium output such that a *reciprocal entry* becomes profitable (Bulow, Geanakoplos, and Klemperer 1985). More formally, see that entry reduces the incumbent's sales and thereby leaves him with unused capacity. As the opportunity cost of unused capacity is smaller than the opportunity cost of used capacity, the incumbent will retaliate entry if the expected profits exceed the reduced opportunity costs (van Wegberg and van Witteloostuijn 1991). Thus, initial entry provokes reciprocal entry (Calem 1988) and this is exactly what DT does by offering an IPTV service.

Apart from retaliation, other reasons for reciprocal entry are also plausible. Watson (1982), for example, argues that firms might enter a potential entrant's home market (prior to actual entry) in order to be able to better protect their own home market. Such counter-competitive actions have especially been effective in the industries characterized by economies of scale. By pro-actively extending competition into the rival's home market, a firm is able to lower its unit costs and thereby able to better fight the potential entrant in one's own home market.[25] Furthermore, Karnani and Wernerfelt (1985) identify a *mutual foothold equilibrium*, where each potential entrant establishes a foothold in the rival's home market in order to signal the possibility of direct retaliation.[26]

A Prisoners' Dilemma

Since I consider facilities-based entry only, reciprocal entry is limited to the two network operators and their respective home markets, yielding a *reciprocal duopoly* market structure. It is

---

[25]Watson especially considers geographically distinct markets and finds empirical evidence for this strategy in the information technology industry.

[26]Here the difference to the prisoner's dilemma situation (see below) is that firms do not actually engage in large scale entry leading to a price war, but make a credible threat by small-scale market entry. Thus, the mutual foothold equilibrium is the first step towards mutual forbearance, discussed in Section 6.3.

easy to see that the reciprocal duopoly situation is pareto dominated by the situation where both firms would have stayed in their isolated monopolies: Suppose, each firm makes a monopoly revenue of R^m and a duopoly profit of R^d. Then it generally holds that $R^m > 2R^d$, because some revenue is foregone in the friction created by competition. Also notice that this is a very strong proposition, because it holds irrespective of scale or scope economies and costs of entry. Consequently, under digital convergence myopic firms face a prisoners' dilemma: Each firm is individually better off by entering the neighboring service market, but as entry provokes re-entry, both firms will end up in the reciprocal duopoly, yielding lower overall profits than before. However, as each firm maximizes its short-term profits myopically, neither firm can commit not to enter each others territory and thus reciprocal entry is inevitable.[27] In Krämer, Berninghaus, and Weinhardt (2006), I show that this prisoners' dilemma situation is not prone to the duopoly and prevails for an arbitrary number of firms with home markets.

2.2.2 Multi-Market and Multi-Product Competition

The story of reciprocal entry, and thus competition under digital convergence, is tied closely to the literature on *multi-market* or *multi-product competition*. The terms *multi-market* and *multi-product* competition are inherently ambiguous and their difference hinges upon the definition of the market. Generally, one can say that if each new product constitutes a new market (with possibly other consumers or a different demand function), then multi-market and multi-product competition coincide. If, however, each new product is a close substitute to the other, then a multi-product firm must not necessarily be active in multiple product markets.[28] While it is impossible to give a comprehensive overview over this broad strand of literature, I will nevertheless try to pin down some of the papers most influential to the present context.[29]

The early literature on the topic sought to explain why multi-product firms arise in the first place. The traditional explanation has been motivated by cost-side effects, in particular the presence of economies of scope (Panzar and Willig 1981). Teece (1980, 1982), however, argues that the existence of economies of scope alone cannot explain why "joint production must be organized within a single multi-product enterprise", because the same could be achieved by contracts. In his view multi-product firms are rather able to economize on transactions

---

[27] In Section 6.3 I will reconsider this argumentation.

[28] That is, if one accepts market boundaries to be defined through demand-substitutability.

[29] The multi-market or multi-product literature dealing with product differentiation or bundling will be discussed in great detail in Chapter 3.

costs–much in the sense of Williamson (1979)–e.g. through avoiding repeated negotiations and hazards of opportunism. In this sense, the efficiency of multi-product organization comes from economies of scope in factor allocation (i.e. contracting) and not necessarily from economies of scope in production (Haber and Levy 1988).

In a different vein, Wolinsky (1986) gives a demand-side explanation for multi-product firms. In his model, firms offer multiple products in equilibrium only if they face imperfect competition. Wolinsky argues that "imperfect competition in a market for a single product often leads to firms' excess capacity". Excess capacity, however, may in turn be interpreted as a form of "quasi-public input", which gives rise to economies of scope. In this way, Wolinksy is able to relate the demand-side explanation with the cost-side explanation of multi-product firms.

Among others, Schmalensee (1978), Scherer (1979) and Brander and Eaton (1984) have shown that diversification cannot only be an optimal choice for a firm because it exploits economies of scope, but also as a strategic preemptive weapon against potential rivals. Kreps and Wilson (1982) and Milgrom and Roberts (1982) argue from a different perspective, that multi-product firms may be able to deter entry in market A by developing a reputation for being aggressive in market B. In a sense these papers present a formalization of the counter-competitive actions described before. Furthermore Srinivasan (1991) shows that an incumbent which operates in multiple markets is able to raise entry barriers by limit pricing across markets. On the contrary, Judd (1985) remarks that entry deterrence through brand proliferation involves a credibility-problem, because a firm producing a line of substitutable products might be highly vulnerable to entry. In fact, whenever exit barriers are low, the incumbent might find it more profitable to leave the market under attack and thereby raise prices in all markets.

Shaked and Sutton (1990), finally, abstract from any cost-side considerations and provide a framework that explains multi-product firms in terms of an *expansion* and *competition effect*. Therein the expansion effect measures the monopolist's relative gain from producing an additional good, whereas the competition effect reflects the profit loss due to increased rivalry. Equilibria of multi-product settings are then characterized by a balance of these two opposing effects.[30]

Concerned with multi-market competition, Bulow, Geanakoplos, and Klemperer (1985) of-

---

[30]Myopic firms, however, first see the short-term expansion effect only. The above prisoners' dilemma situation then arises when the subsequent competition effect overcompensates the benefits received through expansion.

fer a different parameterization of the nature of competition into *strategic complements and strategic substitutes*. The authors investigate a game where one firm operates in a monopoly and a duopoly market. Although demands are not interrelated across markets, they show that a change in one market may nevertheless have ramifications on the other market if costs are interdependent. The critical issue in determining the nature of the interaction is determined by whether competitors regard products as strategic substitutes or complements. If products are strategic complements, a more aggressive behavior of one firm in a market will elicit an aggressive response from its competitors, whereas strategic substitutes refers to a more lenient behavior in response to more aggressive play. The characterization of oligopolistic competition in strategic substitutes and complements is a very substantial one and essentially relates to the slope of the reaction function. For example, under Cournot competition firms reaction functions are usually downward sloping, i.e. as one firm expands its quantity the other firm will lower its output (strategic substitutes). On the contrary, under Bertrand competition reaction functions are generally upward sloping such that an decrease in price by one firm will provoke a price decrease by the other firm (strategic complements), resulting in the well-know Bertrand price war.

Many other models of multi-market competition consider geographically distinct markets of the same product (Anderson and Fischer 1989; Calem 1988; Pinto 1986; Krugman 1980; Venables 1990; Veugelers 1995; Lommerud and Sorgard 2003). It is also in these models where the effects of reciprocal entry have first been studied. Brander and Krugman (1983), for example, find a similar prisoners' dilemma situation while concerned with reciprocal dumping.[31] Other authors focused on hit-and-run entry between contestable markets (Anderson and Fischer 1989; Calem 1988; Venables 1990).

While all of these models capture some sort of multi-market (or multi-product) effect, either on the demand or on the cost side, they are not able to reflect the digital convergence phenomenon. What makes it different from the multi-product literature is that the firms' services (i.e. voice or video) are not demand-substitutes. In the multi-product literature consumers choose exactly one product from a variety of substitutes comprising *one* market. On the other hand, the multi-market literature is concerned with (geographically) distinct consumer markets of the *same* product. In the present scenario, however, the same consumers are present on *all* service markets, willing to purchase exactly one service from each.

---

[31] *Dumping* denotes the observation that international firms may charge a lower price for their products in foreign markets (net transportation costs) than in their home market.

2.2.3 Competition under Digital Convergence: A Survey

Only very few scholars have investigated the economic consequences of the digital convergence phenomenon by means of a rigorous formal analysis.[32] Firstly, Greenstein and Khanna (1997) and Greenstein (1999) provide a starting point by distinguishing two kinds of convergence: *convergence in complements* and *convergence in substitutes*.

Convergence in complements means that "products work better together than separately" or "work better together now than they worked together formerly" (Greenstein and Khanna 1997). This definition suggests that consumers derive greater value from the package of the two complementary products than from the sum of each product separately or, put differently, that products become increasingly compatible. With convergence in complements, ceteris paribus competition should detensify. It is doubtful, however, if the convergence of different services into one service package (like Triple Play) really proves to be a case of convergence in complements on the consumer side. In fact, there is no convincing argument why a TV service subscription should substantially raise the value of one's voice telephony service, although service providers might want us to think so (cf. Kabel Deutschland GmbH 2006; Kabel Baden Wuerttemberg AG 2006). The reduction of transaction costs at least, seems to be a rather weak argument and it is the aim of this dissertation to show that service bundling can be motivated by much stronger means.[33]

Furthermore, Greenstein and Khanna (1997) argue that digital convergence is an example of convergence in complements at the *distribution* stage, because voice, video and data can be send simultaneously over the same wire. Again, I cannot follow this argument and would rather advocate this as economies of scope.

Convergence in substitutes, on the contrary, refers to the case where two previously distinct products or technologies become increasingly interchangeable to consumers. A case in point is the *fixed-mobile convergence (FMC)*: Whereas until recently the mobile voice telephony service was viewed as a luxury complementary service to fixed-line telephony (Feijoo et al. 2006), today both services are rather viewed as substitutes (Welfens 2006, p. 77; OECD 2007c, p.26 ff.). Moreover, digital convergence has lead to convergence in substitutes in the sense that

---

[32]There is an array of strategic management literature which partly or fully addresses digital convergence (e.g. Fransman 2007; Pennings and Puranam 2001 or Warf 2003). These papers either provide general definitions and empirical data of digital convergence and are cited elsewhere or lie outside the focus of the present analysis and are therefore omitted.

[33]Compare Chapter 3.

consumers view the same services provided over different platforms as close substitutes. For example, according to Maldoom et al. (2005, Section 5.1.1) "subscribers saw little difference between DSL and cable modem services." The authors provide several examples that "most consumers are platform agnostic", including two econometric studies by Crandall, Sidak, and Singer (2002) and Rappoport et al. (2002).

Of course, with convergence in substitutes, ceteris paribus competition between the two convergent products intensifies, resulting in market consolidations in the form of merges and acquisitions (Warf 2003), or artificial differentiation strategies, such as bundling. However, bundling of different services can only relax competition if the competitor is not able to offer a matching bundle himself. Thus, for the two network operators bundling alone cannot be a way out of this dilemma. In Chapter 3, I will therefore show that differentiation along the quality dimension can have the desired effects.

Shy (2000, 2001) is the first (to the best of my knowledge) to provide a game-theoretic model of digital convergence. In a similar spirit to the model presented here, Shy studies whether bundling of communications services may lead to market dominance or even fore-closure. His model relies upon four central assumptions. First, firms' (homogeneous) services are horizontally (and not vertically) differentiated through switching costs. Second, markets are asymmetric.Third, services are perfect complements and fourth service provision is cost-less. In particular, there are three firms in the market $1, 2, 3$ and two distinct consumer types θ_1, θ_2. Firms 1 and 2 provide a different service (say voice telephony) than firm 3 (say video). Moreover, the θ_i consumers are biased towards firm i, e.g. through switching costs, and would therefore cope to pay a higher price if they could purchase the service from their desired firm.[34] Consumers wish to purchase one unit of each service. Three different regulatory regimes are investigated: (i) Regulation: Firms are not allowed to offer a service other than their home service. (ii) Partial Deregulation: Only firm 1 is permitted to enter firm 3's home market. (iii) Full Deregulation: Firm 1 and firm 2 are allowed to enter firm 3's market. However, Shy does not allow for reciprocal entry.

Under the regulatory regime (i.e. firms sell their services separately), two equilibria are feasible. Either the voice telephony providers charge high prices and the video service provider a low price *or* voice telephony prices are low whereas the video service price is high. Shy argues that the voice telephony providers have a first-mover advantage in the communications market and therefore the former equilibrium seems more likely.

---

[34]Shy makes the implicit assumption that services are sufficiently differentiated.

Under partial deregulation, firm 1 provides a bundle of voice telephony and video service for the same price as the sum of the prices firm 2 and firm 3 charge for their services individually. Thus, since prices are equal, only the consumer's bias determines who buys which offer. Unfortunately, given a multiplicity of equilibria, Shy is not able to say whether this raises or lowers firm 1's profits as opposed to separate pricing. The merger of firm 1 and firm 3 in order to foreclose firm 2, at least, is not profitable.

Under full deregulation, finally, Shy finds that in the unique equilibrium, both firm 1 and firm 2 provide a service bundle and thereby drive firm 3 out of the market. Aggregate profits are the same as under separate pricing, thus, if service provision was costly, firms' bundle pricing would not be a profitable strategy. Moreover, from the previous discussion, it seems more likely that firm 3 would try to fight back by reciprocal entry, rather than being passive.

Reisinger (2006), although not building upon or referencing Shy's model, partially addresses these shortcomings. In his model of digital convergence, there are two firms 1 and 2 each providing both of two differentiated services A and B (two duopolies).[35] Consumers are again horizontally differentiated with bias towards one firm for each service. They regard the services as independent (not complementary) and have unit demand for each. Finally, the provision of each service induces some marginal cost.

Reisinger considers different correlations of consumer biases by assigning a one-to-one mapping between the consumers' preferences for each service. In this way, he distinguishes between homogeneous consumers (i.e. their preferences are positively correlated) and heterogeneous consumers (i.e. preferences are negatively correlated). Of course, a one-to-one mapping is not able to capture uncorrelated tastes, however.

Reisinger finds that firms employ bundling as an equilibrium pricing strategy, except if consumers tastes are perfectly positively correlated. In this case consumers have a unique bias towards one of the two symmetric firms, and thus bundling is not necessary to "sort" the consumers. However, while bundling is profitable for homogeneous consumers, firms increasingly slip into a prisoners' dilemma when consumers preferences become heterogeneous. For heterogeneous consumers, price competition is harsh and each firm wishes that both products were sold separately, but none can commit to do so.

While more plausible than Shy's model, Reisinger's model also has some major drawbacks.

---

[35]I do not refer to this structure as a reciprocal duopoly, because neither firm has a home market with some strategic advantage in this setting.

Most importantly, the consumers' bias towards different firms is exogenous and cannot be influenced by the firms. As I have argued before, there is no convincing argument why consumers should have a *bias* towards one firm in market A and another bias towards another firm in market B. It would be more appealing if decisions were driven by real *preferences* stemming from product characteristics (as in vertical product differentiation). If biases are exogenous and positively correlated (i.e. consumers have a strong tendency towards one firm for all services), it is not very surprising that firms can exploit this bias by offering bundles–especially since each consumer *must* buy one unit of each service. Furthermore, Reisinger's framework does not allow him to address the interesting case of uncorrelated preferences. Also does it neither account for economies of scale (but rather suggests positive marginal costs) nor allows to investigate the possibility of market leverage through bundling.

Finally, in independent work Diallo (2006) considers a model of digital convergence where firms can choose the vertical characteristic of their service. Again there are two firms in the industry, 1 and 2, each providing both services A and B. However, only the service in market A is differentiated in either high or low quality. In market B both firms provide the same service quality. Furthermore costs of service quality provision (both fixed and marginal) are zero. Firms cannot endogenously choose their service quality level, but firm 1 is exogenously assigned to be the high-quality provider and firm 2 the low-quality provider in market A. Consumers may purchase either one or zero units of each service that they have independent demand for. The author then considers a two-stage game, where firms first decide on whether to offer their services separately or in a bundle and then compete in prices.

Diallo finds that both firms are better off by pursuing a bundle pricing strategy and therefore emerges as a dominant strategy equilibrium. Unfortunately, this result is false because his analysis is flawed. In fact, only the high-quality provider would be better off by bundling. Although Diallo's framework came to my attention only after the analysis to be presented in Chapter 3 has been complete, I can show that bundling might nevertheless indeed emerge as an equilibrium strategy for both firms. I extend Diallo's framework in many respects. Most notably, I allow for service differentiation in *both markets* and let firms endogenously choose their quality levels. Furthermore, in my setting firms bear costs of quality improvement, such that the optimal quality choice becomes non-trivial. It is also due to these missing "ingredients" that Diallo fails to notice that bundling can have a tremendous effect on the firms' quality choice.

2.3 Digital Convergence and Market Engineering

Weinhardt, Holtmann, and Neumann (2003) define *Market Engineering* as the structured, systematic and theoretically founded procedure of analyzing, designing, introducing and also quality assuring of electronic markets as well as their legal framework regarding simultaneously the market microstructure, infrastructure, and business strategy. The key elements of this definition are summarized by Figure 2.1.

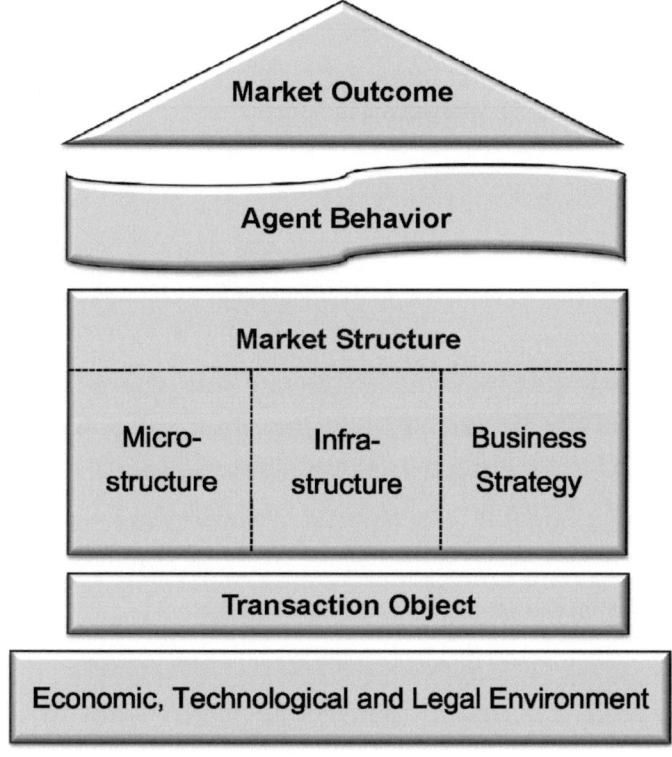

Figure 2.1: *The Market Engineering Framework*

Indeed, the careful reader will already have recognized that Market Engineering and Digital Network Convergence rest upon the same foundation: The Economic, Technological and Legal Environment. In particular, Section 1.1 has provided a detailed discussion of the technological developments that have stimulated and enabled digital convergence as well as a presentation of the current state of the technology employed in the PSTN and CATV network. Moreover, Section 1.2 surveyed the legal developments in the European Union which have shaped the structure and behavior on the communications market. Finally, most of this Chapter (especially Section

2.1) has been devoted to the presentation of the economic characteristics of communications markets.

The interplay between these three components comprises a unique environment which forms the foundation of electronic markets in general and the communications market in particular. The communications services (*transaction objects*) which may be offered on the market are enabled through this environment: They must be technologically feasible, economically appealing and legal in order to be marketable.

In turn, a market is constituted by the provision of different communications services by different firms. The structure of this market is determined by several factors which can be related to the microstructural, infrastructural and business strategy related aspects. The *market microstructure* is e.g. affected by the number of active firms, (historic) market shares or other strategic advantages. Obviously, for the market outcome, it makes a fundamental difference whether the market is monopolistic or oligopolistic or whether one firm has a strategic advantage over the other. Likewise, the firms' *infrastructure* affects their ability to compete on the market. The specific architecture of the CATV network, for example, is tailored to the provision of video and TV broadcasting, but has its disadvantages when employed for data or voice traffic.[36] Similarly, the PSTN relies upon the inferior twisted pair wiring which has been sufficient to transport voice traffic, but is at its limits when required to transmit bandwidth demanding services, such as video. Finally, in the next chapter I will show that also a firm's *business strategy* greatly influences the market. More specifically, I investigate the influence of firms' pricing strategies (separate or bundle pricing) on the market outcome.

The consumer (*agent*), finally, is the last element in the chain of market structure and market environment whose decision eventually determines the market outcome. Whether a particular market outcome is desirable or not may be viewed from different angles. On the one hand, one might take the consumers' point of view and regard market outcomes as favorable if they result in an increase of consumers' surplus. This might well be the case because prices are low or because consumers can choose their optimal service portfolio out of a large variety of offerings. For the firms, on the other hand, the consumers' desires are often contradictory to profit maximization. Generally, producers' surplus is high if competition is low, i.e. there are few competing services and high prices. In Chapter 5, I will provide the reader with a welfare analysis (in terms of producers' and consumers' surplus) of the predicted market outcome.

---

[36]Recall the problem of shared bandwidth, for instance.

Thus, the structure of analysis within this paper follows strictly the Market Engineering methodology, starting from the technological, legal and economic environment, to the analysis of market structure and finally market outcome. It shall, however, be noted that Market Engineering is not a static framework, but requires a dynamic approach. For example, we have already seen that technological convergence has also lead to regulatory convergence which again enabled economic convergence in the form of reciprocal market entry. Hence, altering any one of the key factors comprising the market structure or environment, even changes in the consumers preferences, may lead to different market outcomes and thereby might require a re-engineering of the market as a whole.

Chapter 3

Quality Leverage through Bundling

The previous chapters have pointed out that the communications markets are highly complex in technological, legal and economic terms. No formal mathematical model will be able to capture the full dynamics present in this industry and no model attempts to do so. The beauty of microeconomic modeling rather lies within its power to enable an isolation of strategic effects which might otherwise be overshadowed by other forces, and are thus not necessarily empirically observable. The difficulty of this methodology is to discover and formalize only those parts of the complex whole which are indispensable for the specific features of the model to hold.

In this chapter, a game-theoretic model is presented which considers the effects of bundle offers (such as Triple Play) and quality competition in a *mature* communications industry under digital convergence. In the model, most of the aforementioned communications market characteristics are comprised. In particular, I consider the inter-modal competition of integrated PSTN and CATV network operators (cf. Section 1.1.5) in a reciprocal duopoly (cf. Section 2.2.1). This market structure has been constituted as a consequence of the digital convergence phenomenon and is characterized by a strategic advantage which each firm enjoys in its respective home market (cf. Section 2.1.7). Each firm has invested considerable sunk costs with market entry and thus firms' entry decision is taken as irrevocable (cf. Section 2.1.1). The provision of each distinct communications service exhibits large economies of scale because the production requires mainly fixed costs, whereas marginal costs of supplying an additional consumer are zero (cf. Section 2.1.2).[1] These characteristics constitute considerable barriers to entry and exit and therefore justify to focus on the interaction of the two-firm and two-market

---

[1] In Chapter 4 also economies of scope are considered.

economy proposed by the reciprocal duopoly framework (cf. Section 2.1.3). Each firm offers exactly one distinct service in its home and its secondary market. Moreover firms can choose different qualities of their services (cf. Section 2.1.9).[2] At equal prices, higher service qualities will c.p. induce more demand. However, the costs of service provision also rise (convexly) with the quality level. Thus, firms must trade off between higher service quality and costs. Finally, firms may offer their services separately in each market, or sell a pure bundle of both services instead (cf. Section 2.1.8).

The main accomplishment of the present model is to show that the pricing decision (i.e. separate selling or bundling) can have significant ramifications upon the firms quality choice. More precisely a three-stage game is considered. In the first stage firms select a pricing strategy,[3] then, in a second stage, firms simultaneously choose the quality of their services. Finally, in stage three, firms set flatrate prices for each of their services, or the bundle of them.

I can show that bundle pricing serves as a powerful leverage device. This is achieved through a vertical differentiation effect, which accrues as the firms wish to shield themselves from increased price competition in the market for bundles. Absent bundling, each firm can exploit its limited home market power and obtain quality leadership (associated with higher profits) in its home market. Under bundle pricing, however, one firm emerges as the high-quality, high-profit provider in both markets, whereas the competing firm has to settle for low qualities and profits.

In Section 1.3 I have presented empirical data from OECD countries which shows that in mature communications industries PSTN and CATV network operators are symmetric firms which compete heavily for market share and profits.[4] The aforementioned *quality leverage effect* is remarkable, because it confirms that–everything else being symmetric–bundle pricing affects the firms quality decision, such that for one of the firms it is an effective tool in leveraging home market power over to its secondary market. What distinguishes the present model from previous ones technically is that it provides an integrated analysis of bundle pricing and vertical product differentiation in multiple markets. Moreover it considers a reciprocal duopoly market structure where firms have home markets (cf. Section 2.2.3). Before proceeding to the formal

---

[2]As I have argued before, only facilities-based competition can accommodate for such vertical competition, because only then firms have full control over all quality characteristics of their communications services.

[3]For now firms may only offer pure bundles. The model is later extended to incorporate unilateral mixed bundling as well.

[4]For the course of this book, I will therefore not consider switching costs, because in my model firms neither have asymmetric market-share nor do they compete for repeat purchasers.

model description, I will therefore survey the most relevant and related findings in the literature on vertical differentiation and product bundling first.

3.1 Quality Differentiation under Oligopoly

3.1.1 The Differentiation Principle

The basic structure of the game employed here, where firms in a duopoly decide simultaneously first on quality levels and then on prices, owes much to Shaked and Sutton (1982, 1983, 1984).[5] These early contributions derive the consumers' quality choice from a direct utility function relating different preferences to differences in income. Instead, Tirole (1988, Section 2.1.1) considers an indirect utility function, which introduces a heterogeneous taste parameter that can be interpreted as the marginal rate of substitution between income and quality. Thus, higher income corresponds to higher taste for quality and in this vein Tirole was able to capture the notion of the earlier papers by the same simple (indirect) utility function which I will employ here.[6] These classical contributions have all affirmed that in equilibrium firms will differentiate their products.[7] This *quality differentiation principle* stems from the fact that firms wish to weaken price competition by refraining from offering close substitutes. If firms offered exactly the same product qualities, their products would be perfect substitutes and in the subsequent Bertrand stage prices were driven down to marginal costs. Thus firms will not offer the same product qualities and one firm must emerge as the high- and the other firm as the low quality provider.

However, my analysis departs from the traditional single market, single product setting of the product differentiation literature since I consider firms which provide a distinct service for each of two markets. Surprisingly, despite of its practical relevance, the product differentiation literature concerned with multi-market competition is rather sparse in diversity. Broadly speaking, previous research has either been concerned with (entry deterrence by) multi-product firms (e.g. Eaton and Lipsey 1989; Donnenfeld and Weber 1995; Constantos and Perrakis

---

[5]Previous work on vertical product differentiation has either assumed qualities as exogenous (Gabszewicz and Thisse 1979) or focused on non strategic market structures (Mussa and Rosen 1978).

[6]See also Peitz (1995) for a more elaborate argument. Therein the corresponding direct counterpart of Tirole (1988)'s indirect utility function is constructed and shown that the underlying preference relation satisfies reflexivity, transitivity, completeness and local nonsatiation.

[7]See Choi and Shin (1992) for an explicit solution to the model in Tirole (1988).

1997) or product line rivalry by duopolists (e.g. Brander and Eaton 1984; Champsaur and Rochet 1989; Lal and Matutes 1989; de Fraja 1996; Klemperer 1992; Klemperer and Padilla 1997; Johnson and Myatt 2003). Product line rivalry investigates firms' endogenous choice of product variants on *one* product market, i.e. where the firms' products are close substitutes. Under differing assumptions, the authors then either find market segmentation (each firm offers a range of close substitutes thus maximally differentiating their product lines), or head-to-head competition (each firm matches exactly a substitutive product of her competitor) resulting in minimally differentiated product lines. Quite differently, I consider *two* product markets, whose products are neither substitutes nor complements. Here the only link between the markets is constituted by the firms and consumers being present in both. I will show that in my model firms seek to segment the consumer rather than the product space via the *vertical differentiation effect* of bundling (cf. Section 3.2.2).

3.1.2 The High-Quality Advantage Principle

Most of the classical contributions cited above assume zero or small and decreasing costs of quality improvement. Obviously, consumers are willing to pay more for a product of higher quality. Consequently, if costs of quality improvement are negligible, firms wish to provide a product of the highest possible quality because this allows them to extract maximal consumer rent.[8] By the quality differentiation principle, only one firm can provide the highest feasible quality, however, whereas the other firm must bear to offer some intermediate quality. Here two forces are at work, the balance of which characterizes the equilibrium in such a vertical differentiation framework: First, firms wish to mitigate price competition by maximally differentiating their products. This tends to drive down the quality of the designated low-quality firm. Second the low-quality firm also wishes to extract consumer rent which is higher at higher quality levels, of course. This gives the low-quality firm incentive to increase quality. The equilibrium then obtains when the marginal effects of both forces are equally strong. Moreover, it is easy to understand that the high-quality firm will generally earn the higher profits: Under zero costs of quality improvement, it is always best to provide the highest quality which in turn allows to extract maximal consumer rent.

At a first glance the above *high-quality advantage* principle seems to hinge on the assump-

---

[8]In all models, including the present, consumers' willingness-to-pay is uniformly distributed on some interval. Therefore, results may differ if a skewed distribution is assumed.

tion that costs of quality improvement are negligible. If costs of quality improvement are non-neglegible the high-quality advantage is not as intuitive, but still valid. Some authors (Aoki and Prusa 1996; Boom 1995; Motta 1993; Ronnen 1991) have confirmed the high-quality advantage for specific cost functions. Lehmann-Grube (1997), finally, was able to generalize this result to all cost functions which are increasing and convex in the quality chosen, but independent of the output.[9] Furthermore, Lehmann-Grube shows that if firms choose their quality sequentially in Stackelberg fashion, then the Stackelberg leader will always select the product of higher quality. This result is important for the present context because it provides the central explanation to how the incumbent can exploit its home market advantage. More specifically, I assume that the home-market advantage grants first-mover privileges to the incumbent firm which– according to the high-quality advantage principle– seeks to establish itself as the high-quality provider. By the quality-differentiation principle, the entrant can do no better than offer a product of lower quality, yielding lower profits.

3.2 Bundling and the Leverage Theory

3.2.1 Reasons for Bundling

Beginning with Stigler (1963), the literature on bundling has grown vast and encompasses a magnitude of different themes today. The most comprehensive overview on the topic is provided by Nalebuff (2003), which also claims to be complete. The subsequent survey will focus on the most related literature only. Following Nalebuff there are two main motives which incentivize firms to employ bundling: *efficiency reasons* and *strategic reasons*.

Efficiency Reasons

Economies of Scale and Scope: The naive explanation of bundling is that it reduces costs through economies of scope or scale. Chae (1992), for example, considers the bundling of TV channels to one subscription and notes that the producers' desire to bundle stems from

---

[9]On the contrary, if quality improvement induces an increase of *marginal* costs, the low-quality provider may earn greater profits. Moorthy (1988), for example, shows that this is the case when marginal costs rise at a higher rate than consumers' willingness-to-pay. Also Kuhn (2007) finds a low-quality advantage under positive marginal costs, as long as consumers' utility depends only very little on quality.

the fact that the "distribution technology exhibits an extreme form of economies of scope". Salinger (1995) adds that bundling is especially profitable if economies of scope are coupled with consumers' positively correlated valuations for the goods. Similarily, Bakos and Brynjolfsson (1999, 2000) consider bundling of (digital) information goods. Due to consumers' heterogeneity in valuation for different kinds of information, firms usually find it difficult to set an appropriate price for every individual information item. Therefore, the authors propose large-scale bundling as a profitable strategy, as the law of large numbers levels the consumers' preferences out, such that firms can better predict the demand and optimal price of the bundle. However, large-scale bundling is only feasible because information goods are characterized by zero marginal costs and therefore exhibit large scale economies.

Price Discrimination: The model of Bakos and Brynjolfsson (1999, 2000) also touches upon an earlier theme in the literature. Quite surprisingly, the early literature on bundling was not concerned with the naive cost-side effects, but rather proposed bundling as a price discrimination device. Adams and Yellen (1976) followed Stigler (1963)'s initial thought and were the first to formally show that bundling is profitable to a multi-product monopolist when consumers' reservation prices are negatively correlated. This is best explained by a brief example. Suppose a monopolist sells two goods, A and B to two potential customers 1 and 2. Furthermore, let 1 (2) have a reservation price of 10€ (5€) for good A and 5€ (10€) for good B. If the monopolist was to sell the goods individually, the best he could to was to sell each at 10€ (or 5€) and make a revenue of 20€. If he offered a bundle containing good A and good B at a price of 15€, however, both consumers would still buy and he would make a revenue of 30€. The example points out that bundling is advantageous because it reduces the consumers heterogeneity. While Adams and Yellen (1976) have assumed that consumers' valuations for the goods are negatively correlated, McAfee, McMillan, and Whinston (1989) and Schmalensee (1982, 1984) proved that this result also holds if consumers valuations are uncorrelated or even positively (but not perfectly positively) correlated.

Double Marginalization: In the above setting, firms' products are independent to the consumers. If products are complements, bundling may have an additional effect, because its avoids double marginalization. This results dates far back to Cournot (1838, Chapter ix), who considered two monopolists, each selling a good being a perfect complement to the other (i.e. the goods were only of value if consumed together). Cournot found that if both firms price their products independently, they would set an inefficient high price, because neither firm considered the effect its price has on the demand for the complementary good. If instead, firms would offer the package of both goods at a common bundle price, then (i) prices would fall because firms circumvented double marginalization and (ii) firms' profits would increase because the rise in demand overcompensates the price reduction.[10] Thus, in the end, both consumers' and producers' surplus rises. Of course, this results rests upon some strong assumptions, among which are the complementarity of the goods and the possibility that firms can coordinate (or merge). Even if we agreed that communications services are complementary, the latter assumption cannot be sustained in the present context: Recall that the EC has demanded the PSTN and CATV network operators to be separated into two legal entities. Furthermore the rules of the game are different because firms have already engaged in reciprocal market entry.[11]

Strategic Reasons

The literature concerned with efficiency reasons for bundling focuses on monopolized markets with no strategic interaction. Under oligopoly, bundling can have quite different, strategic effects. For example, depending on consumers' preferences, bundling might either increase or decrease the level of competition (Stole 2003). Thus, in order to determine whether bundling for strategic reasons is profitable, one must weigh such competitive effects with the above efficiency gains.[12]

Entry Deterrence: Among the strategic motives why firms engage in bundling, entry deterrence has been studied first. As Nalebuff (2004) points out, "although price discrimination provides a reason to bundle, the gains are small compared with the gains from the entry-deterrent effect". Entry deterrence changes the level of competition because it alters the market structure. However, the way in which this is achieved is manifold. All models consider a multi-product firm, say 1 which offers two goods, A and B and a single-product firm, say 2, which seeks to enter market B. Whinston (1990), for example, shows that bundling makes the multi-product

---

[10]In fact, Sonnenschein (1968) showed that Cournot's theory of complementary monopolies and his duopoly theory are technically identical. One follows from the other by a reinterpretation of the parameters.

[11]Nevertheless, the presence of this efficiency gain might be of relevance in the context of mutual forbearance, which I will discuss in Section 6.3.

[12]Notice that both incentives to bundle may intersect. Efficiency reasons may also have strategic consequences, for example.

incumbent, 1, more aggressive and thereby discourages entry (or encourages exit even). Whinston's model, however, requires a commitment to bundling by the incumbent, because bundling is not an ex post credible strategy once the market has been foreclosed. Considering the same market structure, Choi and Stefanadis (2001) show that market foreclosure through bundling is also likely if A and B are perfect complements. Since B has no value alone to customers, they can either buy the bundle of firm 1 or must refrain from buying at all. Their model also requires commitment. In a similar way, entry deterrence may also work if products and not perfect complements. Carlton and Waldmann (2002) present a dynamic framework in which the incumbent deters entry by exploiting network effects. By bundling its monopoly network product A with a complementary product B, firm 1 prevents the entrant 2 from achieving sufficient scale in order to be profitable and thereby deters entry. Also in this framework firm 1 faces a commitment problem. Nalebuff (2004), finally is able to resolve the commitment problem. He shows that bundling is most effective as an entry deterrent when consumers' preferences for both goods are positively correlated, but can also be achieved if tastes are uncorrelated.[13]

In my framework, bundling has also the potential to deter entry. Moreover it is credible without any prior commitment. Nevertheless, I will not explicitly consider entry deterrence for two reasons. First, in reality firms' reciprocal entry has already taken place and considerable sunk costs have been invested. Thus, the deterrence perspective would be merely hypothetical. The only question of practical relevance which remains is whether any one firm is able to drive its competitor out of its home market again. Second, in the presence of high sunk entry costs, it is notoriously difficult to determine when the entrant is indeed better off by exiting the market: When it is not possible to deny sales completely to the entrant, he will still find it better to make some surplus which contributes to recouping entry costs, rather than to write off his initial investment altogether. Consequently, to make the assessment of entry deterrence feasible, one must at least incorporate the present static framework into a dynamic context.

Competition Mitigation: If entry has occurred (i.e. firm 1 is monopolist in A and duopolist in B, while firm 2 provides B only) bundling may still be profitable because of its ability to soften competition. Carbajo, de Meza, and Seidmann (1990) and Chen (1997), for instance, show that bundling has the ability to artificially differentiate otherwise homogeneous products. To see this, suppose firms engage in Bertrand competition and the provision of products bears zero marginal costs. Then, if products are sold individually, the Bertrand price war will compete

---

[13]The effect vanishes for perfectly negatively correlated values.

away any profits in market B, leaving firm 1 with its market A revenue only. However, if firm 1 offered its products in a pure $A - B$ bundle, while firm 2 still offers B individually, then both firms can extract some additional consumers' surplus from market B. The bundle differentiates the products. Those consumers which have a high valuation for both goods will buy from firm 1, while some remaining consumers with low valuation buy from firm 2.[14]

Furthermore Seidmann (1991) and Spector (2007) show that bundling may also facilitate (tacit) collusion and thereby mitigate competition. While Seidmann's model rests upon the artificial differentiation principle (and a precommitment to bundling) again, Spector considers a repeated game where firms can explicitly coordinate on a collusive outcome using Nash bargaining.

Gaining Competitive Advantages: Finally, there exists an array of articles which provide further examples of how firms can gain competitive advantages through bundling. Among these are, e.g. Choi (2004), who shows that bundling may reduce rivals' innovation incentives, Choi (2003), who suggests to bundle new products with old to signal quality, or Martin (1999), who provides an example of how bundling can change the substitution relationships between products. Further examples are mentioned in Nalebuff (2003). However, almost all of the strategic reasons to bundling address the broader theory of *market leverage*, i.e. the question whether market power in one product market may be used to gain a competitive advantage in the other market. This question is also of particular importance for the present framework and the next subsection is therefore devoted to a detailed presentation. Furthermore, obviously all of the strategic reasons for bundling immediately raise antitrust concerns and consequently there is also a great body of literature which investigates the basic tension between bundling and welfare. This part of the bundling literature will be surveyed in Section 5.1.

3.2.2 The Leverage Hypothesis

There has been a long dispute in economic literature about whether a firm with market power in its primary market could use bundling as a device in order to gain an advantage in (or through) a secondary market. This *leverage hypothesis* has for a long time been dismissed on the grounds of the *Chicago critique* (cf. e.g. Director and Levi 1956; Bowman 1957; Posner 1976). In a

---

[14]In Carbajo, de Meza, and Seidmann's model consumers preferences are for simplicity perfectly positively correlated.

nutshell, the Chicago argument runs as follows.[15] Consider a multi-product firm which provides product A as a monopolist and product B competitively (i.e. at marginal costs, say c). If market power could be leveraged by (pure) bundling, then there must be a bundle price p^b, which grants higher profits to the monopolist than if he sold A at price p^s and B at a price of c separately. Obviously, since B is provided competitively, consumers can purchase it for c. Consequently, only those consumers will buy the $A - B$ bundle whose reservation price for A exceeds $p^b - c$.[16] However, if the monopolist would have sold A at a price of $p^s = p^b - c$ individually, then the same consumers would have purchased A and he would have made the same profit. Hence, as Whinston (1990) puts it, "there is only one monopoly profit that can be extracted".[17]

The Chicago critique has been so influential that it effectively prevented research on strategic reasons for bundling for more than a decade. Instead, efficiency reasons, such as price discrimination, were put forward as a motivation to bundling. However, in a pathbreaking article, Whinston (1990) was among the first to recognize that the Chicago critique was not as general as believed and hinged upon some critical assumptions. Among these, the most important are that the secondary market is perfectly competitive and that firms have a constant returns-to-scale technology. Obviously, both assumptions fail to hold for the communications industry.

Whinston proposed the (by now well known) market structure, where a multi-product firm holds a monopoly in one product market, but faces imperfect competition in the other. Without noticeable exceptions, subsequently scholars concerned with the resurrection of the leverage theory have adopted this market structure. The most influential among these have been surveyed in the previous subsection.

Quality Leverage

This paper extends the literature on market leverage in two respects.

First, I deviate from Whinston's standard market structure by assuming a duopoly in both markets. This assumption is per se not new to the bundling literature (cf. Matutes and Regibeau

---

[15]The following example is adapted from Whinston (1990).

[16]This is, assuming products A and B are independent.

[17]As a matter of fact, for completeness it shall be noted that under pure bundling the Chicago critique also holds if goods are complements, or if valuations for A and B are not perfectly correlated (Nalebuff 2003).

1992; Anderson and Leruth 1993; Economides 1993; Kopalle, Krishna, and Assuncao 1999),[18] even in the context of digital convergence (Reisinger 2006; Diallo 2006). However, none of these works is concerned with market power leverage. Furthermore, in my model, I do not just consider two duopoly markets, but reciprocal entry. Thereby, the crucial difference is that each firm has a home market in which it enjoys a strategic advantage.

Among the reasons why the reciprocal duopoly setting has not been considered in the leverage literature so far, is that each firm's market power is lessened considerably when its primary market is a duopoly. Also in my setting, ex ante it is not clear whether bundling may facilitate market leverage because the leverage efforts of either firm counteract. Nevertheless, I can show that one firm can leverage its home market advantage over to the secondary market, even if market power is rather limited.

Secondly, I propose a new mechanism through which market leverage is achieved. More specifically, I will show that bundling facilitates the segmentation of consumers into their willingness-to-pay for quality. Whereas under separate selling, each firm exercises its home market advantage by establishing itself as the high-quality provider, under a bundling regime, firms find it profitable to specialize on providing either high- or low quality products in both markets. Thus, bundling serves as a *quality differentiation mechanism*, both on the consumer and the producers' side. Thereby, the firm which engages in bundle pricing first, can achieve to leverage its home market quality dominance over to its secondary market and achieve greater profits than under separate pricing.

Definition (Quality Leverage). *Quality Leverage refers to a mechanism which facilitates a firm's ability to leverage market power from its home market into a secondary market by altering the quality of its products.*

In this work I will provide ample evidence that quality leverage is very viable and, more specifically, that product bundling may act as a quality leverage mechanism. This result is shown to be very robust, as its holds without any prior commitment to bundling and also if consumers quality preferences are uncorrelated. Further extensions, such as unilateral mixed bundling, economies of scope or correlated consumer preferences are also feasible and discussed in Chapter 4.

---

[18]These papers have mainly investigated whether pure bundling or mixed bundling will emerge as an equilibrium strategy and are presented in Section 4.2.

3.3 The Base Model

3.3.1 Principal Assumptions and Game Structure

Having located my framework within the literature, I can finally begin with the presentation of my base model.[19] There are two established firms $i = 1, 2$ in the industry whose home (or primary) markets are denoted by $m = A, B$, respectively. More specifically, a symmetric reciprocal duopoly is assumed, which has been constituted as each firm has entered the other firm's home market (reciprocal entry).[20] Firms provide exactly one service for each market.

Game Structure: The aim of the present model is to show that a firm's pricing strategy (i.e. separate selling or bundling) can have significant ramifications on the quality of all firms' services. In this vein, one firm, say 1, can quality leverage its home market advantage over to its secondary market. To this extend, the following three-stage game is considered: In the first stage, firms decide whether to sell their services as a pure bundle or separately. For ease of exposition, firms choose their pricing strategy sequentially in the first stage: Firm 1 will choose first and firm 2 can observe firm 1's decision before selecting its optimal pricing strategy.[21] In the second stage of the game, firms simultaneously choose the quality for all their services. Each firm has the choice between a high- or low quality service for each market, where quality levels are exogenously given by $q_H \geq 4\, q_L > 0$.[22] Finally, in the third stage, firms simultaneously set continuous positive prices $p \in \mathbb{R}^+$. The solution concept is that of subgame perfectness (Selten 1975).

Notice that the game structure reflects that quality is rather a long term variable which cannot be altered so quickly. Although under facilities-based competition firms have maximal

---

[19]A preliminary version of this model has been published as Krämer (2007a, 2007b). Furthermore, I would like to thank the participants at the 6th Conference on Telecommunication Techno-Economics (CTTE), 2007 and at the 34th Conference of the European Association for Research in Industrial Economics (EARIE), 2007 for valuable comments.

[20]More specifically I take the firms' entry decision as given and sunk, such that exit is prohibitively costly. Thus, I fade out any aspects related to strategic entry deterrence, nor will I further address the question on whether entry should have occurred in the first place.

[21]Later, it is shown that the results are identical under simultaneous decision making, as long as the costs of quality improvement are non negligible.

[22]The choice of $q_H \geq 4\, q_L$ will be motivated later in the text and is not crucial for the quality differentiation effect to hold. In fact, as one will see later, the assumption has been made to ensure existence of subgame equilibria other than the desired.

control over the network and associated quality characteristics, once a decision has been made (e.g. with respect to a certain technology) considerable sunk costs constitute a high level of quality commitment. Hence, in the model, firms' quality decisions (in stage two) are sunk and irrevocable during the Bertrand price competition (in stage three). Furthermore, the main aim of the present model is to investigate the long term impact of bundling as a pricing strategy decision upon the firms' quality decision and subsequent price competition. In this mindset, the pricing strategy decision must take place before the quality decision, i.e. before the quality decision has become sunk.

For the further presentation of the model, it will be convenient to introduce a short-hand notation distinguishing between the four subgames which may emerge after the first stage of the game. In particular, denote by *ss* the subgame that obtains when both firms choose separate pricing, *sb* the subgame where firm 1 chooses separate and firm 2 bundle pricing, *bs* the subgame where firm 1 chooses bundle pricing and firm 2 separate pricing, and finally, *bb*, where both firms choose the bundle pricing strategy. Moreover, I will denote *ss* as the *separate pricing regime*, and all other subgames as *bundle pricing regimes*.

Home Market Advantage: It is at the heart of this model that each firm has a home market in which it can exercise some additional market power over her competitor. In principle, a first-mover-advantage at the quality-decision stage seems to capture this very adequately. Indeed, the incumbent has been in the market before and should therefore be able to decide upon his service quality prior to the entrant. In the absence of cross-market effects, it is a standard result of the vertical differentiation literature that the first-mover will choose to provide the high-quality service, because it is associated with the higher revenues, whereas the entrant has to settle for the low-quality, low-revenue service (high-quality advantage principle). In the reciprocal duopoly setting this means that under the separate pricing regime, each firm will be the high-quality provider in its home market and the low-quality provider in its secondary market. Under any bundle pricing regime, on the contrary, cross-market effects create a joint market in which neither firm can be considered to have an advantage ex ante. Thus, in order not to forestall any leverage results within the otherwise symmetric framework, only the simultaneous choice of qualities can preserve a neutral bias under the bundle pricing regimes. However, prescribing a different decision sequence under the separate pricing regime and the bundle pricing regimes might dilute some of the more subtle effects underlying the transition between them. To solve this problem, I assume simultaneous quality choice under *all* regimes. Nevertheless, under the separate pricing regime each firm's strategic home market advantage can be preserved, when the incumbent firm is exogenously attributed to provide the high-quality service in each market. In this way the strategic dilemma can be overcome.

Demand: Depending on the decision in stage one, each firm either offers its two services in a bundle (b), or separately (s). Furthermore, let $q_i = (q_{Ai}, q_{Bi})$ denote the quality vector of firm i, which has been chosen in the second stage of the game. Finally, let p_i be the corresponding price vector. If firm i has chosen separate pricing in the first stage of the game, the price vector has two elements, $p_i = (p^s_{Ai}, p^s_{Bi})$, one for each service. Otherwise, if bundling has been chosen in stage one, the vector degenerates to a single element, $p_i = p^b_i$, representing the bundle price. Then each firm's *service offer*, $\Gamma_i = (q_i; p_i)$, is fully characterized by the tuple of the quality vector and the price vector. Notice that under the separate pricing regime, Γ_i can be decomposed into the two distinct suboffers $\Gamma_{Ai} = (q^s_{Ai}; p^s_{Ai})$ and $\Gamma_{Bi} = (q^s_{Bi}; p^s_{Bi})$. The services of different firms are perfectly compatible, such that consumers can also mix-and-match suboffers of different firms to obtain their optimal service portfolio.[23]

There is a continuum of consumers normalized to mass 100 who have a positive valuation for exactly one service from each market $m = A, B$. More specifically, consumers differ in their marginal willingness-to-pay for quality, θ, and value a service offer Γ_i with quality q_i at[24]

$$V_\theta(q_i) \equiv \theta \, q_i \tag{3.1}$$

Consequently, consumers with a relatively low θ do not value quality enough in order to find it reasonable to purchase a rather expensive high-quality service, which consumers with a relatively high θ would still find attractive. In contrast to horizontal product differentiation models, however, at equal prices all consumers prefer the service of higher quality. In addition, I allow for the possibility that consumers may have a different willingness-to-pay for each service, i.e. $\theta = (\theta_A, \theta_B)$. Moreover, θ_m is uniformly, independently and identically distributed in the unit

---

[23]However, consumers have positive valuation for exactly one service in each market. Therefore, I assume that consumers will refrain from purchasing superfluous units of services, also if they are bundled together with another service. Thus, in the base model mixing-and-matching will be of relevance under the separate pricing regime only. To the contrary, In Section 4.2, where firms are allowed to employ unilateral mixed bundling, mixing-and-matching will be of central importance. The related mix-and-match literature will be surveyed in Subsection 4.2.1.

[24]As will be seen soon, also θ is a vector.

interval.[25] As a limit case, I assume that tastes are uncorrelated across service types, such that consumers are uniformly distributed on the unit square which is spanned by θ_A and θ_B.[26]

In order to be able to isolate the strategic effect of bundle pricing alone, I assume away any scope economies or consumption dependencies, i.e. complementarity or substitutability across services of different markets.[27] Following an investigation by Crampes and Hollander (2007) this does not pose a limitation: "In the Triple Play case, one can discard the argument of utility super-additivity. Even if the services were complements for the consumer, there is no reason to purchase from a single supplier." Moreover, they note that due to the digital nature of the services, one may assume that the transaction cost argument, by which consumers prefer a 'single bill', is not essential.

Consequently, each consumer's total valuation is linearly separable his valuation for each service. Notwithstanding, since consumers have a positive valuation for exactly one service from each market only, on each market the competitively supplied services are demand substitutes. More precisely, given two distinct service offers $\Gamma_i = (q_i; p_i)$ and $\Gamma_j = (q_j; p_j)$, a consumer, say $\widetilde{\theta}$, will be indifferent between both offers if and only if

$$V_{\widetilde{\theta}}(q_i) - \mathbf{1}p_i = V_{\widetilde{\theta}}(q_j) - \mathbf{1}p_j, \tag{3.2}$$

where $\mathbf{1}$ is a vector of proper length where each element is one.[28] Moreover, the consumers' outside option is normalized to zero, i.e. the consumer indifferent between buying service offer Γ_i (or any suboffer, respectively) and not buying at all, say $\widehat{\theta}$, is determined by:

$$V_{\widehat{\theta}}(q_i) - \mathbf{1}p_i = 0. \tag{3.3}$$

The set of indifferent consumers imposes a demand pattern onto the unit square spanned by θ_A and θ_B. Thus, the demand a firm receives for a specific service (sub-)offer is determined by the area of the unit square in which those consumers are located for whom this offer maximizes utility. In this way, firm i's total demand, $D_i(\Gamma_i, \Gamma_{-i}, \Theta)$ can be represented by a vector, which depends on firm i's own service offer, Γ_i, the service offer of the other firm, Γ_{-i}, and the

---

[25]By this, I implicitly assume that the market is not covered in equilibrium because there will always be some consumers who do not value a given service at its price. This assumption has mainly been made to avoid case differentiations and is not crucial for the the main implications of this model. Incidentally, it also seems reasonable that there are always some consumers which refrain from buying a certain product.

[26]I will argue later in Section 4.3 that uncorrelated tastes are actually a worst-case scenario for the quality sorting effect to occur.

[27]Economies of scope are considered in Section 4.4.

[28]If service offer Γ_i is sold at a bundle price, then $\mathbf{1}$ has one element, otherwise two.

characteristics of the consumers, Θ, which comprises the assumptions about the distribution and correlation of quality preferences. If firm i has chosen a separate pricing strategy, the demand vector contains the demand for every distinct suboffer, $D_i = (D_{Ai}, D_{Bi})$. Conversely, when firm i employs bundle pricing, D_i degenerates to a single value which represents the demand for the pure bundle.

Costs and Profits: I assume that firms' costs of quality improvement fall on fixed costs only (cf. Subsection 2.1.2). Yet, notice that this assumption does not neglect the existence of marginal costs per se, but rather suggests that marginal costs are not influenced by a firm's service quality choice. Clearly, if marginal costs are quality independent, they have no influence on the service quality and merely result in a linear mark-up on prices. Thus, for expositional clarity, I can w.l.o.g. normalize marginal costs to zero. In particular, consider the following cost function for each service:[29]

$$C(q_{mi}) \equiv c\, q_{mi}^{e}, \tag{3.4}$$

where $c > 0$ and $e > 1$ are parameters of the fixed cost function, characterizing its scale and elasticity.[30] Obviously, $C'(\cdot) > 0$ and $C''(\cdot) > 0$, i.e. the cost function is convex such that services of higher qualities are more costly to provide and increasingly so at higher cost levels.

Let $R_i = D_i\, p_i$ be firm i's revenue. Then i's profit, which it seeks to maximize, is given by:

$$\Pi_i \equiv R_i - C(q_{Ai}) - C(q_{Bi}). \tag{3.5}$$

I will relax and deviate from some of the above assumptions in Chapter 4 to show the robustness of my main findings.

It will be convenient to determine the equilibrium of the game specified above in three main steps. First, the separate pricing regime (ss subgame) is considered in isolation, because it forms a special case due to the absence of cross-market effects. Second, the three remaining bundle pricing subgames (bb, bs, and sb) are solved. Third, each firm's equilibrium pricing strategy (stage one of the complete game) is determined on basis of the results of the four subgames.

---

[29] Also in reference to the communications industry, Economides and Lehr (1995) have proposed a similar, although less general, cost function.

[30] I will discuss these latter parameters in more detail shortly.

3.3.2 Separate Pricing Regime

As a point of departure, let us first investigate the subgame that occurs if both firms choose the separate pricing strategy (*ss*). Under this regime, firms assign a separate price to each of their two services such that consumers can mix-and-match an individual service package from the firms' suboffers, possibly containing services of different firms. Clearly, there is no economic link between the markets which could influence firms' or consumers' decisions. Hence, by the home market advantage, the incumbent firm of market m, say h, will provide the high-quality product in m, while the entrant, say l, must content itself with offering the low-quality service here.[31] Consequently, under the separate pricing regime each firm will earn high profits in its home and low profits in its secondary market. Due to the reciprocal market structure with symmetric firms, and in the absence of any cross market effects, firms cannot transport their home market advantage over to their secondary market, and thus both firms will earn identical overall profits.

Proposition 3.1 (Equilibrium and Revenue under Separate Pricing). *Under the separate pricing regime, each firms offers a high-quality service in its home market and a low-quality service in its secondary market. Total revenue is approximated by*

$$R_i^{ss} \approx q_H \left(25 - \frac{28}{3}\mu\right)$$

Proof. The first part follows directly from my assumptions. Thus, the incumbent in market m will be the high-quality provider due to its strategic home market advantage. According to (3.2), the consumer indifferent between assigning to the high and low quality service in market A (B) is located at

$$\widetilde{\theta}_A^{ss} = \frac{p_{A1}^{ss} - p_{A2}^{ss}}{q_H - q_L}, \qquad \left(\widetilde{\theta}_B^{ss} = \frac{p_{B2}^{ss} - p_{B1}^{ss}}{q_H - q_L}\right).$$

Likewise, by (3.3) the consumer indifferent between buying the low-quality service and not buying at all in market A (B) satisfies

$$\widehat{\theta}_{A2}^{ss} = \frac{p_{A2}^{ss}}{q_L}, \qquad \left(\widehat{\theta}_{B1}^{ss} = \frac{p_{B1}^{ss}}{q_L}\right).$$

In particular, it is easy to see that the location of indifferent consumers is independent of the distribution of consumers on the other market. Figure 3.1 visualizes the demand pattern under the separate pricing regime.

---

[31]Recall the differentiation principle which affirms that firms will never choose to offer services of the same quality in equilibrium because this lack of differentiation would otherwise dissipate all profits in the subsequent Bertrand stage.

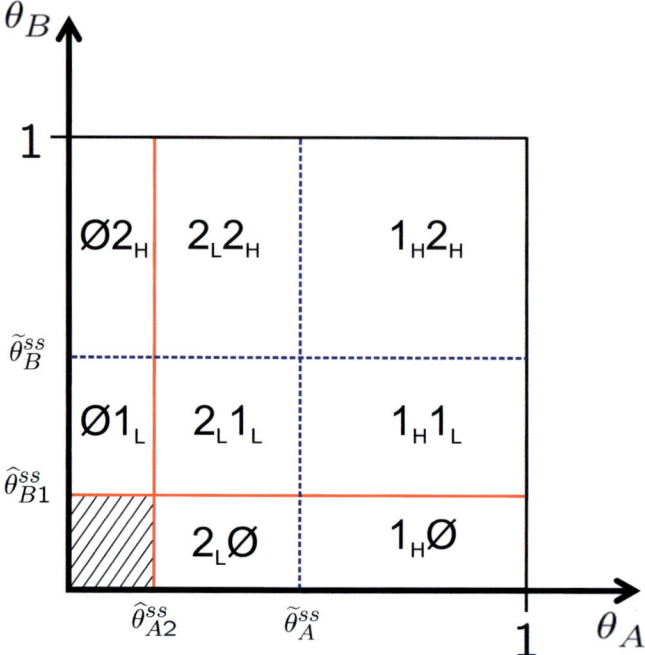

Figure 3.1: *Demand Pattern under the Separate Pricing Regime*

In this and all following visualizations of demand patterns the following convention is made: The first number specifies the firm and service quality (subscript H for high-quality or subscript L for low-quality) which consumers located in this area will buy in market A. Likewise, the second number relates to the firm and service quality bought from the same consumers in market B. If a set of consumers buys nothing in market A (B), then this is denoted by the first (second) number being $\emptyset$.

The absence of cross-market effects allows to consider each market separately. In each market the revenue for the incumbent h (high-quality) and entrant l (low-quality) firm is

$$
\begin{aligned}
R_{mh}^{ss} &= D_{mh}^{ss} \, p_{mh}^{ss} = 100 \quad (1 - \widetilde{\theta}_m^{ss}) \quad p_{mh}^{ss} \\
R_{ml}^{ss} &= D_{ml}^{ss} \, p_{ml}^{ss} = 100 \quad (\widetilde{\theta}_m^{ss} - \widehat{\theta}_{ml}^{ss}) \quad p_{ml}^{ss}.
\end{aligned}
\tag{3.6}
$$

Solving for optimal prices yields:

$$
\begin{aligned}
p_{mh}^{ss*} &= 200 \quad \frac{q_H(q_H - q_L)}{4\,q_H - q_L}, \\
p_{ml}^{ss*} &= 100 \quad \frac{q_L(q_H - q_L)}{4\,q_H - q_L}.
\end{aligned}
\tag{3.7}
$$

By substituting this into the revenue functions, I obtain:[32]

$$
\begin{aligned}
R_{mh}^{ss*} &= 400 \quad \frac{q_H^2(q_H - q_L)}{(4q_H - q_L)^2}, \\
R_{ml}^{ss*} &= 100 \quad \frac{q_H q_L(q_H - q_L)}{(4q_H - q_L)^2}.
\end{aligned}
\tag{3.8}
$$

---

[32] Since each market is considered separately here, this is a standard result (cf. e.g. Motta 1993).

Thus, each firm's total revenue is given by

$$R_i^{ss}(\mu) = R_{mh}^{ss} + R_{ml}^{ss} = q_H \frac{100(1-\mu)(4+\mu)}{(4-\mu)^2}. \tag{3.9}$$

To be able to compare this revenue with others obtained later, I will approximate the revenue function linearly in the feasible range of $\mu \in (0, \frac{1}{4}]$. First, notice that $\frac{\partial R_i^{ss}}{\partial \mu} < 0$. Furthermore $R_i^{ss}(0) = 25 q_H$ and $R_i^{ss}(\frac{1}{4}) = 22\frac{2}{3} q_H$. Thus, under the linear approximation scheme, $R_i^{ss} \approx R_i^{ss}(0) - 4\left(R_i^{ss}(0) - R_i^{ss}(\frac{1}{4})\right)\mu = q_H(25 - \frac{28}{3}\mu)$. $\qquad\square$

I have assumed a rather general cost function in order to show that my results are robust to variations of its parameters. However, to make the analysis yet tractable, I have to consider discrete quality levels as a sacrifice.[33] If firms were to chose quality levels from a continuous set, Lehmann-Grube (1997) has shown that the high-quality advantage principle holds. Consequently, a minimum feasibility requirement one can make is that under the separate pricing regime the high-quality firm earns higher profits than the low-quality provider in any one market. In this vein, I find a constraint governing the relationship between the parameters of the cost function, on the one hand, and the feasible quality levels on the other:

Lemma 3.2 (Feasibility Constraint). *The high-quality advantage principle holds if*

$$\mathscr{C} \equiv \frac{C(q_H) - C(q_L)}{q_H} < 18.75 - 27\mu = \overline{f}(\mu),$$

where $\mu = \frac{q_L}{q_H} \in (0, \frac{1}{4}]$.

Proof. Formally, I must show that under the separate pricing regime the profit of the high-quality provider, Π_{mh}^{ss}, is greater than the profit of the low-quality provider, Π_{ml}^{ss}, for any market m. Substituting the optimal revenue functions (3.8) into the profit functions yields

$$\begin{aligned} \Pi_{mh}^{ss} &= R_{mh}^{ss*} - C(q_H) = 400 \frac{q_H^2(q_H - q_L)}{(4q_H - q_L)^2} - c\, q_H^e, \\ \Pi_{ml}^{ss} &= R_{ml}^{ss*} - C(q_L) = 100 \frac{q_H q_L(q_H - q_L)}{(4q_H - q_L)^2} - c\, q_L^e. \end{aligned} \tag{3.10}$$

To show the lemma I must find a constraint for $\Pi_{mh}^{ss} > \Pi_{ml}^{ss}$, which, by setting $\mu = \frac{q_L}{q_H}$, rewrites to

$$c\, q_H^{e-1}(1 - \mu^e) < 300 \frac{(1-\mu)^2}{(4-\mu)^2}. \tag{3.11}$$

For later comparison, I employ the linear approximation scheme again. To this extend, set $f(\mu) = 300 \frac{(1-\mu)^2}{(4-\mu)^2}$ and notice that $\frac{\partial f}{\partial \mu} < 0$. Furthermore $f(0) = 18.75$ and $f(\frac{1}{4}) = 12$. Thus, the feasibility constraint function, f may be well approximated from above by $\overline{f}(\mu) \approx f(0) - 4\left(f(0) - f(\frac{1}{4})\right)\mu = 18.75 - 27\mu$ and the lemma obtains. $\qquad\square$

---

[33]I will show later that my results also hold if firms choose quality levels endogenously.

Cost Relevance Measure $\mathscr{C}$: Notice that $\mathscr{C} = \frac{C(q_H) - C(q_L)}{q_H}$, which will be in the center of my analysis, is the difference in costs between the high-quality service and the low-quality service, expressed in units of q_H. As such, $\mathscr{C}$ measures how relevant costs are in a firm's decision process. If $\mathscr{C}$ is very small, i.e. the costs for high- and low-quality services differ only very little, firms will offer high-quality services, no matter what the market conditions are, since high-quality services promise higher profits by the high-quality advantage principle. Consequently, if costs are *negligible*, the analysis becomes trivial, because firms must not trade off between revenue and costs.

Conversely, it is in the interest of this model to analyze those settings where costs are *non negligible*.[34] However, intuitively it is also clear, that there should be an upper bound to $\mathscr{C}$, at which costs are so prevalent that the high-quality advantage principle fails to hold and no firm finds it profitable to continue business. Such a bound is identified by Lemma 3.2.

Finally, it is annotated that $\mathscr{C}$ may also be interpreted as a convexity measure of the cost function. To this extend, rewrite $\mathscr{C} = c\, q_H^{e-1}(1 - \mu^e)$. Thereby q_H^{e-1} reflects the convexity of the cost function and c the general magnitude of costs. Obviously, the higher $\mathscr{C}$, the costlier it is for firms to improve their quality. For low values of $\mathscr{C}$, costs rise only slowly with quality because either convexity is mild or costs are generally small, or both. Thus, firms will be able to operate profitably here and high-quality providers generally earn more than their low-quality competitors. As $\mathscr{C}$ increases, cost considerations become increasingly prevalent, until eventually costs are unfeasibly high, i.e. $\mathscr{C} \geq \overline{f}$.

3.3.3 Bundle Pricing Regimes

In contrast to the separate pricing regime, which did not evoke any cross-market effects, bundle pricing of any one firm creates externality on the other market. In order to compare a service bundle with competing service offers, consumers cannot consider each market separately anymore, but must simultaneously assess all offers on the converged markets. I can show that this externality acts as a *quality-leverage device*, which enables one firm to provide a high-quality service on both markets.

Due to the completely symmetric set-up of the model, ex ante either one of the two firms can potentially achieve quality leverage. Hence, there exist at least two symmetric equilibria, which

---

[34]The negligibility threshold is defined later in Proposition 3.8 precisely.

are identical up to permutations of the firms' indices. To fix ideas, I denote the firm which is believed to achieve quality leverage by 1. In other words, for the remainder of this chapter the following hypothesis shall be under consideration:

Hypothesis (Quality Leverage Hypothesis). *Firm 1 achieves greater payoffs under service bundling than under separate selling because bundling enables firm 1 to leverage its quality leadership in market A over to its secondary market B.*

To this extend, asymmetry is introduced into the model in the following two respects:

1.) Firm 1 will choose its pricing decision first, firm 2 can observe firm 1's decision and react optimally. This assumption reflects that firm 1 actively seeks to achieve leverage through its pricing decision. It is annotated that this assumption is not crucial for the quality leverage effect to be feasible. In fact, at the end of my analysis I will show that the equilibrium properties are not altered if firms select their pricing decision simultaneously, as long as costs of quality improvement are non negligible.

2.) Under all bundle pricing regimes, firm 1 is fixed as the high- and firm 2 as the low-quality provider in market A. This assumption resolves the multiplicity of Nash equilibria. It is important to notice, however, that the assumption is without loss of generality. Due to the quality-differentiation principle, firms must differentiate their service qualities in at least one market in equilibrium. Otherwise, if all services would have the same quality, firms would fall prey of the Bertrand price war and obtain zero profits.

Since the quality assignment is being fixed for market A, it is now at the core of this section to investigate the quality choice of firms in market B when firm 1 has chosen a bundle pricing strategy. In total, four scenarios are possible:

Scenario LH: Certainly, if bundling had no effect on the firms' quality decision, firm 1 would choose q_L and firm 2 would choose q_H in market B in equilibrium again. Denote this scenario by LH.

Scenario HL: Conversely, the equilibrium scenario which supports the quality leverage hypothesis the strongest is denoted by HL. Here, firm 1 is able to establish itself as the high-quality seller in market A and B, while simultaneously forcing the other firm into providing a low-quality service in *both* markets.

Scenario HH: Also scenario HH supports the quality leverage hypothesis, although not as strongly as HL. Firm 1 achieves to be the high-quality seller in both markets, but cannot prevent firm 2 from providing a high-quality service in B as well. However, firm 1's profits are expected to be lower than under scenario HL, because firms fail to differentiate their services in market B, which leads to intensified price competition in turn. Call this scenario HH.

Scenario LL: Finally, if both firms choose a low-quality service in equilibrium in market B, scenario LL obtains. Obviously, scenario LL is not very desirable to the firms for two reasons. First, neither firm can benefit from the high-quality advantage in market B. Second, firms do not differentiate their services in market B, like in scenario HH, such that price competition will intensify and lead to diminishing profits. Due to this strategic similarity between scenario HH and LL, it will often be convenient to subsume the two under *scenario XX*.

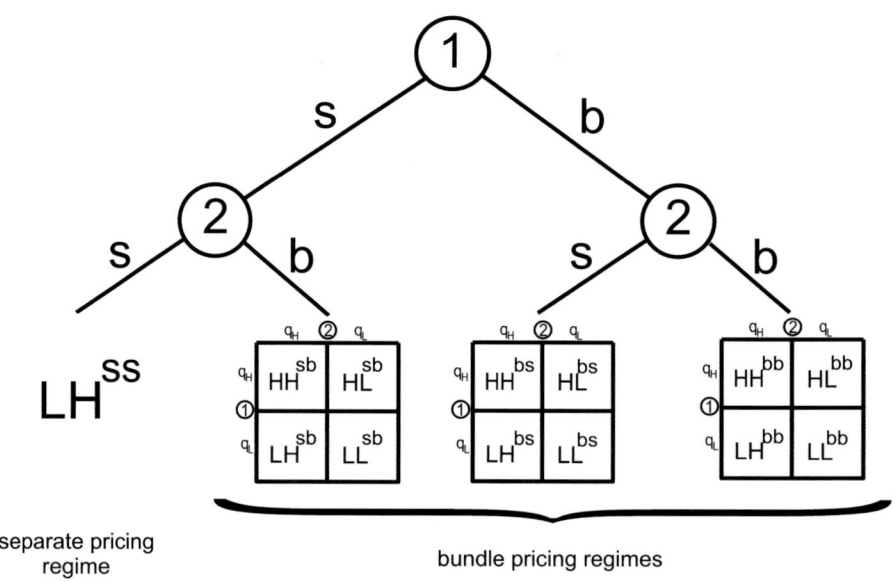

Figure 3.2: *Stylized Game Tree under Sequential Pricing-Strategy Decisions*

With the help of this notation, the whole game can be represented by the stylized game tree shown in Figure 3.2, which can be interpreted as follows: First, firm 1 decides upon its pricing strategy, i.e. whether to bundle (b) or to sell its services separately (s). Subsequently firm 2 can observe this decision and choose its pricing strategy as well. The firms' pricing strategy decision in stage one constitutes either one of the four subgames *ss*, *sb*, *bs* or *bb*. In each subgame, firms decide simultaneously about the quality levels of their services. In the *separate pricing regime (ss)*, there are no cross-market effects and each firm can play out its home market advantage. Thus, in market B, firm 1 is forced into choosing q_L and firm 2 will choose q_H. Therefore only scenario LH is feasible here. In contrast, under the *bundle pricing regimes (sb, bs, bb)* the effect of each firm's respective home market advantage cannot be isolated ex ante and is thus determined endogenously within the game. Since the quality assignment for services in market A is fixed exogenously, the firms' quality decision in each bundle pricing subgame degenerates to a normal form game, which reflects the firm's quality decision in market B. Each of these normal form games can be represented by a bimatrix like Table 3.1. Finally, given the quality decision in each subgame, firms simultaneously choose

Market	Firm 2	
B	q_H	q_L
Firm 1 q_H	$\Pi_1(HH)$ $\Pi_2(HH)$	$\Pi_1(HL)$ $\Pi_2(HL)$
q_L	$\Pi_1(LH)$ $\Pi_2(LH)$	$\Pi_1(LL)$ $\Pi_2(LL)$

Table 3.1: *Bundle Pricing Subgame: Quality Decisions in Market B*

prices, either for the pure bundle or for each service separately. In this way, LH^{ss} as well as each scenario of each bundle pricing subgame implies an underlying Bertrand price game. Thus, in total 13 Bertrand price subgames have to be investigated. This is a very tedious and cumbersome task and therefore I have abandoned parts of the proof to the appendix for the sake of readability. Within the following subsections, I will consider each bundle pricing subgame separately.

Bundle vs. Bundle Pricing Regime

In this subsection, I consider the subgame where both firms have chosen a bundle pricing strategy in the first stage of the game (*bb*). Before I can investigate each of the four scenarios (HH, HL, LH, LL) independently, I must introduce some common notation. First, as already mentioned, I set $q_{A1} = q_H$ and $q_{A2} = q_L$ under all bundling regimes w.l.o.g. in order to avoid multiplicity of equilibria. Of course all results also hold for the symmetric case where firm 2 would be the designated high-quality firm in market B. The consumers indifferent between firm 1's and 2's bundle lie on the line

$$\widetilde{\theta}_B^{bb} = \frac{p_1^{bb} - p_2^{bb}}{q_{B1} - q_{B2}} - \theta_A \frac{q_H - q_L}{q_{B1} - q_{B2}},$$

where p_i^{bb} denotes the price of firm i's bundle. The consumers indifferent between buying bundle 1 or 2 at all are located along

$$\widehat{\theta}_{B1}^{bb} = \frac{p_1^{bb}}{q_{B1}} - \theta_A \frac{q_H}{q_{B1}} \qquad \text{and}$$

$$\widehat{\theta}_{B2}^{bb} = \frac{p_2^{bb}}{q_{B2}} - \theta_A \frac{q_L}{q_{B2}},$$

respectively. The locus of consumers indifferent between all three choices (if existent) is $L^{bb} = (L_A^{bb}, L_B^{bb})$, with

$$L_A^{bb} = \frac{p_1^{bb} \, q_{B2} - p_2^{bb} \, q_{B1}}{q_H \, q_{B2} - q_L \, q_{B1}} \qquad \text{and}$$

$$L_B^{bb} = \frac{p_2^{bb} \, q_H - p_1^{bb} \, q_L}{q_H \, q_{B2} - q_L \, q_{B1}}.$$

Notice that the indifferent consumers are now determined by their tastes for *both* service types. These cross-market effects are responsible for the existence of the quality leverage effect.

Next, I will try to give some intuition for the price competition evolving in each of the scenarios. I will employ the visualizations of the demand patterns here to undermine my analysis. The quantitative results are summarized by the subsequent lemmas whose proofs may be found in the appendix.

Scenario LH^{bb}: I start with the investigation of the LH^{bb} scenario because it represents a short-term transition stage between the separate- and bundle pricing regime which would obtain if firms did not alter quality-levels but only prices. Figure 3.3 shows the corresponding demand pattern. I addition to the already introduced notation labeling the different demand areas, I use the convention to put parenthesis around the two numbers if the service is offered in a bundle. Scenario LH^{bb} is characterized by perfect symmetry. Each firm is the high-quality provider in its home market and the low-quality provider in its foreign market. The corresponding bundles are therefore a mix of high-and low quality services and very similar in nature. Consequently, price competition is rather intense, because a small change in price may induce many consumers to switch bundles. However, due to symmetry, in equilibrium both firms must offer the same price for their bundles and will consequently earn the same profits. The consumers being

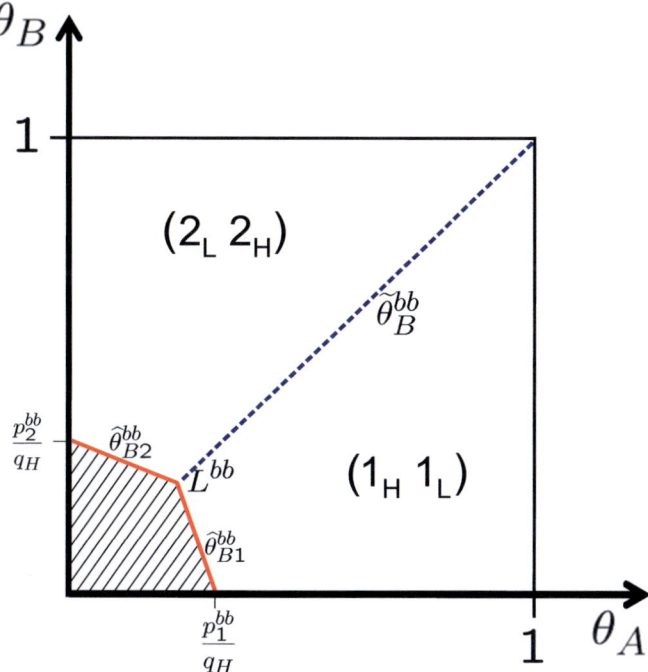

Figure 3.3: *Bundle Pricing Subgame: Scenario LH^{bb}*

Bundles offers are denoted by parenthesis in this and all following visualizations of demand patterns.

indifferent between both service bundles are thus located along the angle bisecting line. Furthermore, the lack of differentiation in the vertical dimension will keep prices and consequently revenues rather low.

Scenario HL^{bb}: Next, assume the quality-sorting effect holds and firm 1 emerges as the high- and firm 2 the low-quality provider in both markets. Then the demand pattern looks as in Figure 3.4. In this scenario price competition is much weaker than under LH^{bb} because firms' bundles are now maximally differentiated. One firm has specialized on serving the low-quality end of the market, whereas the other firm serves the high-quality loving consumers. This segmentation of the consumer space allows for more inelasticity in prices. Of course, due to the high-quality advantage principle, the revenues of both firms are not equal anymore and firm 1 will be much better off than firm 2. I will soon show, however, that this setting can nevertheless be achieved by firm 1 in equilibrium when it pursues a bundle pricing strategy.

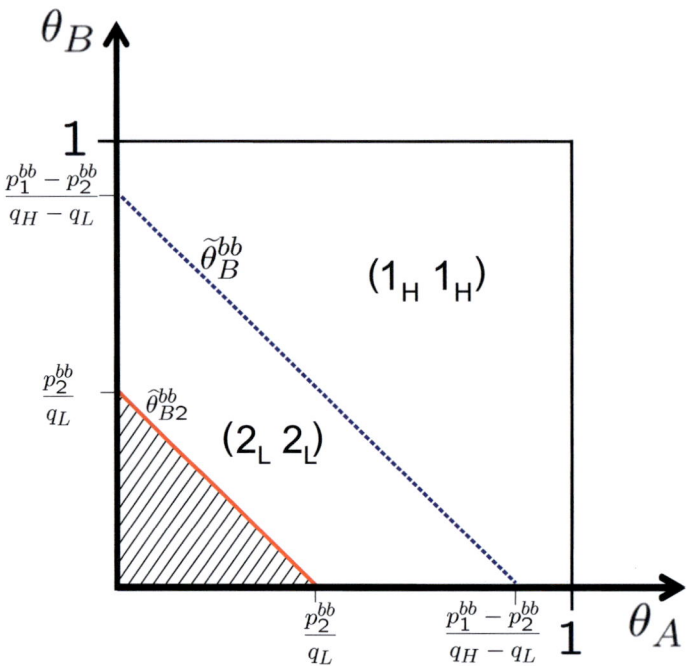

Figure 3.4: *Bundle Pricing Subgame: Scenario HL^{bb}*

Scenarios HH^{bb} and LL^{bb}:   Finally, I must consider the case where firms do not differentiate their products in market B. Say both firms provide a service of quality $q_X \in \{q_H, q_L\}$ in B.
The corresponding demand pattern is given by Figure 3.5. In this scenario, the consumers indifferent between both scenarios are all characterized by the same taste for quality in market A,
because firms fail to differentiate their services in market B. Price competition is at an intermediate level and largely determined the by the degree of differentiation in market A. Of course,
due to the high-quality advantage principle, scenario HH generates higher revenues than scenario LL. However, for price equilibria to exist in these scenarios, at least firms' services in
market A must be sufficiently differentiated.

Lemma 3.3 shows that the existence of interior price equilibria for these four scenarios
generally requires a minimum amount of service differentiation.

Lemma 3.3 (Price Equilibrium Feasibility Constraints: Pure Bundling). *Interior price equilibria exist only if quality levels are sufficiently differentiated. Scenario HL^{bb} is feasible for
$q_H > 1.77\, q_L$, scenario HH^{bb} for $q_H > 2.31\, q_L$, scenario LH^{bb} for $q_H > q_L$ and scenario
LL^{bb} for $q_H > 3.73\, q_L$.*

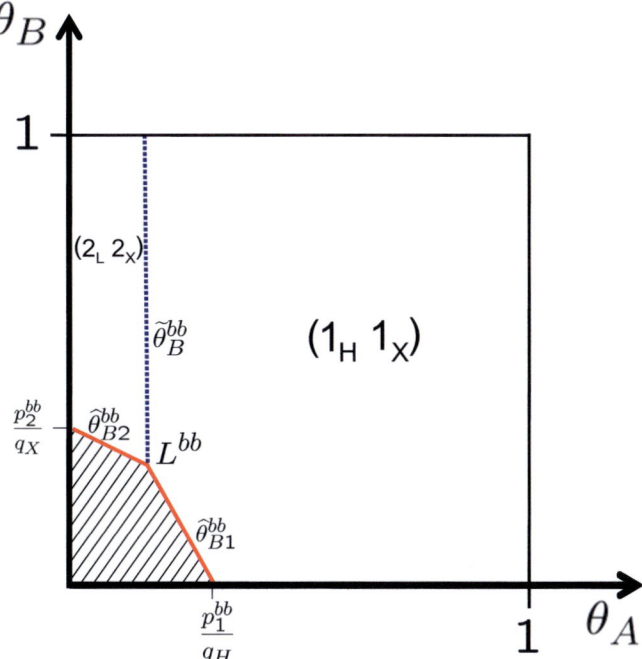

Figure 3.5: *Bundle Pricing Subgame: Scenarios HH^{bb} and LL^{bb}*

Proof. See Appendix. □

The reader may now understand why $q_H \geq 4\, q_L$ is actually an unfavorable assumption, because it ensures the existence of all four scenarios of the *bb* subgame. As q_L approaches q_H further, the equilibria where both firms provide the same service quality in market B gradually cease to exist. This is intuitively clear, since services must be sufficiently differentiated in market A, if firms fail to distinguish their services in market B. Scenarios HL^{bb} and LH^{bb}, on the contrary, continue to hold under significantly less service differentiation. Also keep in mind that the conditions in Lemma 3.3 are only necessary, because quality levels are exogenous. If firms would choose quality levels freely, the classical literature on vertical differentiation has shown that sufficient differentiation arises endogenously, such that interior price equilibria generally exist.

Now, let us turn to a more quantitative analysis of the *bb*-subgame.

Lemma 3.4 (Revenues in the *bb*-subgame). *The revenue of firm i in each scenario of the bb-*

subgame, denoted by R_i^{bb}, can be well approximated by

$$
\begin{aligned}
R_1^{bb}(HH) &= q_H\,(36.88 - 28\mu) & , & \quad R_2^{bb}(HH) &= q_H\,(6.71 - 1.54\mu) \\
R_1^{bb}(HL) &= q_H\,(54.41 - 29.06\mu) & , & \quad R_2^{bb}(HL) &= q_H\,8.62\,\mu \\
R_i^{bb}(LH) &= q_H\,(17.16 - 3.84\mu) \\
R_1^{bb}(LL) &= q_H\,(25 - 1.50\mu) & , & \quad R_2^{bb}(LL) &= q_H\,14.54\,\mu
\end{aligned}
$$

Proof. See Appendix. □

In particular notice that firms' revenue depends on q_H and $q_L = \mu\,q_H$ only and generally increases with quality. In order to determine the quality equilibrium of the bundle pricing regime subgames, I must now define a function $BR_i(q_{-i})$, which returns firm i's best quality response in market B, given the quality decision of her opponent, $-i$. The pure quality Nash-equilibrium of each subgame is then given by a set of qualities (q_i, q_{-i}), from which neither firm wishes to deviate unilaterally, i.e. $BR_i\left(BR_{-i}(q_i)\right) = q_i, \forall i$.

Lemma 3.5 (Best Quality Responses in the bb-subgame)**.** *In the bb-subgame, each firms best quality response function BR_i^{bb} is*

$$
\begin{aligned}
BR_1^{bb}(q_L) &=
\begin{cases}
q_H, & \text{if} \quad \mathscr{C} \le \bar{r}_1^{bb}(q_L) = 29.41 - 27.56\mu \\
q_L, & \text{otherwise}
\end{cases} \\[2mm]
BR_1^{bb}(q_H) &=
\begin{cases}
q_H, & \text{if} \quad \mathscr{C} \le \bar{r}_1^{bb}(q_H) = 19.72 - 24.16\mu \\
q_L, & \text{otherwise}
\end{cases} \\[2mm]
BR_2^{bb}(q_L) &=
\begin{cases}
q_H, & \text{if} \quad \mathscr{C} \le \bar{r}_2^{bb}(q_L) = 17.16 - 18.37\mu \\
q_L, & \text{otherwise}
\end{cases} \\[2mm]
BR_2^{bb}(q_H) &=
\begin{cases}
q_H, & \text{if} \quad \mathscr{C} \le \bar{r}_2^{bb}(q_H) = 6.71 - 10.16\mu \\
q_L, & \text{otherwise}
\end{cases}
\end{aligned}
$$

For all $\mu \in (0, \frac{1}{4}]$ it holds that the threshold functions, $\bar{r}$, can be uniquely ranked as $\bar{r}_2^{bb}(q_H) < \bar{r}_2^{bb}(q_L) < \bar{r}_1^{bb}(q_H) < \bar{r}_1^{bb}(q_L)$.

Proof. The best response function determines whether it is best to reply with a high- or low quality service, given the quality level of the opponents' service. Consider firm 1, for example. If firm 2 offers a service of quality $q_X \in \{q_H, q_L\}$ in market B, firm 1 will respond with a high-quality service iff $\Pi_1(HX) \ge \Pi_1(LX)$. Rearranging this inequality yields

$$
c\,(q_H^e - q_L^e) \le R_1(HX) - R_1(LX)
$$

Moreover, we know from Lemma 3.4 that the revenue functions follow the basic form of $R_i = q_H\, g_i(\mu)$, such that a division by q_H together with substituting $q_L = \mu\, q_H$ yields

$$c\, q_H^{e-1}(1 - \mu^e) \leq \bar{r}_1,$$

where the left hand side is $\mathscr{C} = \frac{C(q_H) - C(q_L)}{q_H}$ and the right hand side corresponds to the threshold function $\bar{r}_1 = \frac{R_1(HX) - R_1(LX)}{q_H}$. Of course, the same holds analogously for firm 2. The lemma then follows trivially from Lemma 3.4. To see how well the linear approximations of Lemma 3.4 resemble the original function, Figure A.1 in the appendix shows a comparison of both. □

Lemma 3.4 has two important implications.

First, notice that the threshold functions may be uniquely ranked in terms of $\mathscr{C}$, however independent of μ and e. Consequently, the Nash-equilibrium of the bb-subgame depends only on the general size of the cost relevance measure, $\mathscr{C}$, and not on the precise relationship between q_H and q_L. Consequently, although I have simplified the analysis by fixing the quality levels exogenously, I obtain qualitatively identical results as if quality levels were chosen endogenously. This gives rise to the following corollary.

Corollary 3.6 (Exogeneity Independence). *The pure quality strategy equilibria of the bb-subgame are independent of whether quality levels are exogenously given or endogenously chosen from a continuous set.*

Second, note that the feasibility constraint function identified by Lemma 3.2, $\bar{f}$, satisfies

$$\bar{r}_2(q_H) < \bar{f} < \bar{r}_1(q_H) < \bar{r}_1(q_L), \qquad \forall \mu \in (0, \tfrac{1}{4}]$$

which means that the range of feasible $\mathscr{C}$-values is cut-off at a level below the threshold functions, $\bar{r}_1$, of firm 1. The next corollary follows immediately.

Corollary 3.7 (High-Quality Commitment). *For all feasible values of $\mathscr{C}$, firm 1 chooses q_H in market B as a dominant strategy in the bb-subgame.*

Corollary 3.7 refers to the *high-quality commitment* effect of bundle pricing. Providing a high-quality service in market B is a credible strategy for the high-quality provider in market A, irrespective of the precise fixed cost function. This shows very impressively how powerful the bundle pricing strategy may act as a *quality leverage device*.

In an effort to determine the pure strategy Nash equilibria of the bb-subgame, I will consider all feasible settings of $\mathscr{C}$ in turn. If costs are negligible, i.e $\mathscr{C} < \bar{r}_2^{bb}(q_H)$, the HH^{bb} scenario is the unique equilibrium. Here costs have only small impact on the quality decision and thus both firms strive toward offering a high-quality service, i.e. $BR_i(q_H) = q_H, \forall i$.

When $\mathscr{C}$ increases, such that $\bar{r}_2^{bb}(q_H) < \mathscr{C} \le \min\{\bar{r}_2^{bb}(q_L), \bar{f}\}$,[35] cost considerations become more prominent, such that scenario HL is the robust unique equilibrium outcome of the bundle pricing bb-subgame for all remaining settings: More precisely, if $\bar{r}_2^{bb}(q_H) < \mathscr{C} \le \bar{r}_2^{bb}(q_L)$, firm 2 will reply with $BR_2(q_H) = q_L$ and $BR_2(q_L) = q_H$ in this parameter range. However, since firm 1 will offer a high-quality service as a dominant strategy, HL^{bb} is the unique equilibrium scenario here. Likewise, should $\bar{r}_2^{bb}(q_L) < \mathscr{C} < \bar{f}$ hold, firm 2 will provide a low-quality service in market B as a dominant strategy, irrespective of firm 1's quality choice. That is, in this parameter range firm 1's high-quality commitment effect is coupled with a *low-quality commitment effect* of firm 2. Consequently, scenario HL^{bb} remains the unique quality equilibrium of the bb-subgame here, even in dominant strategies.

Proposition 3.8 (Quality Equilibria of the bb-subgame).

Non Negligible Costs: *If costs of quality improvement are non negligible, i.e. $\mathscr{C} > \bar{r}_2^{bb}(q_H)$,* ***Scenario*** HL^{bb}*obtains as the unique pure strategy quality equilibrium of the bb-subgame.*

Negligible Costs: *If costs of quality improvement are negligible, i.e. $\mathscr{C} \le \bar{r}_2^{bb}(q_H)$,* ***Scenario*** HH^{bb}*obtains as the unique pure strategy quality equilibrium of the bb-subgame.*

Bundle vs. Separate Pricing Subgame

In order to show that the strong results obtained under a bundle vs. bundle pricing regime extend to hybrid pricing regimes, I consider the bundle vs. separate pricing subgame next. Here firm one has chosen a bundle pricing strategy, whereas firm 2 seeks to counteract the leverage efforts of firm 1 by selling its services separately. Since the course of proofs is analogous to the bb-subgame, I will keep the analysis as concise as possible.[36] All variables of this subgame will be denoted by a superscript bs to indicate the *bundle vs. separate* pricing regime.

---

[35]Precisely, $\min\{\bar{r}_2^{bb}(q_L), \bar{f}\} = \bar{r}_2^{bb}(q_L)$ iff $\mu < 0.18$ and $\bar{f}$ otherwise.

[36]Of course, details are available in the appendix.

In this subgame consumers have the choice of five different service portfolios: They may buy firm 1's bundle, firm 2's services separately (either one or both) or refrain from purchasing any service. I must therefore distinguish the following indifferent consumers:[37]

Consumers indifferent between buying firm 1's bundle and firm 2's A-service satisfy

$$\widetilde{\theta}_B^{bs+} = \frac{p_1^{bs} - p_{A2}^{bs}}{q_{B1}} - \theta_A \frac{q_H - q_L}{q_{B1}}.$$

Consumers indifferent between buying firm 1's bundle and firm 2's B-service only are located at

$$\widetilde{\theta}_B^{bs++} = \frac{p_1^{bs} - p_{B2}^{bs}}{q_{B1} - q_{B2}} - \theta_A \frac{q_H}{q_{B1} - q_{B2}}.$$

Consumers indifferent between buying firm 1's bundle and each of firm 2's services separately lie along

$$\widetilde{\theta}_B^{bs+++} = \frac{p_1^{bs} - p_{A2}^{bs} - p_{B2}^{bs}}{q_{B1} - q_{B2}} - \theta_A \frac{q_H - q_L}{q_{B1} - q_{B2}}.$$

Finally, the locus of consumers indifferent between buying firm 1's bundle and either firm 2's A-service or both services of firm 2, i.e. where $\widehat{\theta}_B^{bs+} = \widehat{\theta}_B^{bs+++}$ is given by $L^{bs} = (L_A^{bs}, L_B^{bs})$, where

$$L_A^{bs} = \frac{q_{B2} \left(p_1^{bs} - p_{A2}^{bs} \right) - q_{B1} \, p_{B2}^{bs}}{(q_H - q_L) \, q_{B2}}, \qquad\qquad L_B^{bs} = \frac{p_{B2}^{bs}}{q_{B2}}.$$

Figure 3.6 shows the demand patterns for each of the scenarios of the bs-subgame. Before I turn to the quantitative analysis of the above scenarios, I will try to give some qualitative intuition concerning the nature of the price competition again.

This time the LH^{bs} scenario is not perfectly symmetric because the firms employ different pricing strategies. Although both firms offer a high-quality service in their home market and a low-quality service in their secondary market, the use of different pricing strategies creates some artificial differentiation between the firms' service portfolios. Hence, we may already conclude from Figure 3.6(a) that price competition is less intense than under LH^{bb}. However, by offering its services separately, firm 2 induces some self-inflicted competition among its own services. We may thus conjecture that firm 2's revenues are lower under LH^{bs} as compared with LH^{bb}. Consequently, counteracting firm 1's bundling strategy by a separate selling strategy may not be firm 2's best choice when it simultaneously tries to prevail its high-quality leadership in market B.

---

[37]Not all of these indifferent consumers may be of importance in all of the subsequent scenarios. Recall that quality assignments in market A are held fixed as $q_{A1} = q_H$ and $q_{A2} = q_L$.

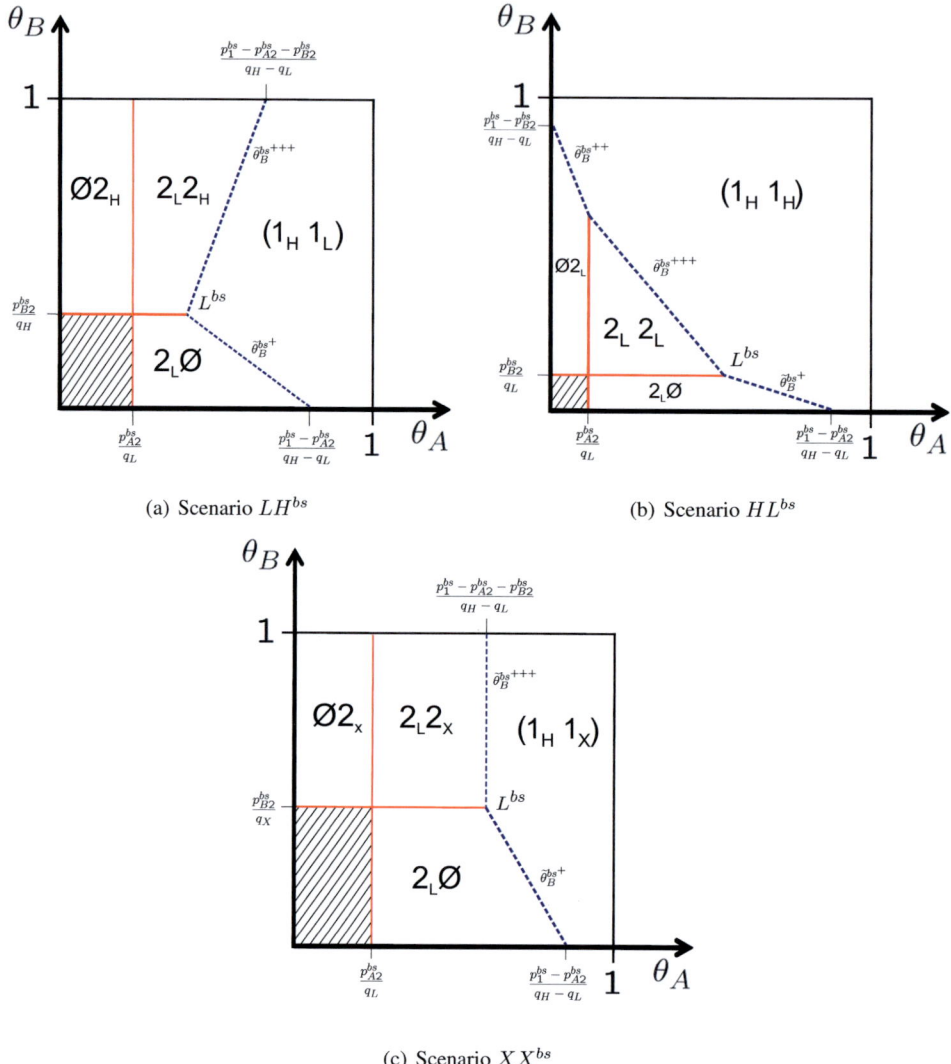

(a) Scenario LH^{bs} (b) Scenario HL^{bs}

(c) Scenario XX^{bs}

Figure 3.6: *Bundle Pricing Subgame: (a) Scenario LH^{bs}, (b) Scenario HL^{bs} (c) Scenarios HH^{bs} and LL^{bs}*

Next, consider scenario HL^{bs}. Figure 3.6(b) shows that although firm 1's bundle competes against more distinct service portfolios, the nature of competition is very similar to that from HL^{bb}: Firm 1 serves the high-quality consumer segment, whereas firm 2 offers low-quality services. By offering its services separately, firm 2 induces some self-inflicted competition again, however, on the other side it also seems to capture some more consumers by doing so (especially those with extreme differences in θ across markets). In summary, we can expect revenues akin to those in HL^{bb}.

Similar holds for the scenarios XX^{bs}, where firms offer the same service quality in market B. Again, firm 1 is able to attract the most valuable consumers with high θ values in both markets and will therefore achieve higher revenues. By its separate pricing strategy, firm 2 is able to steal some demand in the low θ_B segment, but also suffers from self-inflicted competition again.

The corresponding quantitative analysis may be found in the appendix and is summarized by the following lemmas.

Lemma 3.9 (Revenues in the bs-subgame). *The revenue of firm i in each scenario of the bs-subgame can be well approximated by*

$$
\begin{aligned}
R_1^{bs}(HH) &= q_H\,(36.9 - 30.56\mu) &,\quad R_2^{bs}(HH) &= q_H\,(6.71 - 3.28\mu) \\
R_1^{bs}(HL) &= q_H\,(54.41 - 31.36\mu) &,\quad R_2^{bs}(HL) &= q_H\,6.65\,\mu \\
R_1^{bs}(LH) &= q_H\,(35.09 - 27\mu) &,\quad R_2^{bs}(LH) &= q_H\,(5.88 - 1.69\mu) \\
R_1^{bs}(LL) &= q_H\,(25 - 0.95\mu) &,\quad R_2^{bs}(LL) &= q_H\,13.47\,\mu
\end{aligned}
$$

Proof. See Appendix. □

Lemma 3.10 (Best Quality Responses in the bs-subgame). *In the bs-subgame, each firm's best quality response function is*

$$
BR_1^{bs}(q_L) = \begin{cases} q_H, & \text{if} \quad \mathscr{C} \leq \bar{r}_1^{bs}(q_L) = 29.41 - 30.41\mu \\[2mm] q_L, & \text{otherwise} \end{cases}
$$

$$
BR_1^{bs}(q_H) = \begin{cases} q_H, & \text{if} \quad \mathscr{C} \leq \bar{r}_1^{bs}(q_H) = 1.81 - 3.56\mu \\[2mm] q_L, & \text{otherwise} \end{cases}
$$

$$
BR_2^{bs}(q_L) = \begin{cases} q_H, & \text{if} \quad \mathscr{C} \leq \bar{r}_2^{bs}(q_L) = 5.88 - 15.16\mu \\[2mm] q_L, & \text{otherwise} \end{cases}
$$

$$
BR_2^{bs}(q_H) = \begin{cases} q_H, & \text{if} \quad \mathscr{C} \leq \bar{r}_2^{bs}(q_H) = 6.71 - 9.93\mu \\[2mm] q_L, & \text{otherwise} \end{cases}
$$

For all $\mu \in (0, \frac{1}{4}]$ it holds that the threshold functions, $\bar{r}$, can be uniquely ranked as $\bar{r}_1^{bs}(q_H) < \bar{r}_2^{bs}(q_L) < \bar{r}_2^{bs}(q_H) < \bar{f} < \bar{r}_1^{bs}(q_L)$.

Proof. Analogous to Lemma 3.5 □

Lemma 3.10 reveals two major differences of the sb-subgame compared to the bb-subgame.

First, due to the asymmetry and resulting weak price competition in scenario LH^{bs}, firm 1 is able to achieve much higher revenues here. Consequently, LH^{bs} is much more appealing to firm 1 such that $BR_1^{bs}(q_H) = q_L$ at small $\mathscr{C}$ values already. Likewise, compared to LH^{bb}, firm 2 is worse off in scenario LH^{bs}, which in turn raises the attractiveness of scenario LL^{bs} for firm 2. Therefore $BR_2^{bs}(q_L) = q_L$ holds for much lower values of $\mathscr{C}$ than before. The remaining best response functions have changed only little in comparison to the bb-subgame.

Second, the diminishing revenue differences across neighboring scenarios also disposes firm 1's high quality commitment effect. In fact, $BR_1^{bs}(q_H) = q_L$ already holds for very relatively low values of $\mathscr{C}$, such that scenario LH^{bs} obtains as the equilibrium of the bs-subgame in the range $\bar{r}_1^{bs}(q_H) < \mathscr{C} \leq \bar{r}_2^{bs}(q_L)$.

If cost considerations become more prominent, i.e. $\mathscr{C} > \bar{r}_2^{bs}(q_L)$, scenario HL^{bs} is the unique equilibrium of the sb-subgame again. To see this consider $\bar{r}_2^{bs}(q_H) > \mathscr{C} > \bar{r}_2^{bs}(q_L)$ first. Here scenario LH^{bs} cannot be sustained in equilibrium anymore, because firm 2 wishes to deviate into LL^{bs}. LL^{bs} is not an equilibrium either, however, as $BR_1^{bs}(q_L) = q_H$, leads to scenario HL^{bs}. When costs rise further to $\bar{f} > \mathscr{C} > \bar{r}_2^{bs}(q_H)$, firm 2's low-quality commitment effect is viable again and HL^{bs} can be sustained in equilibrium as firm 1 will choose $BR_1^{bs}(q_L) = q_H$ while firm 2 responds with $BR_2^{bs}(q_H) = q_L$.

Finally, notice that there exists no pure strategy quality equilibrium in the range $\bar{r}_2^{bs}(q_L) < \mathscr{C} \leq \bar{r}_2^{bs}(q_L)$. The borderline between negligible and non negligible cost levels as specified by Proposition 3.8, namely $\bar{r}_2^{bb}(q_H)$, also falls in this range. This proves the following proposition.

Proposition 3.11 (Equilibria of the bs-subgame).

Non Negligible Costs: *If costs of quality improvement are non negligible (in the sense of Proposition 3.8)* **Scenario HL^{bs}** *obtains as the unique pure strategy quality equilibrium of the bs-subgame.*

Negligible Costs: *The unique pure strategy quality equilibrium is constituted by* **Scenario LH^{bs},** *if $\bar{r}_1^{bs}(q_H) < \mathscr{C} \leq \bar{r}_2^{bs}(q_L)$. Otherwise, if $\mathscr{C} \leq \bar{r}_1^{bs}(q_H)$,* **Scenario HH^{bs}** *obtains.*

Separate vs. Bundle Pricing Regime

The separate vs. bundle pricing regime (sb-subgame) obtains when firm 1 chooses a separate pricing strategy and firm 2 a bundle pricing strategy.

Lemma 3.12 (Revenues in the sb-subgame). *Revenues in the bs-subgame can be well approximated by*

$$
\begin{aligned}
R_1^{sb}(HH) &= q_H\,(25 - 11.32\mu) & , & \quad R_2^{sb}(HH) &= q_H\,(8\mu) \\
R_1^{sb}(HL) &= q_H\,(50.72 - 27.43\mu) & , & \quad R_2^{sb}(HL) &= q_H\,6.09\,\mu \\
R_1^{sb}(LH) &= q_H\,(5.88 - 1.69\mu) & , & \quad R_2^{sb}(LH) &= q_H\,(35.09 - 27\mu) \\
R_1^{sb}(LL) &= q_H\,(25 - 13.58\mu) & , & \quad R_2^{bs}(LL) &= q_H\,7.26\,\mu
\end{aligned}
$$

Proof. First notice that scenario LH^{sb} is identical to scenario LH^{bs}, just with the role of each firm interchanged. Thus, equilibrium revenues in LH^{bs} can be derived from Lemma 3.9 and by interchanging firms' indices. The rest of the proof may be found in the appendix. $\qquad\square$

Furthermore, best responses are given by:

Lemma 3.13 (Best Quality Responses in the sb-subgame). *In the sb-subgame, each firm's best quality response function is*

$$
\begin{aligned}
BR_1^{sb}(q_L) &= \begin{cases} q_H, & \text{if} \quad \mathscr{C} \le \bar{r}_1^{sb}(q_L) = 25.72 - 13.85\mu \\[2mm] q_L, & \text{otherwise} \end{cases} \\[4mm]
BR_1^{sb}(q_H) &= \begin{cases} q_H, & \text{if} \quad \mathscr{C} \le \bar{r}_1^{sb}(q_H) = 19.12 - 9.63\mu \\[2mm] q_L, & \text{otherwise} \end{cases} \\[4mm]
BR_2^{sb}(q_L) &= \begin{cases} q_H, & \text{if} \quad \mathscr{C} \le \bar{r}_2^{sb}(q_L) = 35.09 - 34.26\mu \\[2mm] q_L, & \text{otherwise} \end{cases} \\[4mm]
BR_2^{sb}(q_H) &= \begin{cases} q_H, & \text{if} \quad \mathscr{C} \le \bar{r}_2^{sb}(q_H) = 1.91\mu \\[2mm] q_L, & \text{otherwise} \end{cases}
\end{aligned}
$$

For all $\mu \in (0, \frac{1}{4}]$ it holds that the threshold functions, $\bar{r}$, can be uniquely ranked as $\bar{r}_2^{sb}(q_H) < \bar{f} < \bar{r}_1^{sb}(q_H) < \bar{r}_1^{sb}(q_L) < \bar{r}_2^{sb}(q_L)$.

Proof. Analogous to Lemma 3.5 $\qquad\square$

In particular notice, that firm 1 will choose q_H as a dominant strategy for all feasible values of $\mathscr{C}$. The next proposition then follows immediately.

Proposition 3.14 (Equilibria of the sb-subgame).

Non Negligible Costs: *If costs of quality improvement are non negligible (in the sense of Proposition 3.8)* **Scenario HL^{sb}** *obtains as the unique pure strategy quality equilibrium of the sb-subgame.*

Negligible Costs: *The unique pure strategy quality equilibrium is constituted by* **Scenario HH^{sb}**, *if $\mathscr{C} \leq \bar{r}_2^{sb}(q_H)$. Otherwise,* **Scenario HL^{bs}** *obtains.*

3.3.4 Equilibrium Pricing Strategies

The previous two subsections have established the pure strategy price equilibria (stage three) and quality equilibria (stage two) for all feasible values of the cost relevance measure $\mathscr{C}$. These results are summarized by Table 3.2 Therein, six different regions of $\mathscr{C}$ from zero to $\overline{f}$ are differentiated. Each of these regions represents a different set of quality equilibrium scenarios, comprised from each of the four subgames. In particular, note that regions V and VI represent the interval of $\mathscr{C}$ where costs are considered non negligible in the sense of Proposition 3.8. Conversely, regions I through IV represent the interval where firms consider costs negligible, i.e. $\mathscr{C} \leq \bar{r}_2^{bb}(q_H)$.

Costs			Pricing Subgame			
		$\mathscr{C}$	bb	bs	sb	ss
negligible	I:	$\mathscr{C} \leq \bar{r}_2^{sb}(q_H)$	HH^{bb}	HH^{bs}	HH^{sb}	LH^{ss}
	II:	$\bar{r}_2^{sb}(q_H) < \mathscr{C} \leq \bar{r}_1^{bs}(q_H)$	HH^{bb}	HH^{bs}	HL^{sb}	LH^{ss}
	III:	$\bar{r}_1^{bs}(q_H) < \mathscr{C} \leq \bar{r}_2^{bs}(q_L)$	HH^{bb}	LH^{bs}	HL^{sb}	LH^{ss}
	IV:	$\bar{r}_2^{bs}(q_L) < \mathscr{C} \leq \bar{r}_2^{bb}(q_H)$	HH^{bb}	N/A	HL^{sb}	LH^{ss}
	V:	$\bar{r}_2^{bb}(q_H) < \mathscr{C} \leq \bar{r}_2^{bs}(q_H)$	HL^{bb}	N/A	HL^{sb}	LH^{ss}
	VI:	$\bar{r}_2^{bs}(q_H) < \mathscr{C} < \overline{f}$	HL^{bb}	HL^{bs}	HL^{sb}	LH^{ss}

Table 3.2: *Overview of Quality Equilibrium Scenarios*

Table 3.2 displays which equilibrium scenario will obtain in each of the four possible pricing strategy subgames for each of the six feasible regions of $\mathscr{C}$. In order to determine each firm's equilibrium pricing strategy, it is convenient to examine the case of non negligible cost and negligible costs separately.

Non Negligible Costs

Consider the case of non negligible costs of quality improvement first, i.e $\mathscr{C} > \bar{r}_2^{bb}(q_H)$. Table 3.2 shows quite impressively that scenario HL will obtain under *all* bundle pricing regimes. In other words, whenever *any* of the two firms chooses a bundle pricing strategy, firm 1 will emerge as the high-quality provider in market A and B, while firm 2 provides low-quality services in both markets. Only the separate pricing regime results in a symmetric quality distribution as each firm provides a high-quality service in its home and a low-quality service in its secondary market. However, due to the high-quality advantage, firm 1 is much better off in any of the HL scenarios than under separate pricing. This is expressed by the following lemma.

Lemma 3.15 (Dominance of Bundle Pricing under Non Negligible Costs). *Firm 1 will choose bundle pricing as a dominant strategy if costs of quality improvement are non negligible.*

Proof. Obviously firm 1 faces the same costs in all HL scenarios, such that higher revenues translate directly into higher profits. Thus, by Lemmas 3.4, 3.9 and 3.12 $\Pi_1^{bb}(HL) > \Pi_1^{bs}(HL) > \Pi_1^{sb}(HL)$. Finally, by Lemmas 3.12 and 3.4 see that $\Pi_1^{sb}(HL) > \Pi_1^{ss}(LH)$ iff $q_H(50.72 - 27.43\mu) - 2cq_H^e > q_H(25 - 9.33\mu) - cq_H^e(1 - \mu^e)$. The inequality is satisfied iff $\mathscr{C} < 25.72 - 18.1\mu$, which holds for all feasible $\mathscr{C}$. Thus, firm 1 is best off by a bundle pricing strategy, irrespective of firm 2's pricing decision. $\qquad\square$

Given Lemma 3.15 the next proposition is straight forward.

Lemma 3.16 (Pricing Equilibrium under Non Negligible Costs). *If costs are non negligible, both firms choose bundle pricing in the unique pricing equilibrium.*

Proof. Since bundle pricing is a dominant strategy by firm 1, firm 2 compares $\Pi_2^{bb}(HL) > \Pi_2^{bs}(HL)$, which trivially holds by Lemmas 3.4 and 3.9. $\qquad\square$

Lemma 3.15 bears yet another important implication. Since firm 1 chooses bundle pricing in equilibrium irrespective of firm 2's pricing decision, the sequence of decision making is irrelevant.

Corollary 3.17 (Irrelevance of Decision Sequence under Non Negligible Costs). *Under non negligible costs, the sequence of the firms' bundle pricing decision in stage one of the game is irrelevant for the equilibrium of the game.*

Put differently, under negligible costs, scenario HL^{bb} constitutes the unique equilibrium of the game also if firms choose their pricing strategy *simultaneously*. Moreover, in region VI this remains true, even if firm 2 would select its pricing strategy first.

Negligible Costs

If costs are negligible, the leverage result is not as obvious, because firm 2 will generally continue to provide a high-quality service in market B. Moreover, bundle pricing is not a dominant strategy for firm 1 anymore. This is mainly because scenario HL^{sb} remains viable at almost all cost levels. As a consequence, under negligible costs, the sequence of firms' pricing decisions matters.

Lemma 3.18 (Pricing Equilibrium under Negligible Costs). *If costs are negligible, both firms choose bundle pricing in the unique pricing equilibrium.*

Proof. Consider each of the four regions of $\mathscr{C}$ in turn.

In region I, costs are irrelevant and thus under the bundle pricing regimes, both firms will offer a high-quality service in market B. Obviously, if firm 1 chose a bundle pricing strategy here, firm 2 compares $\Pi_2^{bb}(HH) > \Pi_2^{bs}(HH)$ and would choose bundle pricing as well. Conversely, if firm 1 chose separate pricing, firm 2 compares $\Pi_2^{sb}(HH) < \Pi_2^{ss}(LH)$ and would choose separate pricing. Consequently, firm 1 compares $\Pi_1^{bb}(HL) > \Pi_1^{ss}(LH)$, which holds for all feasible values $\mathscr{C} < \overline{f}$. Therefore, both firms choose bundle pricing and HH^{bb} obtains in equilibrium.

In region II, the previous analysis is changed only if firm 1 chooses separate pricing first. Then firm 2 compares $\Pi_1^{sb}(HL) < \Pi_2^{ss}(LH)$, which holds for all feasible $\mathscr{C}$ and would still choose separate pricing. Hence, for firm 2 nothing has changed and HH^{bb} obtains again.

Next, suppose firm 1 choose bundle pricing in region III. Then, firm 2 would choose bundle pricing as well, because $\Pi_2^{bb}(HH) > \Pi_2^{bs}(LH)$. If firm 1 chose separate pricing first, then firm 2 would choose separate pricing as well (compare region ii). Thus, HH^{bb} is also the unique equilibrium in region iii.

Finally, in region IV, firms cannot coordinate on a pure-strategy quality equilibrium in the bs-subgame. Even if they did, firm 2 would still choose a bundle pricing strategy, since $\Pi_2^{bb}(HH) > \max\{\Pi_2^{bs}(HH), \Pi_2^{bs}(LH), \Pi_2^{bs}(HL), \Pi_2^{bs}(LL)\}$. Thus, the analysis is qualitatively identical to the one pursued for region iii and the lemma obtains. □

Finally, it is annotated that subgame sb is not to be very tempting for firm 1, since $R_1^{sb}(XY) \leq R_1^{bb}(XY), \forall \mu \in (0, \frac{1}{4}]$, where $X, Y \in \{H, L\}$. In particular, this means that the bb-subgame is *ex post credible* because firm 1 would never wish to deviate into the sb- subgame, once the quality decision has been fixed.[38] This is important, because in my model, I show that the pricing strategy (which includes little commitment) has influence upon the firms' quality decision (which requires sunk investments and thus high commitment). Hence, if firm 1 can force firm 2 into the bb-subgame, and influence it to provide a low-quality service through the quality differentiation mechanism of bundling, then ex post credibility ensures that firm 1 has no incentive to deviate from its pricing strategy, once the beneficial quality configuration has been obtained.[39] Consequently, contrary to Whinston (1990), in my model firm 1 does not need any exogenous commitment to bundling in order to achieve market leverage. Bundle pricing remains an equilibrium strategy, even after it has altered the nature of competition in the market.

3.3.5 Quality Leverage through Bundling

Having fully characterized all equilibria of the game at all feasible cost levels, I can finally turn to the interpretation of the results.

First see that bundle pricing emerges an an equilibrium pricing strategy for firm 1 at all cost levels. Interestingly, also firm 2 chooses bundle pricing as its unique equilibrium pricing strategy. In this sense, one can say that firms find it beneficial to adopt a *symmetric pricing strategy*.[40] That is, the model provides evidence that offering Triple Play bundles is indeed a pure Nash-equilibrium strategy for the integrated network operators, because it poses a best response to the bundling strategy of the opposing firm.

---

[38]It is easy to see that similar holds for a deviation from the bs-subgame to the separate pricing regime (ss).

[39]Since firm 2 is the second-mover it will always choose the optimal pricing strategy in response to firm 1, of course, and thus the problem of ex post credibility does not arise here.

[40]Also recall from the proof of Lemma 3.18 that firm 2 will always follow the pricing strategy of firm 1 under negligible costs.

This insight, however, does not yet explain why one firm offers a pure bundle of its services in the first place. To this extend, recall that if both firms offer their services separately, consumers can self-select their optimal services from markets A and B, possibly comprising an individual package which contains services of both firms. Thus, a consumer's decision in market A has no ramifications on his decision in market B and firms experience no cross-market effects in demand. As a consequence, each firm can play out its limited market power and establish itself as the high-quality service provider in its home market. In this way, either firm provides high-quality in the foreign market and low-quality in the secondary market (scenario LH).

When any firm offers its services in a pure bundle, consumers are unequivocally forced to optimize their service portfolio decision for both markets simultaneously. This creates externality in the market which leads the firms to alter the quality of their service offerings. In particular, the above analysis has revealed that the precise quality constellation depends on how prominently costs affect firms' decision making.

If costs of of quality improvement are non negligible scenario HL^{bb} constitutes the unique equilibrium of the game. The HL^{bb} scenario is so appealing to the firms because it allows them to affectively shield themselves from the aggressive Bertrand price competition by segmenting the market into low- and high-quality buyers. By the high-quality advantage, in scenario HL^{bb} firm 1 is much better and firm 2 worse off than under the separate pricing regime. Conversely, if under the all bundle pricing regime firms would have continued to provide a high-quality service in their home market and a low-quality service in their secondary market (LH^{bb} scenario), price competition would have intensified compared to the separate pricing strategy because bundles became relatively close substitutes. Thus, both firms would rather price their products separately than choosing LH^{bb} under a bundle pricing strategy.

If costs considerations become negligible, scenario HH^{bb} obtains. In fact, costs are so small that firm 1 cannot prevent firm 2 from participating of the high-quality advantage itself, which is in turn so large that it even recoups the losses incurred from intensified price competition. This eventually leads to higher profits than under separate pricing.

The main result of this chapter is summarized by the next proposition.

Proposition 3.19 (Bundling and Quality Leverage). *Both firms will choose a bundle pricing strategy and differentiate their bundles in equilibrium. Let w.l.o.g firm 1 provide a high-quality* *service and firm* 2 *provide a low-quality service in market* A. *Then bundle pricing affects the firms' quality decision such that*

- *firm* 1 *and firm* 2 *will provide a high-quality service in market* B, *if costs are negligible (scenario* HH^{bb})

- *only firm* 1 *will provide a high-quality service in market* B *(while firm* 2 *provides a low-quality service in market* B*) if costs are non negligible (scenario* HL^{bb}).

In all cases, firm 1 *achieves greater payoffs than under a separate pricing regime because the quality leverage effect of bundling enables firm* 1 *to leverage its quality leadership, which is associated with higher profits, from its primary market* A *to its secondary market* B.

Example

To exemplify Proposition 3.19, consider the following values for q_H, q_L, e and c.

Cost Function: Suppose $C(q_{mi}) = \frac{1}{2}q_{mi}^2$, i.e. $c = \frac{1}{2}$ and $e = 2$. This particular cost function has been chosen, because it has been frequently employed in the quality differentiation literature (cf. e.g. Motta 1993; Aoki and Prusa 1996).

Quality Levels: Quality levels are set at $q_H = 25$ and $q_L = 5$. These values are not chosen at random, but result from Lemma 4.9 in Chapter 4.3, where quality levels have been endogeneized, given the above specification of the cost function. More specifically, if firms would choose their quality levels freely from the continuous set $[0, \infty)$ under a bundle pricing regime, they would elicit $q_H^* = 25.33$ and $q_L^* = 4.82$ as the optimal qualities.

Notice that all necessary assumptions are satisfied for these parameter values. First, quality levels are sufficiently differentiated as $\mu = \frac{1}{5} < \frac{1}{4}$. Second, costs are non negligible, but yet feasible, since $\bar{r}_2^{bb}(q_H) = 4.68 < \mathscr{C} = 12 < \overline{f} = 13.35$.

Let firm 1 be the high-quality provider in market A, then firms receive a payoff of

$$\Pi_i^{ss}(LH) = R_i^{ss} - \frac{1}{2}(25^2 + 5^2) = 253.35$$

(a) Bundle vs. Bundle Pricing Regime

bb-subgame (market B)	Firm 2 q_H	q_L
Firm 1 q_H	$\Pi_1^{bb}(HH) = 157.00$ $\Pi_2^{bb}(HH) = -164.95$	$\Pi_1^{bb}(HL) = 590.00$ $\Pi_2^{bb}(HL) = 18.10$
Firm 1 q_L	$\Pi_1^{bb}(LH) = 84.80$ $\Pi_2^{bb}(LH) = 84.80$	$\Pi_1^{bb}(LL) = 292.50$ $\Pi_2^{bb}(LL) = 47.70$

(b) Bundle vs. Separate Pricing Regime

bs-subgame (market B)	Firm 2 q_H	q_L
Firm 1 q_H	$\Pi_1^{bs}(HH) = 144.70$ $\Pi_2^{bs}(HH) = -173.65$	$\Pi_1^{bs}(HL) = 578.45$ $\Pi_2^{bs}(HL) = 8.25$
Firm 1 q_L	$\Pi_1^{bs}(LH) = 417.25$ $\Pi_2^{bs}(LH) = -186.45$	$\Pi_1^{bs}(LL) = 295.25$ $\Pi_2^{bs}(LL) = 42.35$

(c) Separate vs. Bundle Pricing Regime

sb-subgame (market B)	Firm 2 q_H	q_L
Firm 1 q_H	$\Pi_1^{sb}(HH) = -56.60$ $\Pi_2^{sb}(HH) = -285.00$	$\Pi_1^{sb}(HL) = 505.85$ $\Pi_2^{sb}(HL) = 5.45$
Firm 1 q_L	$\Pi_1^{sb}(LH) = -186.45$ $\Pi_2^{sb}(LH) = 417.25$	$\Pi_1^{sb}(LL) = 232.1$ $\Pi_2^{sb}(LL) = 11.30$

Table 3.3: *Example Payoffs for the Bundle Pricing Subgames*

in the separate pricing subgame, where qualities are determined through the firms relative home market advantage. In the remaining three bundle pricing subgames, firms face the following quality decision in market B: Obviously, scenario HL is the unique quality equilibrium in all bundle pricing subgames. Since $\Pi_1^{bb}(HL) > \Pi_1^{bs}(HL) > \Pi_1^{sb}(HL) > \Pi_1^{ss}(LH)$ and $\Pi_2^{ss}(LH) > \Pi_2^{bb}(HL) > \Pi_2^{bs}(HL) > \Pi_2^{sb}(HL)$ both firms will choose bundle pricing in equilibrium, independent of the sequence of decision making. Therefore, scenario HL^{bb} will obtain in equilibrium. Therein, firm 1 receives a payoff of 590, while firm 2 only makes a profit of 18.10. Under the separate pricing regime both firms would have received 253.35 instead. Thus, in this case, the quality leverage effect of bundle pricing enables firm 1 to more than double its profit compared to the separate pricing regime.

Chapter 4

Model Extensions: Unilateral Mixed Bundling, Correlated Preferences and Economies of Scope

In this chapter I extend and deviate from the base model with respect to several central assumptions. Thereby, I can show that the main results are unaffected by these variations. To facilitate the distinction between the base model and its extensions, I denote the most critical assumptions of the former as follows:

(A1) Firms provide exactly one service per market

(A2) Firms cannot employ unilateral mixed bundling

(A3) Consumers' preferences are uncorrelated across markets

(A4) Firms are symmetric

(A5) Firms must choose from discrete exogenous quality levels

(A6) Firms' technology exhibits no scope economies

In following, I will relax any one of these assumptions.

4.1 Monopoly and Optimal Quality Differentiation

First, I show that firms will never find it profitable to offer more than one service per market. This proves that assumption (A1) is not binding. To make the analysis as simple and precise as possible, imagine that reciprocal entry has not yet taken place such that each firm is an unconstrained monopolist in its home market. Certainly, if under the given conditions already a monopolistic firm does not find it profitable to introduce a second service quality into the market, this would be strong evidence that the same holds under oligopoly. In particular, let θ again denote the consumers' willingness-to-pay for quality which is uniformly distributed on the unit interval and let $U(\theta, q^m, p^m) = \theta \, q_i^m - p_i^m$ be each consumers' utility function for the monopolist's service variant i. If the monopolist offered a single product, the marginal consumer indifferent between buying and not buying this service would be $\widehat{\theta}^m = \frac{p^m}{q^m}$. Hence, given the same cost function as before, i.e. $C(q^m)$ for each service, the firm's profit function is

$$\Pi_1^m = (1 - \frac{p_1^m}{q_1^m})p_1^m - C(q_1^m)$$

Solving for the optimal price yields $p_1^{m*} = \frac{q_1^m}{2}$. Put differently, in the absence of competition, a monopolistic firm would choose a quality deflated price of $\frac{p_1^m}{q_1^m} = \frac{1}{2}$, and thereby serve only half of the consumers. Consequently, the single service monopolist makes a profit of

$$\Pi_1^{m*} = \frac{q_1^m}{4} - C(q_1^m)$$

Introducing a second quality, say $q_2^m < q_1^m$, changes the monopolist's profit function to

$$\Pi_2^m = (1 - \widetilde{\theta}^m)p_1^m + (\widetilde{\theta}^m - \widehat{\theta}^m)p_2^m - C(q_1^m) - C(q_2^m),$$

where $\widetilde{\theta}^m = \frac{p_1^m - p_2^m}{q_1^m - q_2^m}$ denotes the consumer indifferent between purchasing service 1 or 2 from the monopolist. Again, optimal prices are given by $p_1^{m*} = \frac{q_1^m}{2}$ and $p_2^{m*} = \frac{q_2^m}{2}$, such that the profit function becomes

$$\Pi_2^{m*} = \frac{q_1^m}{4} - C(q_1^m) - C(q_2^m),$$

because the low-quality service does not receive any demand at these prices. Consequently, the introduction of another service variant just causes costs without any revenue gains, such that $q_2^{m*} = 0$.

Proposition 4.1. *The unconstrained monopolist never finds it profitable to introduce a second service quality.*

4.2 Unilateral Mixed Bundling

Next, I allow for unilateral mixed bundling as a more flexible pricing strategy and thereby relax $(A2)$. Of course, it should be in the discretion of each firm whether it pursues a pure bundling or a unilateral mixed bundling strategy. As mentioned before, the latter is especially common in the communications market and refers to the firms practice of tying the sale of the secondary service to the purchase of the home service, while simultaneously allowing the separate purchase of the home service. Obviously, unilateral mixed bundling subsumes pure bundling because firms can always choose to set the price for the individual purchase of their home service arbitrarily high, thereby establishing a de-facto pure bundling regime. Likewise, mixed bundling (i.e. offering the bundle and *both* service types separately) subsumes unilateral mixed bundling.

4.2.1 Mixed Bundling vs. Pure Bundling

Mix-and-Match

When firms offer their home services individually, consumers have the ability to *mix-and-match* services from different providers. Obviously, this is possible only because service types are taken to be fully compatible (cf. Section 2.1.5). There exists a small body of literature which has investigated whether product compatibility is indeed advantageous to firms. Foremost, Matutes and Regibeau (1988)–whose model has subsequently been extended by Economides (1989)– consider a duopoly market in which each firm offers both of two complementary products. More precisely, the firms play a two stage game in which they first decide whether to produce compatible products and then compete in prices. If firms agree on a compatibility standard, consumers can mix-and-match products from different suppliers. Conversely, if firms choose to provide incompatible products the situation is akin to pure bundling, since consumers must buy the whole set of products from one firm. Interestingly, the authors find that firms are in fact inclined to offer compatible products, because compatibility reduces the level of competition in the duopoly market and thereby allows for higher prices. Also Einhorn (1992) finds similar results while extending Matutes and Regibeau's framework (where consumers have uncorrelated horizontal preferences for each good) to a model with vertical differentiation (where firms offer products of different qualities). In particular, Einhorn shows that compatibility mitigates competition because it increases the aggregate degree of product differentiation in the market.

Equilibrium Pricing Strategies

As compatibility of services is in the firms' best interest, consumers will generally be able to mix-and-match their optimal service portfolio from different suppliers. The previously mentioned mix-and-match literature does not account for mixed bundling, however, i.e. consumers cannot be given a bundle discount if they purchase both products from one supplier. This issue is addressed in another body of literature investigating mixed bundling in duopoly. Unfortunately, the authors disagree on whether mixed bundling actually raises firms profits or at least emerges as an equilibrium pricing strategy in comparison to separate pricing or pure bundling. Economides (1993), for example, finds in a linear demand model that mixed bundling forces firms into a prisoners' dilemma. Thus, although mixed bundling is chosen as a dominant strategy in equilibrium, it leads to lower profits than separate pricing. On the contrary, using a logit demand model, Anderson and Leruth (1993) show that separate pricing (weakly) dominates pure or mixed bundle pricing: Here firms are reluctant to mixed bundling because it induces self inflicted competition, while pure bundling, on the other hand, forgoes the ability to price discriminate between both products. Also Matutes and Regibeau (1992) extend their mix-and-match model by a third stage (located between the compatibility decision and the price competition stage) in which firms can choose their pricing strategy (i.e. either pure bundle -, mixed bundle -, or separate pricing). The authors find that the separate selling strategy dominates the pure bundling strategy as firms generally wish to make their products compatible. Moreover, they show that the optimal pricing strategy of firms producing compatible products depends on the consumers' reservation price for their ideal product portfolio: If it is low, both firms choose mixed bundling and earn less than if they would have chosen separate pricing. This resembles the prisoners' dilemma situation also found by Economides (1993). At intermediate reservation prices, one firm chooses mixed bundling and the other separate pricing, and at high reservation prices both firms choose separate pricing. Kopalle, Krishna, and Assuncao (1999) extend the framework of Anderson and Leruth (1993) by introducing an additional "no purchase" option. They allow for all three pricing strategies, but show that pure bundling will never be an equilibrium strategy by either firm. Their key finding, however, is that the equilibrium bundling strategy depends on the scope for market expansion. When the probability of purchase is low (i.e. there is scope for market expansion) firms are likely to employ mixed bundling, but as the scope for market expansion decreases firms favor to price products independently. Finally, also McAfee, McMillan, and Whinston (1989) briefly comment on the optimal pricing strategy in a multiproduct duopoly setting and find that independent pricing cannot be more profitable than (mixed) bundling if reservation prices for the two products are independently distributed.

In summary, it seems that the optimal (equilibrium) pricing strategy hinges upon the precise model assumptions – in particular the demand structure. In the literature, at least, no robust setting in favor of any bundling strategy could be identified. In my model, bundle pricing is always preferred over separate pricing. Moreover, I can show that pure and (unilateral) mixed bundle pricing strategies can simultaneously coexist in equilibrium. This is a remarkable finding, as recently, Vaubourg (2006) has criticized that the previous literature on equilibrium bundling strategies cannot explain this phenomenon, despite its practical relevance. Although my model is distinct from Vaubourg's, we both share the assumption that products are independent in demand, whereas the earlier models have assumed a complementary relationship.

4.2.2 The Unilateral Mixed Bundle Pricing Regime

In following, I extend the base model by allowing for a unilateral mixed bundle pricing strategy instead of a pure bundle pricing strategy in the first stage of the game. From Chapter 3 we know that firms tend to use the same pricing strategies, such that the bb-regime emerges as unique equilibrium subgame under pure bundling. I will therefore limit the investigation to the unilateral mixed bundle pricing vs. unilateral mixed bundle pricing regime, denoted by superscript uu. Moreover, firms individual (home service) prices are p_{A1}^{uu} and p_{B2}^{uu}, respectively; all other variables are as before. Before proceeding, however, I must specify the location of some indifferent consumers again:

Consumers indifferent between buying firm 1's pure bundle and firm 2's home service only are located at

$$\widetilde{\theta}_B^{uu+} = \frac{p_1^{uu} - p_{B2}^{uu}}{q_{B1} - q_{B2}} - \theta_A \frac{q_H}{q_{B1} - q_{B2}}.$$

Likewise, the consumers indifferent between buying firm 1's home service and firm 2's pure bundle satisfy

$$\widetilde{\theta}_B^{uu++} = \frac{p_2^{uu} - p_{A1}^{uu}}{q_{B2}} + \theta_A \frac{q_H - q_L}{q_{B2}},$$

and consumers indifferent between firm 1's and firm 2's bundle lie at

$$\widetilde{\theta}_B^{uu+++} = \frac{p_1^{uu} - p_2^{uu}}{q_{B1} - q_{B2}} - \theta_A \frac{q_H - q_L}{q_{B1} - q_{B2}}.$$

Furthermore, the consumers indifferent between buying bundle 1 or 2 at all are located along

$$\widehat{\theta}_{B1}^{uu} = \frac{p_1^{bb}}{q_{B1}} - \theta_A \frac{q_H}{q_{B1}} \qquad \text{and}$$

$$\widehat{\theta}_{B2}^{uu} = \frac{p_2^{bb}}{q_{B2}} - \theta_A \frac{q_L}{q_{B2}},$$

respectively. Let the locus of consumers indifferent between buying either bundle or not buying anything at all, i.e. $\widetilde{\theta}_B^{uu^{+++}} = \widehat{\theta}_{B1}^{uu} = \widehat{\theta}_{B2}^{uu}$, if existent, be $L^{uu} = (L_A^{uu}, L_B^{uu})$, with

$$L_A^{uu} = \frac{p_1^{uu} q_{B2} - p_2^{uu} q_{B1}}{q_H q_{B2} - q_L q_{B1}} \qquad \text{and}$$

$$L_B^{uu} = \frac{p_2^{uu} q_H - p_1^{uu} q_L}{q_H q_{B2} - q_L q_{B1}}.$$

Finally, denote the locus of consumers indifferent between buying firm 1's bundle, firm 2's bundle or firm 1's home service separately, i.e. $\widetilde{\theta}_B^{uu^{++}} = \widetilde{\theta}_B^{uu^{+++}}$, by $P^{uu} = (P_A^{uu}, P_B^{uu})$, with

$$P_A^{uu} = \frac{p_{A1}^{uu} - p_2^{uu}}{q_H - q_L} + \frac{p_1^{uu} - p_{A1}^{uu}}{q_H - q_L} \frac{q_{B2}}{q_{B1}} \qquad \text{and}$$

$$P_B^{uu} = \frac{p_1^{uu} - p_{A1}^{uu}}{q_{B1}}.$$

Again, I will first provide the reader with some intuition concerning the nature of competition in each of the four scenarios. The tedious quantitative analysis is mostly executed in the appendix and summarized by Lemmas 4.2 through 4.4.

Scenario LH^{uu}: Once more, let us begin with the investigation of scenario LH. If firms can employ unilateral mixed bundling instead of pure bundling (cf. Figure 3.3) the demand pattern changes to the one depicted in Figure 4.1. One can already conclude from the demand pattern that competition is much less intense in LH^{uu} as compared to LH^{bb}. As each firm sells its high-quality home service separately, the consumers with the highest willingness-to-pay (i.e. the most profitable consumers) are able to compile an all-high-quality service portfolio themselves. In this vein, both firms evenly profit from the individual offering of their home services by contributing exactly one service to this most-valued service portfolio. Hence firms' home services are viewed as complementary by these consumers and thus price competition is very weak in the individual service segment. On the contrary, firms' pure bundles remain to be demand substitutes, evoking rather harsh price competition in the bundle segment. However, since only those consumers with medium willingness-to-pay in both markets are directly indifferent between the firms' bundles, the effect of small price changes onto firms' profits is not as pronounced as in LH^{bb}. Overall, one can say that scenario LH^{uu} seems to combine the

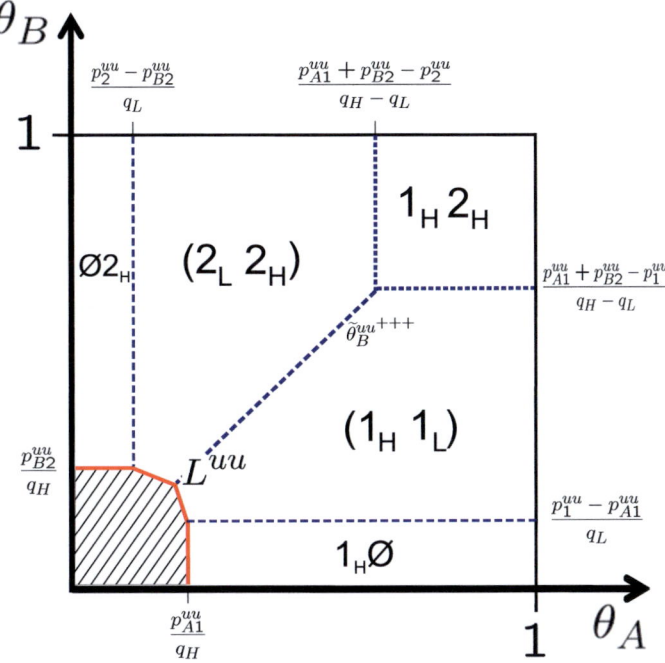

Figure 4.1: *Unilateral Mixed Bundle Pricing Subgame: Scenario LH^{uu}*

best of the two regimes: On the one hand, individual home service offerings allow to single out the most valued customers by allowing them to compile their optimal service portfolio, the revenue of which is evenly shared. On the other hand, competing bundle offerings compromise on the amount of self-inflicted price competition in lieu of substitutive price competition. Taken together, we can thus expect symmetric revenues which are well above the level of LH^{bb} and might even exceed those achieved under the separate pricing regime.

Scenario HL^{uu}: The expected demand pattern under scenario HL^{uu} is drawn in Figure 4.2(a). Since firm 1 is the high-quality service provider in both markets in this scenario, its bundle offering is especially appealing to the most valued customers, and therefore very profitable. In contrast to scenario LH^{uu}, the individually compiled service portfolio now attracts only some medium valuable customers, and thus cannot serve as a source of high revenues. In fact, the additional revenue generated by this portfolio is not able to compensate firm 2 for the self-inflicted competition caused between its individual home service and its bundle offering. Hence, firm 2 refrains from selling its home service separately (i.e. it sells it at a price equal or above the bundle price), leading to the demand pattern depicted in Figure 4.2(b). Of course, with

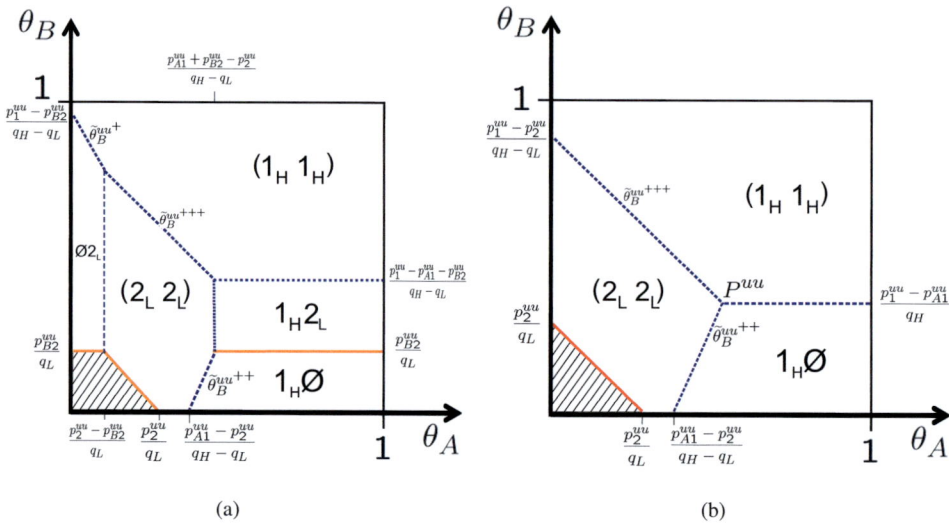

Figure 4.2: *Unilateral Mixed Bundle Pricing Subgame: Scenario* HL^{uu}

the discontinuation of 2's home service, two distinct demand areas drop out, leaving consumers with three potential service offerings; the two bundles and firm 1's home service. It turns out that selling its home service separately remains profitable for firm 1, because the revenue gain from stealing some of 2's demand (weakly) exceeds the losses incurred through self-inflicted competition with its own bundle. This latter revenue gain is not very strong, however, and we can thus expect revenues at about the same magnitude as in HL^{bb}, but with a slight increase (decrease) in firm 1's (2's) revenues.

Scenarios HH^{uu} and LL^{uu}: Finally, consider the demand pattern shown by Figure 4.3, which obtains if both firms select the identical quality level for their B-service. At first glance, it is evident that only very little has changed compared to scenario XX^{bb}. Mainly, this is because there is no reason for the customers to compile an individual service portfolio from each firm's individual home service offerings in this scenario: Due to the lack of service differentiation in market B, all possible service portfolios consisting of two services are covered by the firms' bundles already. Consequently, since bundles are by definition cheaper than the sum of their components, no consumer can benefit from assembling services of different firms. Moreover, each firm's separate home service offering appeals only to customers with extreme differences in their willingness-to-pay for quality across service types. The quantitative analysis will show that the value generated by these customers cannot countervail the negative effects created by

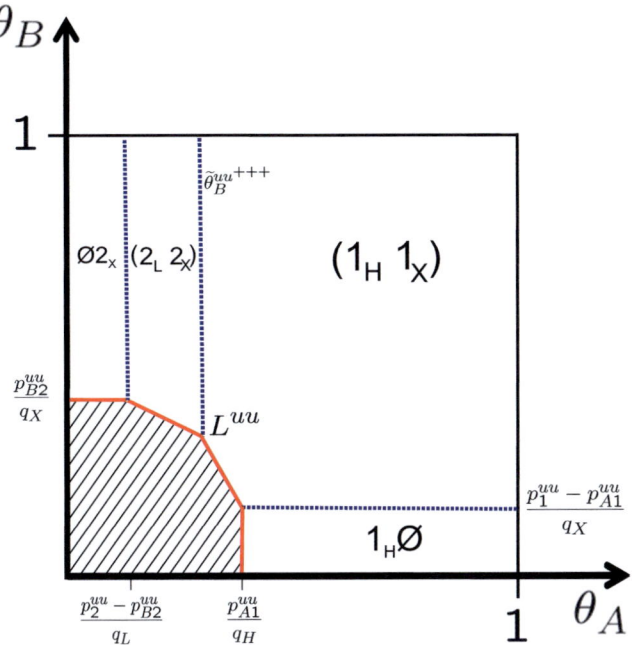

Figure 4.3: *Unilateral Mixed Bundle Pricing Subgame: Scenarios HH^{uu} and LL^{uu}*

self-inflicted competition between each firm's individual and bundled services. Consequently, in this scenario, both firms choose not to offer their home services separately, resulting in the very same situation as in XX^{bb}.

For the quantitative analysis, I begin by deriving the the price equilibrium feasibility constraints for the unilateral mixed bundle pricing regime. Since there are generally more distinct demand regions in this regime, quality levels must therefore also be generally more differentiated in order to ensure existence of an interior price equilibrium. However, since scenario LL^{bb} (which has been the limiting case in the base model) and scenario LL^{uu} (which remains to be the limiting case in this extension) turn out to be identical in both settings, the assumption of $q_H \geq 4q_L$ is still justified and ensures the feasibility of all four scenarios.

Lemma 4.2 (Price Equilibrium Feasibility Constraints: Unilateral Mixed Bundling). *Under unilateral mixed bundling interior price equilibria exist only if quality levels are sufficiently differentiated. Scenario HL is feasible for $q_H > 2.12\,q_L$, scenario HH for $q_H > 2.31\,q_L$, scenario LH for $q_H > 2.46\,q_L$ and scenario LL for $q_H > 3.73\,q_L$.*

Proof. See Appendix. □

Furthermore, the following lemma confirms the findings of the above intuitive interpretation.

Lemma 4.3 (Revenues in the uu-subgame). *The revenue of firm i in each scenario of the uu-subgame can be well approximated by*

$$
\begin{aligned}
R_1^{uu}(HH) &= q_H\,(36.88 - 28\mu) & , \quad R_2^{uu}(HH) &= q_H\,(6.71 - 1.54\mu) \\
R_1^{uu}(HL) &= q_H\,(54.62 - 29.45\mu) & , \quad R_2^{uu}(HL) &= q_H\,8.58\,\mu \\
R_i^{uu}(LH) &= q_H\,(25 - 8.92\mu) & & \\
R_1^{uu}(LL) &= q_H\,(25 - 1.50\mu) & , \quad R_2^{bb}(LL) &= q_H\,14.54\,\mu
\end{aligned}
$$

Proof. See Appendix. $\qquad\square$

With the exception of LH^{uu}, revenues have changed only very little with respect to the bb-subgame. However, the softening of price competition in scenario LH^{uu} has significant impact on the firms' best response functions. In particular, firm 1 is now less inclined to choose q_H (especially at high cost levels, in response to a high-quality B-service offering of firm 2) because LH^{uu} is much more attractive than LH^{bb} used to be. Likewise, for the same reason, firm 2 is less willing to give into providing a low-quality service in response to a high service quality offering by firm 1.

Lemma 4.4 (Best Quality Responses in the uu-subgame). *In the uu-subgame, each firm's best quality response function is*

$$
BR_1^{uu}(q_L) =
\begin{cases}
q_H, & \text{if} \quad \mathscr{C} \leq \bar{r}_1^{uu}(q_L) = 29.62 - 27.95\mu \\
q_L, & \text{otherwise}
\end{cases}
$$

$$
BR_1^{uu}(q_H) =
\begin{cases}
q_H, & \text{if} \quad \mathscr{C} \leq \bar{r}_1^{uu}(q_H) = 11.88 - 19.08\mu \\
q_L, & \text{otherwise}
\end{cases}
$$

$$
BR_2^{uu}(q_L) =
\begin{cases}
q_H, & \text{if} \quad \mathscr{C} \leq \bar{r}_2^{uu}(q_L) = 25 - 23.45\mu \\
q_L, & \text{otherwise}
\end{cases}
$$

$$
BR_2^{uu}(q_H) =
\begin{cases}
q_H, & \text{if} \quad \mathscr{C} \leq \bar{r}_2^{uu}(q_H) = 6.05 - 10.12\mu \\
q_L, & \text{otherwise}
\end{cases}
$$

For all $\mu \in (0, \frac{1}{4}]$ it holds that the threshold functions, $\bar{r}$, can be uniquely ranked as $\bar{r}_2^{uu}(q_H) < \bar{r}_1^{uu}(q_H) < \bar{f} < \bar{r}_2^{uu}(q_L) < \bar{r}_1^{uu}(q_L)$.

Proof. Analogous to Lemma 3.5 $\qquad\square$

Lemmas 4.3 and 4.4 show that unilateral mixed bundling as ambiguous effects with respect to strengthening firm 2's position in counteracting firm 1's leverage efforts. On the one side, it helps (both firms) to relax the ruinous price competition characterizing scenario LH, but on the other side, it worsens (or has no impact on) the situation in the remaining scenarios. This ambivalence also shows in the next proposition.

Proposition 4.5 (Equilibria of the uu-subgame). *The equilibrium outcomes of the unilateral mixed bundle pricing subgame are virtually identical to those of the pure bundle pricing subgame, with an exception if costs are very high ($\mathscr{C} > \bar{r}_1^{uu}(q_H)$). At this level, next to scenario HL^{uu}, scenario LH^{uu} can also be sustained in equilibrium and firms must coordinate on one of the two equilibria.*

Proof. For very low values of $\mathscr{C}$, the the high-quality advantage lets both firms strive towards offering a high-quality of service in market B again, yielding HH^{uu}. When costs increase to $\bar{r}_2^{uu}(q_H) < \mathscr{C} \leq \bar{r}_1^{uu}(q_H)$, firm 2 finds it more profitable to give in into being the low-quality provider in both markets (scenario HL^{uu}) rather than trying to compete with firm 1 in HH^{uu}. Finally, if costs are such that $\mathscr{C} > \bar{r}_1^{uu}(q_H)$ a coordination problem arises, because both firms would rather refrain from offering the high-quality service in market B, should the opponent choose to do so. Thus, both HL^{uu} and LH^{uu} constitute an equilibrium. $\square$

From Lemmas 3.16 and 3.18 and noticing that the revenues of both firms are virtually identical under unilateral mixed bundle pricing and pure bundle pricing, with the exception of scenario LH^{uu}–where both firms are better off than under LH^{bb}–I can directly conclude that both firms will employ the bundle pricing strategy in equilibrium again, at all cost levels.

Corollary 4.6 (Equilibrium of the Unilateral Mixed Bundle Pricing Game). *Under a unilateral mixed bundle pricing regime, the high quality seller in market A is likely to leverage its quality dominance over to market B and thereby earn greater profits than under a separate pricing regime. Even if quality leverage is not achieved, both firms' profits are higher than under separate selling.*

4.3 Correlation of Consumer Preferences

In the base model I have considered the limit case where consumers' preferences were uncorrelated. In fact, with respect to the quality differentiation mechanism, uncorrelated preferences represent a worst-case scenario, because there is demand in every 'niche' of the market. Graphically, this is represented by a uniform distribution of consumers in the unit square. As consumers' tastes become more (positively) correlated, consumer mass is concentrated around the angle bisecting line (grey shaded area in Figure 4.4). Intuitively, as consumers' preferences

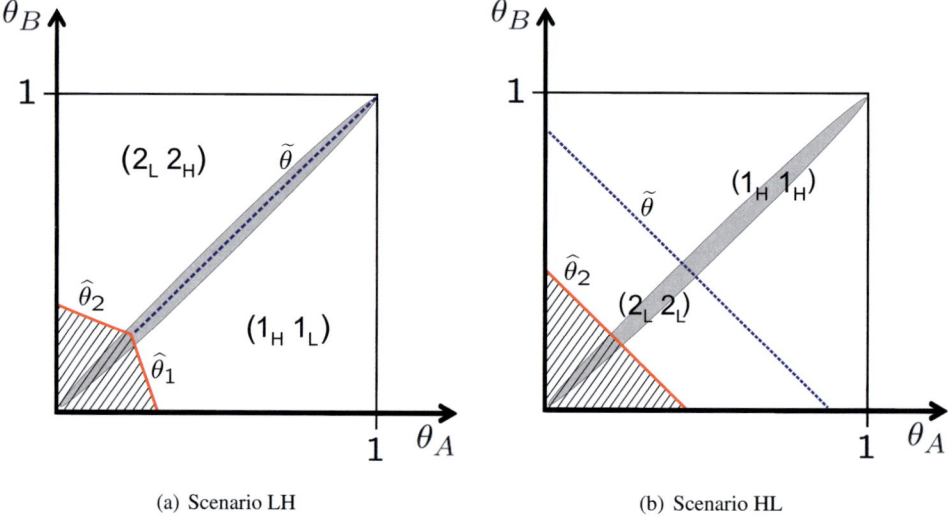

(a) Scenario LH   (b) Scenario HL

Figure 4.4: *Bundle Pricing Regimes under Correlated Consumers' Preferences*

become positively correlated, price competition in the LH scenario must inevitably intensify under the bundle pricing regime, as a small change in either firm's price will now induce an even greater number of consumers to switch providers. Eventually, when consumers' tastes are perfectly positively correlated, the symmetric LH scenario (Figure 4.4(a)) cannot constitute an equilibrium anymore, because either provider can attract *all* consumers by an infinitesimal small drop in price. On the contrary, in the HL scenario (Figure 4.4(b)) demand is much more inelastic as the consumers being indifferent between both bundles lie 'orthogonally' to the angle bisecting line around which consumer mass is concentrated. Thus, as consumers' preferences become positively correlated, scenario HL becomes increasingly attractive to the firms and the results obtained earlier should rather be strengthened.

In this section I deviate from the base model with respect to (A3) - (A6) as follows:

(A3') Consumers' preferences are perfectly positively correlated across service types.

116

(A4') Each firm has a cost advantage (or disadvantage) in its home market, i.e.

$$C''(q_{mi}) = \begin{cases} \frac{1}{2}q_{mi}^2, & \text{if } m \text{ is firm i's home market} \\[2mm] \frac{\sigma}{2}q_{mi}^2, & \text{if } m \text{ is firm i's secondary market,} \end{cases}$$

with $\sigma > 0$.[1]

(A5') Firms choose quality levels, q, endogenously from the continuous interval $[0, \infty)$.

Formally, by $(A3')$ I impose that there is a one-to-one mapping between consumers' preferences for quality across service types, such that $\theta = \theta_A = \theta_B$. Note that θ_m can be interpreted as the marginal rate of substitution between income and quality. Consumers with a higher income have a lower marginal utility of income and thus a higher θ_m (cf. Tirole 1988, p.96). Of course, all consumers can be uniquely ordered according to their income and since the same consumers are present on both markets, there is good reason to believe that this ordering is identical (or at least highly positively correlated) across markets.

Furthermore, I introduce some cost asymmetry in each market and allow firms to choose the quality level of each of their services freely. This allows me to analyze the effect of bundling on equilibrium quality levels in the presence of cost (dis-)advantages.[2]

4.3.1 Separate Pricing Regime

Recall from Section 3.3.2 that there are no cross-market effects under the separate pricing regime. Therefore, we can consider each market separately again. I denote the present separate pricing regime by superscript s. Otherwise the notation is the same as before. Hence, let firm h be the high-quality provider and firm l be the low-quality provider in market m, such that $q_h^s > q_l^s$. Optimal prices are given by[3]

$$\begin{aligned} p_h^{s*} &= 200 \; \frac{q_h^s(q_h^s - q_l^s)}{4 \, q_h^s - q_l^s}, \\[2mm] p_l^{s*} &= 100 \; \frac{q_l^s(q_h^s - q_l^s)}{4 \, q_h^s - q_l^s}. \end{aligned} \tag{4.1}$$

and, consequently, revenues amount to

$$\begin{aligned} R_h^{s*} &= 400 \; \frac{q_h^{s\,2}(q_h^s - q_l^s)}{(4 \, q_h^s - q_l^s)^2}, \\[2mm] R_l^{s*} &= 100 \; \frac{q_h^s q_l^s(q_h^s - q_l^s)}{(4 \, q_h^s - q_l^s)^2}. \end{aligned}$$

---

[1]For expositional clarity I economize on parameters by setting $c = \frac{1}{2}$ and $e = 2$.

[2]I have imposed that a firm's cost advantage in one market is equal to its cost disadvantage in the other market. The analysis trivially extends to the case where firms are not symmetric across both markets.

[3]Cf. Motta (1993).

With the introduction of cost asymmetry, firms' profit functions become:

$$\Pi_h^s = R_h^{s*} - \tfrac{1}{2}q_l^{s2}$$
$$\Pi_l^s = R_l^{s*} - \tfrac{\sigma}{2}q_l^{s2}.$$

Substituting $q_l^s = \mu\, q_h^s$, $\mu \in (0,1)$ into the first order conditions and after some rearranging one obtains that μ is uniquely determined by

$$8\sigma\mu^3 - 12\sigma\mu^2 + (16\sigma + 7)\mu - 4 = 0. \tag{4.2}$$

By implicit differentiation, one can easily check for $\frac{\partial \mu}{\partial \sigma} < 0$, which implies that $\mu \in (0, \frac{4}{7})$ for $\sigma > 0$ and also reveals the previously mentioned *quality differentiation principle*. In particular, for symmetric firms (i.e. $\sigma = 1$) $\mu \approx 0.19$. This provides further evidence that the assumption of $\mu \in (0, \frac{1}{4})$, which has been made in the base model, is most naturally met if quality levels are chosen from a continuous set.

Solving for μ and substituting this back into the first order conditions yields the following optimal qualities:[4]

$$q_h^{s*} = 400 \; \frac{2\mu^2 - 3\mu + 4}{64 - 48\mu + 12\mu^2 - \mu^3}$$
$$q_l^{s*} = \frac{100}{\sigma} \; \frac{4 - 7\mu}{64 - 48\mu + 12\mu^2 - \mu^3}. \tag{4.3}$$

It is easy to see that the *high-quality advantage principle* is confirmed at these quality levels, as the high-quality provider, firm h, achieves a higher payoff than firm l. However, in order to show that this candidate equilibrium is indeed Nash, it remains to be verified whether q_l^{s*} is actually a best response to q_h^{s*} by the designated low quality firm, or whether it has an incentive to *high quality leapfrog* by providing a higher quality than the designated high quality firm.[5] In the this case, the game would have no equilibrium. *Low quality leapfrogging*, on the contrary, is only relevant if the low quality firm earns higher payoffs than the high quality firm (Lehmann-Grube 1997), and can therefore be neglected here.

For symmetric firms, Motta (1993) has shown that high-quality leapfrogging is never advantageous. I allow for asymmetric firms, including those cases where the designated low-quality firm is more efficient than the designated high-quality firm, i.e. where $\sigma < 1$. It turns out that high-quality leapfrogging can be ruled out as long as the low-quality firm's cost advantage is

---

[4]The reader may easily verify that both second order conditions fulfill $\frac{\partial^2 \Pi_{mi}^s}{\partial^2 q_{mi}^s} < 0$ given $q_h^s > q_l^s$.

[5]This has not been necessary before because quality leapfrogging is not possible when there are only two discrete quality levels.

not too predominant, such that $\sigma > \underline{\sigma} \approx 0.63.$[6] Hence for all $\sigma > \underline{\sigma}$ the above candidate equilibrium is subgame perfect Nash, otherwise there exists no equilibrium.

Furthermore, the following lemma sheds some light on the impact of cost asymmetry on competition and equilibrium quality levels.

Lemma 4.7 (Cost Asymmetry under Separate Pricing). *Under separate pricing, an increase (decrease) in the firms' cost asymmetry will c.p. lead to a decrease (increase) in each firm's equilibrium quality. Overall, services will be more (less) differentiated than before, thereby softening (tightening) competition and resulting in an increase (decrease) of the quality deflated prices $\frac{p_i^s}{q_i^s}$.*

Proof. First, recall that $\frac{\partial \mu}{\partial \sigma} < 0$ and $\mu \in (0, \frac{4}{7})$ for $\sigma > 0$. This immediately proves the second part of the lemma. Differentiating q_h^s with respect to σ yields $\frac{\partial q_h^s}{\partial \sigma} = \frac{800 \frac{\partial \mu}{\partial \sigma} \mu(80 - 36\mu + 3\mu^2 - \mu^3)}{(64 - 48\mu + 12\mu^2 + \mu^3)^2}$, which must be smaller than zero because of $\frac{\partial \mu}{\partial \sigma} < 0$. Consequently, $\frac{\partial q_l^s}{\partial \sigma} = \frac{\partial (\mu q_h^s)}{\partial \sigma} = \frac{\partial \mu}{\partial \sigma} q_h^s + \frac{\partial q_h^s}{\partial \sigma} < \frac{\partial q_h^s}{\partial \sigma} < 0.$ $\square$

Finally, notice that although firms are asymmetric in each market, across both markets firms are symmetric again, such that each firm will earn the same overall profit under separate pricing.[7]

4.3.2 Bundle Pricing Regime

Next, consider the bundle pricing regime where firms compete against each other by offering pure bundles. Consequently, the consumer indifferent between firm 1's and firm 2's bundle is located at:[8]

$$\widetilde{\theta}^b = \frac{p_1^b - p_2^b}{\underbrace{(q_{A1}^b + q_{B1}^b)}_{q_1^b} - \underbrace{(q_{A2}^b + q_{B2}^b)}_{q_2^b}}.$$

In following, I use the shorthand notation $q_i^b = q_{Ai}^b + q_{Bi}^b$ to denote the *aggregate quality* of firm i's bundle. Obviously, since preferences are perfectly correlated, consumers care only

---

[6]Formally, I must check whether there exists a quality level $\overline{q} > q_h^{s^*}$, such that

$$R_h^{s^*}(q_h^{s^*}, \overline{q}) - \frac{\sigma}{2}\overline{q}^2 > R_l^{s^*}(q_h^{s^*}, q_l^{s^*}) - \frac{\sigma}{2}q_l^{s^{*2}}.$$

A brief numerical analysis reveals that there exists no such $\overline{q}$ as long as $\sigma > \underline{\sigma} \approx 0.6296$

[7]Of course, if one firm has a cost advantage in the provision of both service types, it will also earn higher overall profits than its less efficient competitor.

[8]Superscript b denotes the bundling regime.

about the aggregate quality level and not how it is distributed among the service types. Thus, in order to make positive revenue, firms must differentiate their aggregate quality levels and I can assume w.l.o.g. that $q_1^{b*} > q_2^{b*}$ in equilibrium. It is easy to see that with the help of this short hand notation, the derivation of equilibrium prices is analogous to the separate pricing regime. Consequently, firms' optimal prices and profits can be written as

$$
\begin{aligned}
p_1^{b*} &= 200 \ \frac{q_1^b(q_1^b - q_2^b)}{4 \ q_1^b - q_2^b}, \\
p_2^{b*} &= 100 \ \frac{q_2^b(q_1^b - q_2^b)}{4 \ q_1^b - q_2^b}.
\end{aligned}
\tag{4.4}
$$

$$
\begin{aligned}
\Pi_1^b &= 400 \ \frac{q_1^{b \, 2}(q_1^b - q_2^b)}{(4 \ q_1^b - q_2^b)^2} - \tfrac{1}{2}q_{A1}^{b}{}^2 - \tfrac{\sigma}{2}q_{B1}^{b}{}^2, \\
\Pi_2^b &= 100 \ \frac{q_1^b q_2^b(q_1^b - q_2^b)}{(4 \ q_1^b - q_2^b)^2} - \tfrac{\sigma}{2}q_{A2}^{b}{}^2 - \tfrac{1}{2}q_{B2}^{b}{}^2.
\end{aligned}
$$

From two of the four first order conditions, I can directly deduce the following *inter market relationships*:

$$
\begin{aligned}
q_{B1}^{b*} &= \tfrac{1}{\sigma} \ q_{A1}^{b*} \\
q_{B2}^{b*} &= \sigma \ q_{A2}^{b*}.
\end{aligned}
\tag{4.5}
$$

The corresponding *intra market relationship* (for market A) is derived by setting $q_{A2}^{b*} = \nu \ q_{A1}^{b*}$, with $\nu \in [0,1]$ and solving simultaneously for all four first order conditions:[9]

$$
8(\sigma\nu)^3 - 12(\sigma\nu)^2 + 23\sigma\nu - 4 = 0,
\tag{4.6}
$$

In fact, see that the solution to this equation must be of the form $\nu = \frac{K}{\sigma}$, where K is a constant independent of σ. Moreover, notice that (4.6) coincides with (4.2) for $\sigma = 1$, such that $K = \mu(1) \approx 0.19$.

Resolving ν and substituting it along with (4.5) into one of the first order conditions yields the following equilibrium quality levels for service type A:[10]

$$
\begin{aligned}
q_{A1}^{b*} &= 400 \ \frac{2(\nu\sigma)^2 - 3(\nu\sigma) + 4}{64 - 48(\nu\sigma) + 12(\nu\sigma)^2 - (\nu\sigma)^3} \\
q_{A2}^{b*} &= \frac{100}{\sigma} \ \frac{4 - 7(\nu\sigma)}{64 - 48(\nu\sigma) + 12(\nu\sigma)^2 - (\nu\sigma)^3}.
\end{aligned}
\tag{4.7}
$$

Proposition 4.8 (Quality Leverage Under Correlated Preferences). *Under the bundle pricing regime with perfectly positively correlated preferences, firms specialize on providing either*

---

[9]The reader may be assured that (4.6) has only one real root in the relevant parameter range.

[10]Second order conditions for a maximum are fulfilled. Furthermore, high-quality leapfrogging by firm 2 is not feasible. That is, there exists no $\bar{q}_2^b = \bar{q}_{A2}^b + \bar{q}_{B2}^b > q_1^{b*}$, such that

$$
\begin{aligned}
\Pi_2^{b*}(q_1^{b*}, q_2^{b*}) &= 100 \ \frac{q_1^{b*} q_2^{b*}(q_1^{b*} - q_2^{b*})}{(4q_1^{b*} - q_2^{b*})^2} - \tfrac{\sigma}{2}q_{A2}^{b*}{}^2 - \tfrac{1}{4}q_{B2}^{b*}{}^2 \ < \\
\Pi_2^{b*}(q_1^{b*}, \bar{q}_2^b) &= 400 \ \frac{\bar{q}_2^{b \, 2}(\bar{q}_2^b - q_1^{b*})}{(4\bar{q}_2^b - q_1^{b*})^2} - \tfrac{\sigma}{2}\bar{q}_{A2}^b{}^2 - \tfrac{1}{2}\bar{q}_{B2}^b{}^2.
\end{aligned}
$$

high-or low-quality service types in both markets (HL scenario) in the unique equilibrium. Thereby one firm can achieve market leverage, even in the presence of cost disadvantages in its secondary market.

Proof. We know that $q_{A1}^b > q_{A2}^b$ as long as $\nu = \frac{\mu(1)}{\sigma} < 1 \Leftrightarrow \sigma > \mu(1) \approx 0.19$. From (4.5) it follows that $q_{B1}^b > q_{B2}^b \Leftrightarrow \frac{1}{\sigma} q_{A1}^b > \sigma q_{A2}^b \Leftrightarrow \sigma < \frac{1}{\mu(1)} \approx 5.26$. Thus, the lemma obtains if the cost asymmetry is not too predominant. □

Finally, I can investigate the impact of bundle pricing on equilibrium quality levels.

Lemma 4.9 (Equilibrium Quality Levels and Bundle Pricing Under Correlated Preferences). *Under bundle pricing, an increase in the firms' cost disadvantage in providing their secondary service will increase (decrease) the quality differentiation on the high-quality seller's home (secondary) market. The overall level of competition, reflected by the quality deflated price $\frac{p_i^b}{q_i^b}$, will remain constant, however.[11]*

Proof. Obviously, since $\nu = \frac{\mu(1)}{\sigma}$ it holds that $\frac{\partial \nu}{\partial \sigma} = -\frac{\nu}{\sigma} < 0$. Thus, an increase of σ will lead to more service differentiation in market A. In particular, differentiating q_{A1}^b with respect to σ yields $\frac{\partial q_{A1}^b}{\partial \sigma} = \frac{2\nu\sigma(5+\nu\sigma)(\nu+\sigma\frac{\partial \nu}{\partial \sigma})}{(\sigma\nu-4)^4} = 0$, and consequently $\frac{\partial q_{A2}^b}{\partial \sigma} = \frac{\partial(\nu q_{A1}^b)}{\partial \sigma} = \frac{\partial \nu}{\partial \sigma} q_{A1}^b + \frac{\partial q_{A1}^b}{\partial \sigma} = -\frac{q_{A2}^b}{\sigma} < 0$. This means that under the bundle pricing regime, firm 1 does not change its equilibrium quality level in market A, such that the increase in differentiation stems from a decrease in firm 2's equilibrium quality level only. This contrasts the results obtained under the separate pricing regime (cf. Lemma 4.7), where both firms adjust their quality levels downwards in response to an increase of cost asymmetry. Thus, I can compute $q_{A1}^{b*} = 25.33$ as the unique equilibrium value, independent of σ.

Conversely, in market B, I find that $\frac{\partial q_{B2}^b}{\partial \sigma} = \frac{\partial(\sigma q_{A1}^b)}{\partial \sigma} = 0$ and $\frac{\partial q_{B1}^b}{\partial \sigma} = \frac{\partial(\frac{1}{\sigma} q_{A1}^b)}{\partial \sigma} = -\frac{q_{B1}^b}{\sigma} < 0$. Hence, quality levels in market B become less differentiated as only firm 1 alters its service quality downwards, thereby approaching firm 2's quality level. Moreover, $q_{B2}^{b*} = 4.82$ in equilibrium, independent of σ. This proves the first part of the lemma.

For the second part of the lemma, differentiate the quality deflated prices with respect to σ

---

[11]Of course, if one firm enjoys a cost advantage in both markets, or if its cost advantage in one market overcompensates its cost disadvantage in the other, then the level of competition will be softened as the overall asymmetry increases.

and substitute the above results, yielding

$$\frac{\partial \frac{p_1^b}{q_{A1}^b + q_{B1}^b}}{\partial \sigma} = \frac{3}{\sigma} \frac{q_{A1}^b \, q_{B1}^b - q_{A2}^b \, q_{B2}^b}{(4(q_{A1}^b + q_{B1}^b) - (q_{A2}^b + q_{B2}^b))^2} = 0$$

and

$$\frac{\partial \frac{p_2^b}{q_{A2}^b + q_{B2}^b}}{\partial \sigma} = \frac{6}{\sigma} \frac{q_{A1}^b \, q_{B1}^b - q_{A2}^b \, q_{B2}^b}{(4(q_{A1}^b + q_{B1}^b) - (q_{A2}^b + q_{B2}^b))^2} = 0,$$

because of (4.5) and $q_{A2}^b = \nu \, q_{A1}^b$. $\qquad\qquad\qquad\qquad\qquad\qquad\qquad\quad$ $\square$

To conclude, the following corollary, which follows directly from the fact that (4.2) and (4.6) coincide for $\sigma = 1$, shows that bundling has no impact on the equilibrium quality levels if firms are symmetric, as assumed in the base model.[12]

Corollary 4.10. *If firms are symmetric such that they have identical costs of quality improvement for both service types, bundling has no effect on the equilibrium service quality levels.*

4.4 Economies of Scope

As I have argued before (cf. Section 2.1.2), the provision of digital goods is characterized by large scale and scope economies. While the cost function employed in the base model has accounted for economies of scale, economies of scope have deliberately been neglected. In this section, I relax the assumption (A6) by assuming that the total cost of quality are only constituted by the service of higher quality, i.e.

$$C(q_A, q_B) = \max\{C(q_A), C(q_B)\}.$$

Indeed, such an extreme form of scope economies seems reasonable in the present context, since costly infrastructure upgrades are usually necessitated by the most demanding service only.

Of course, a change of the cost structure has no effect on the final price competition stage where the firms' quality decisions are sunk already. However, the decision structure at the quality decision stage is altered. In particular, it is easy to see that firm 1, which is assumed to provide the high quality service in market A already, will always provide a high-quality service in market B also, because it can do so at no additional costs. Hence,

$$BR_1(q_H): \qquad \Pi_1(HH) > \Pi_1(LH) \quad \Leftrightarrow \quad R_1(HH) > R_1(LH) \qquad \text{and}$$
$$BR_1(q_L): \qquad \Pi_1(HL) > \Pi_1(LL) \quad \Leftrightarrow \quad R_1(HL) > R_1(LL)$$

---

[12]Further investigations concerning the impact of the pricing strategy on equilibrium quality levels will be undertaken in Section 5.3.

holds for all μ in all bundling subgames. Consequently, firm 1 chooses q_H in market B as a dominant strategy under all bundle pricing regimes. Notice that this rules out the possibility that scenario LH or LL may emerge in equilibrium.

Likewise, under all bundle pricing regimes, $BR_2(q_H)$ and $BR_2(q_L)$ are not altered through economies of scope, as firm 2 faces the principal decision of whether it wants to provide a high-quality service at all. The following proposition follows immediately.

Proposition 4.11 (Equilibria Under Economies of Scope). *If costs of quality improvement are non negligible, i.e. $\mathscr{C} > \bar{r}_2(q_H)$, scenario HL is the unique equilibrium in all bundle pricing regimes (of pure or unilateral mixed bundling) with economies scope. Otherwise scenario HH obtains in equilibrium.*

Therefore, the existence of economies of scope even encourages the quality leverage effect of bundling and strengthens my previous results.

Chapter 5

Quality Leverage and Welfare

5.1 Bundling and Welfare: A Brief Survey

The economic literature on bundling is vast (cf. Section 3.2) and therefore eludes a complete presentation of the normative implications it has put forth. Moreover, as I will exemplify in this section, the welfare consequences of bundling are found to be highly ambiguous and can hardly be generalized. Consequently, I will limit my attention to some exemplary findings of those themes which seem to be most relevant and well supported in literature.[1]

It greatly facilitates the presentation of the welfare effects of bundling to distinguish between monopoly and oligopoly settings. However, this is not to say that any of the following effects are viable under either market structure only. Under monopoly, at least, there is a consensus that bundling will almost certainly raise producers' surplus. In the absence of strategic effects, the monopolistic producer can choose freely whether or not to bundle, and will obviously only do so if it is deemed profitable. The effect of bundling on consumers' surplus, on the contrary, is not as clear. First, recall that under monopoly bundling has been mainly motivated through efficiency reasons (e.g. in production or pricing). Thus, ex-ante bundling must not necessarily be detrimental to consumers' welfare if firms would pass some of these efficiency gains on to the consumers. However, Adams and Yellen (1976) find that bundling rather diminishes consumers' surplus when employed as a price discrimination device, because it allows the monopolist to better sort customers according to their reservation values and thereby enables the extraction of additional consumers' surplus. Furthermore, Adams and Yellen suggest that

---

[1]A more detailed survey on the impact of bundling of communications services may be found in Papandrea, Stoeckl, and Daly (2003). Inevitably, their overview and mine partially overlap.

bundling generally leads to both *distributive and allocative inefficiencies*: The former stemming from the fact that bundling often forces consumers into buying more than they would have desired in the presence of individual offerings, whereas the latter denote that consumers can Pareto improve by selling their superfluous units on an aftersales market. In the present context, only distributive inefficiency will be of relevance, however, since a communications services bundle generally cannot be dismantled in a way that allows consumers to sell any one of its components separately. The same holds for information goods and in this vein also Bakos and Brynjolfsson (2000) find that large scale bundling of zero-marginal-cost goods increases producers' surplus in lieu of consumers' surplus, as it allows to better predict consumers' reservation prices at no additional costs. Among others, Salinger (1995), on the other hand, argues that "the effect of bundling on consumers' surplus depends on the precise distribution of reservation values". In particular, he identifies two independent welfare effects of bundling. First, the pure *bundling effect* refers to the distributive inefficiencies described above. Since these efficiencies are created through excessive purchases, the pure bundling effect will always have a negative impact on consumers' surplus. Second, there is a *price effect*, which is provoked by the difference between the bundle price and the sum of the component prices under separate pricing. As the bundle price is contingent upon the correlation of consumers' reservation prices, it may either exceed or undercut the sum of component prices and thereby have either negative or positive effects on consumers' welfare. Thus, whether consumers are better or worse off under bundling depends on whether the price effect can offset the pure bundling effect. As will soon be seen, the welfare implications of my model will also be driven by these two (opposing) effects.

Under oligopoly the welfare effects of bundling are even more ambiguous because strategic effects can additionaly forfeit the welfare enhancements on the producers' side. To this extend, recall the models of Matutes and Regibeau (1992), Economides (1993) or Reisinger (2006), for example, which have all identified settings in which bundling has forced firms into a prisoners' dilemma, leaving them worse off than under separate pricing. At the same time, although it is not specifically addressed in Matutes and Regibeau (1992) and Economides (1993), one can presume that consumers' surplus could potentially rise in these models as the prisoners' dilemma situation leads to lower prices (i.e. a positive price effect). Reisinger (2006), however, finds that the price effect is not strong enough to compensate for the pure bundling effect and therefore attests bundling a negative overall effect on welfare.

Mitchell and Vogelsang (1991, p. 110) annotate that whenever bundling mitigates competition (as in Carbajo, de Meza, and Seidmann 1990, or Chen 1997) or facilitates collusion (as in Seidmann 1991 and Spector 2007), consumers' surplus will generally be reduced since the price effect is likely to be negative. In these cases, the effect on total welfare depends on whether producers' surplus is increased or decreased. At least Chen (1997) affirms that in his model "profits of all firms in the industry are higher but welfare is unambiguously reduced".

Also when bundling deters entry, Whinston (1990) comments that "the normative implications are not clear", but concludes that consumers should generally be worse off as they face less variety and most likely higher prices after successful monopolization. Similarly, Peitz (2006) also finds that bundling can blockade entry and thereby reduce overall welfare. Likewise other means of market leverage are also found to decrease overall welfare (cf. e.g. Choi 2004; Martin 1999). Yet, Brennan (2005), while analyzing the welfare implications of Nalebuff (2004)'s model, which highlights bundling as an entry deterrent, finds that not only producers', but also consumers' surplus (and thus total welfare) are increased in this framework.

To conclude, the effects of (market leverage through) bundling on welfare are highly ambiguous. Nevertheless, the majority of the models support a tendency towards negative influences on consumers' and total welfare. In this context, the results of my model are very interesting as they provide a wide range of settings in which bundling will unambiguously enhance both consumers' and producers' surplus. In particular, if firms are symmetric, or consumers' preferences are uncorrelated, bundling is confirmed to have positive welfare effects. Only if the entrant has a cost disadvantage and consumers' preferences are perfectly positively correlated, bundling is found to be welfare decreasing on the consumers' *and* producers' side.

5.2 Uncorrelated Preferences

At first, I will investigate the welfare effects of bundling when consumers' preferences for quality are uncorrelated across service types. As usual, welfare (W) is given by the sum of consumers' (CS) and producers' surplus (PS). In the previous chapters I have shown that the HL scenario emerges as the (unique) equilibrium under the bundle pricing regime for almost all parameter settings. Thus, in following, I will focus on the welfare comparison between the separate pricing regime and scenario HL.

5.2.1 Pure Bundling

In this subsection I compare the separate pricing regime with the HL^{bb} scenario.

Consider producers' welfare first and recall that by Proposition 3.1 firms earn equal profits under the separate pricing regime, because both provide a high- and a low-quality service in each market. Under bundle pricing, however, firms specialize on serving either the low- or high-quality end of the market (scenario HL^{bb}), leading to an increase of firm 1's profit at the expense of firm 2's, compared to the profits under separate pricing. Thus, ex-ante it is not clear whether producers' surplus is raised or lowered in the transition. Obviously, since the same service qualities are offered in the economy in both scenarios, just by different providers, cost differences cannot account for a prospective change in producers' surplus. Therefore, the results obtained here are not peculiar to the specifics of the cost function.

Lemma 5.1 (Producers' Surplus under Pure Bundling). *Producers' surplus is higher under the bundle pricing regime (HL^{bb} scenario) than under the separate pricing regime.*

Proof. Since overall costs are identical under HL^{bb} and the separate pricing regime, I must merely show that

$$\Delta PS^{ss}_{bb}(HL) \equiv R^{bb}_1(HL) + R^{bb}_2(HL) - 2(R^{ss}_h + R^{ss}_l) > 0$$

In particular, by Proposition 3.1 and Lemma 3.4, I can directly conclude that $\Delta PS^{ss}_{bb}(HL) \approx q_H(4.41 - 1.77\mu) > 0$ for $\mu \in (0, \frac{1}{4}]$. □

Consequently, although firm 2 is worse off under HL^{bb}, the quality sorting effect of bundling mitigates competition such that overall producers' surplus is increased. However, when taking a course of action, regulators are usually more concerned with consumers' surplus or at least total welfare. More precisely, whether consumers' surplus is increased or decreased hinges upon the direction and size of the price and the bundling effect. In the present setting, the price effect is positive, because the prices for the low- and high-quality bundle are smaller under HL^{bb} than their corresponding counterparts under individual pricing (Figure 5.1). Thus, at least the customers buying these service packages under both regimes are better off under bundling. Although this finding reflects the intuitive notion of a bundle discount, the economic interpretation must moreover explain why firms' profits can rise (Lemma 5.1) while prices drop. Both can be attributed to the *bundling effect*.

On the one hand, selling bundles leaves consumers with less options: Under separate pricing each consumer can compile his optimal service package, possibly consisting of low- and high-quality services from different firms. In total, consumers can choose between nine different

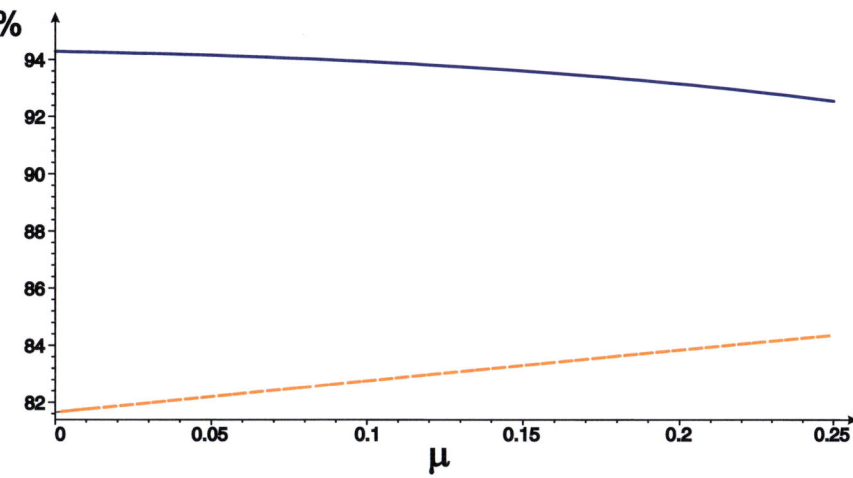

Figure 5.1: *Positive Price Effect: Prices of the low- (solid line) and high-quality bundle (dashed line) in per cent of the price for the corresponding service package under separate pricing.*

service combinations, including the no-buy option. Under the bundle pricing regime, however, consumers have only three options left – to buy the service package of either firm, or not to buy anything at all. As a consequence, many consumers are forced into buying a high-quality service bundle they would not have purchased before. In this way, the bundling effect negatively influences consumers' welfare, but increases producers' surplus.

On the other hand, the consumers' lack of choice is also a lack of differentiation on the providers' side. Whereas under the separate pricing regime a small change in price would have induced consumers to switch their provider for only one service type, a similar price change might provoke consumers to switch their provider altogether under the bundle pricing regime. Hence, bundling evokes an all-or-nothing effect which leads to increased price competition and thereby lower prices.[2]

Lemma 5.1 has confirmed that the bundling effect outweighs the price effect for the providers. Conversely, Lemma 5.2 reveals that the same price effect offsets the welfare losses incurred by the bundling effect on the consumers' side.

Lemma 5.2 (Consumers' Surplus under Pure Bundling). *Consumers' surplus is higher under the bundle pricing regime (HL^{bb} scenario) than under the separate pricing regime.*

---

[2]That is, prices are lower than for the corresponding service package under separate pricing. Recall that among the scenarios of the bundle pricing regimes, prices are among the highest in the HL^{bb} scenario.

Proof. I must show that

$$\Delta CS^{ss}_{bb}(HL) \equiv CS^{bb}(HL) - CS^{ss} > 0,$$

where $CS^{ss}_{bb}(HL)$ and CS^{ss} is the consumers' surplus under HL^{bb} and separate pricing, respectively.

First, recall the demand pattern under separate pricing from Figure 3.1. Knowing that both markets are completely symmetric, consumers' welfare can be computed as

$$CS^{ss} = \quad CS^{ss}_{\emptyset,1_L} + CS^{ss}_{\emptyset2_H} + CS^{ss}_{2_L\emptyset} + CS^{ss}_{1_H\emptyset} +$$
$$CS^{ss}_{2_L1_L} + CS^{ss}_{2_L2_H} + CS^{ss}_{1_H1_L} + CS^{ss}_{1_H2_H},$$

with

$$CS^{ss}_{\emptyset1_L} = CS^{ss}_{2_L\emptyset} = 100 \int_{\widehat{\theta}^{ss}}^{\widetilde{\theta}^{ss}} \int_0^{\widehat{\theta}^{ss}} (\theta^{ss}_A q_L - p^{ss}_l)\, d\theta^{ss}_B\, d\theta^{ss}_A$$

$$CS^{ss}_{1_H\emptyset} = CS^{ss}_{\emptyset2_H} = 100 \int_{\widetilde{\theta}^{ss}}^{1} \int_0^{\widehat{\theta}^{ss}} (\theta_A q_H - p^{ss}_h)\, d\theta_B\, d\theta_A$$

$$CS^{ss}_{1_H1_L} = CS^{ss}_{2_L2_H} = 100 \int_{\widetilde{\theta}^{ss}}^{1} \int_{\widehat{\theta}^{ss}}^{\widetilde{\theta}^{ss}} (\theta_A q_H - p^{ss}_h + \theta_B q_L - p^{ss}_l)\, d\theta_B\, d\theta_A$$

$$CS^{ss}_{2_L1_L} = 100 \int_{\widehat{\theta}^{ss}}^{\widetilde{\theta}^{ss}} \int_{\widehat{\theta}^{ss}}^{\widetilde{\theta}^{ss}} (\theta_A q_L - p^{ss}_l + \theta_B q_L - p^{ss}_l)\, d\theta_B\, d\theta_A$$

$$CS^{ss}_{1_H2_H} = 100 \int_{\widetilde{\theta}^{ss}}^{1} \int_{\widetilde{\theta}^{ss}}^{1} (\theta_A q_H - p^{ss}_h + \theta_B q_H - p^{ss}_h)\, d\theta_B\, d\theta_A$$

such that

$$CS^{ss} = q_H \frac{100(16 + 16\mu - 5\mu^2)}{(4 - \mu)^3}.$$

Furthermore, consumers' surplus in the HL^{bb} scenario is given by (cf. Figure 3.4):

$$CS^{bb}(HL) = CS^{bb}_{(1_H1_H)}(HL) + CS^{bb}_{(2_L2_L)}(HL)$$

$$CS^{bb}_{(1_H1_H)}(HL) = 100 \left[\int_0^{\frac{p^{bb}_1 - p^{bb}_2}{q_H - q_L}} \int_{\widehat{\theta}^{bb}_B}^{1} (\theta_A q_H + \theta_B q_H - p^{bb}_1)\, d\theta_B\, d\theta_A + \right.$$
$$\left. \int_{\frac{p^{bb}_1 - p^{bb}_2}{q_H - q_L}}^{1} \int_0^{1} (\theta_A q_H + \theta_B q_H - p^{bb}_1)\, d\theta_B\, d\theta_A \right]$$

$$CS^{bb}_{(2_L2_L)}(HL) = 100 \left[\int_0^{\frac{p^{bb}_2}{q_L}} \int_{\widehat{\theta}^{bb}_{B2}}^{\widehat{\theta}^{bb}_B} (\theta_A q_L + \theta_B q_L - p^{bb}_2)\, d\theta_B\, d\theta_A + \right.$$
$$\left. \int_{\frac{p^{bb}_2}{q_L}}^{\frac{p^{bb}_1 - p^{bb}_2}{q_H - q_L}} \int_0^{\widetilde{\theta}^{bb}_B} (\theta_A q_L + \theta_B q_L - p^{bb}_2)\, d\theta_B\, d\theta_A \right]$$

130

It turns out that $\Delta CS_{bb}^{ss}(HL) = q_H \, \omega^{bb}(\mu)$, where $\frac{\partial \omega^{bb}}{\partial \mu} < 0$ and $\omega^{bb}(0) = 2.4552$ and $\omega^{bb}(\frac{1}{4}) = 1.2431$, which proves the lemma. Figure 5.2 visualizes numerically exact solutions of $\Delta CS_{bb}^{ss}(HL)$ (dashed line), $\Delta PS_{bb}^{ss}(HL)$ (dotted line) and $\Delta W_{bb}^{ss}(HL) = \Delta PS_{bb}^{ss}(HL) + \Delta CS_{bb}^{ss}(HL)$ (solid line) in units of q_H for different values of μ. $\square$

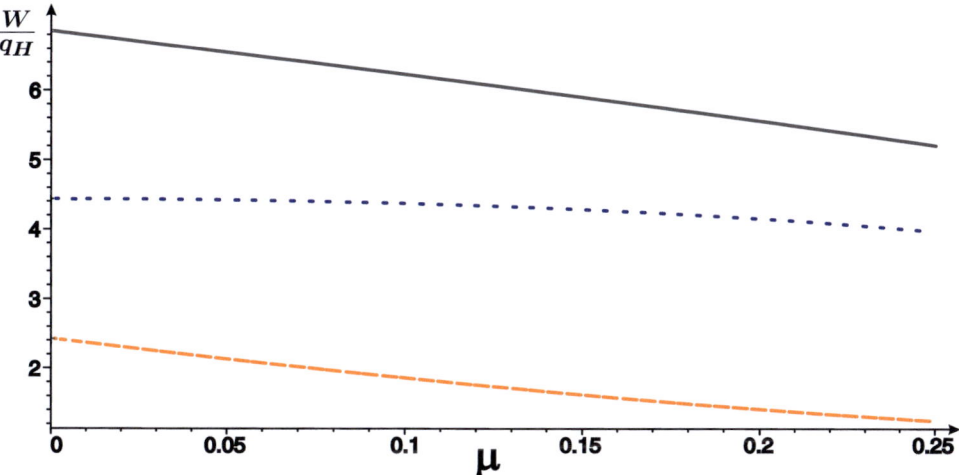

Figure 5.2: *Absolute Difference of Consumers' (dashed line), Producers' (dotted line) and Total Welfare (solid line) Between the Bundle and the Separate Pricing Regime in Units of q_H.*

The next proposition then follows trivially.

Proposition 5.3 (Total Welfare under Pure Bundling). *Total welfare is higher under the bundle pricing regime (HL^{bb} scenario) than under the separate pricing regime.*

5.2.2 Unilateral Mixed Bundling

For completeness, I pursue the same welfare analysis for the unilateral mixed bundle pricing regime (scenario HL^{uu}) instead of HL^{bb}. In general, one can say that there is only little difference to the previous results.

Lemma 5.4 (Producers' Surplus under Unilateral Mixed Bundling). *Producers' surplus is higher under the unilateral mixed bundle pricing regime (HL^{uu} scenario) than under the separate pricing regime.*

Proof. Again, since overall costs are identical under HL^{uu} and the separate pricing regime, I must only show that

$$\Delta PS^{ss}_{uu}(HL) \equiv R^{uu}_1(HL) + R^{uu}_2(HL) - 2(R^{ss}_h + R^{ss}_l) > 0$$

In particular, by Proposition 3.1 and Lemma 4.3, I can directly conclude that $\Delta PS^{ss}_{uu}(HL) \approx q_H(4.62 - 2.20\mu) > 0$ for $\mu \in (0, \frac{1}{4}]$. $\qquad\square$

Overall one can observe that $\Delta PS^{ss}_{uu}(HL) > \Delta PS^{ss}_{bb}(HL)$. This is because the price effect is weaker (i.e. prices are higher) for the high-quality bundle. On the contrary, since firm 2 faces more competition, the price effect for the low-quality bundle is stronger, but cannot off-set the increase in surplus of firm 1. Hence, unilateral mixed bundling allows producers to extract some additional rent over pure bundling.

Lemma 5.5 (Consumers' Surplus under Unilateral Mixed Bundling). *Consumers' surplus is higher under the unilateral mixed bundle pricing regime (HL^{uu} scenario) than under the separate pricing regime.*

Proof. I must show that

$$\Delta CS^{ss}_{uu}(HL) \equiv CS^{uu}(HL) - CS^{ss} > 0,$$

where $CS^{ss}_{uu}(HL)$ and CS^{ss} is the consumers' surplus under HL^{uu} and separate pricing, respectively.

Consumers' surplus in the HL^{uu} scenario is given by (cf. Figure 4.2(b)):

$$CS^{uu}(HL) = CS^{uu}_{1_H\emptyset}(HL) + CS^{uu}_{(1_H1_H)}(HL) + CS^{uu}_{(2_L2_L)}(HL)$$

$$CS^{uu}_{1_H\emptyset}(HL) = 100 \;\Big[\int_{\frac{p^{uu}_{A1}-p^{uu}_2}{q_H-q_L}}^{p^{uu}_A} \int_0^{\tilde{\theta}^{uu++}_B} (\theta_A\, q_H - p^{uu}_{A1})\; d\theta_B\, d\theta_A \;+$$

$$\int_{p^{uu}_A}^{1} \int_0^{\frac{p^{uu}_1-p^{uu}_{A1}}{q_H}} (\theta_A\, q_H - p^{uu}_{A1})\; d\theta_B\, d\theta_A\Big]$$

$$CS^{uu}_{(1_H1_H)}(HL) = 100\; \Big[\int_0^{p^{uu}_A} \int_{\tilde{\theta}^{uu+++}_B}^{1} (\theta_A\, q_H + \theta_B\, q_H - p^{uu}_1)\; d\theta_B\, d\theta_A \;+$$

$$\int_{p^{uu}_A}^{1} \int_{\frac{p^{uu}_1-p^{uu}_{A1}}{q_H}}^{1} (\theta_A\, q_H + \theta_B\, q_H - p^{uu}_1)\; d\theta_B\, d\theta_A\Big]$$

$$CS^{uu}_{(2_L2_L)}(HL) = 100 \quad [\int_0^{\frac{p^{uu}_2}{q_L}} \int_{\hat{\theta}^{uu}_{B2}}^{\tilde{\theta}^{uu+++}_B} (\theta_A\,q_L + \theta_B\,q_L - p^{uu}_2)\;d\theta_B\,d\theta_A \quad +$$

$$\int_{\frac{p^{uu}_2}{q_L}}^{\frac{p^{uu}_{A1}-p^{uu}_2}{q_H-q_L}} \int_0^{\tilde{\theta}^{uu+++}_B} (\theta_A\,q_L + \theta_B\,q_L - p^{uu}_2)\;d\theta_B\,d\theta_A +$$

$$\int_{\frac{p^{uu}_{A1}-p^{uu}_2}{q_H-q_L}}^{P^{uu}_A} \int_{\tilde{\theta}^{uu++}_B}^{\tilde{\theta}^{uu+++}_B} (\theta_A\,q_L + \theta_B\,q_L - p^{uu}_2)\;d\theta_B\,d\theta_A]$$

Here $\Delta CS^{ss}_{uu}(HL) = q_H\,\omega^{uu}(\mu)$, where $\frac{\partial\omega^{uu}}{\partial\mu} < 0$ and $\omega^{uu}(0) = 1.6970$ and $\omega^{uu}(\frac{1}{4}) = 1.2132$, which proves the lemma. $\qquad\square$

Conversely, due to the decrease in the high-quality price effect, consumers are now worse off under HL^{uu} compared to HL^{bb}. Obviously, the prices for the high-quality services generally have a greater impact on welfare and therefore overall consumers' surplus falls, although the low-quality service bundle is cheaper than under pure bundling. In sum, the total welfare improvement of unilateral mixed bundling over separate selling is a little less pronounced than under pure bundling as some welfare gain is shifted from consumers to producers.

Proposition 5.6 (Total Welfare under Unilateral Mixed Bundling). *Total welfare is higher under the unilateral mixed bundle pricing regime (HL^{uu} scenario) than under the separate pricing regime.*

5.3 Perfectly Positively Correlated Preferences

Next, consider the case where consumers' preferences for quality are perfectly positively correlated. Furthermore, as a starting point, assume $\sigma = 1$, i.e. neither firm has a cost advantage in the provision of any service type. In this perfectly symmetric setting, we know from Lemma 4.9 and Corollary 4.10 that bundling has no effect on equilibrium qualities. Moreover, consumers have to pay exactly the same for the bundle than for the sum of individual services under separate pricing, such that the same consumers will buy the same services at the same quality, and consequently, bundling will have no effect on welfare.

Proposition 5.7 (Welfare Neutrality of Bundling Under Symmetric Costs). *In the absence of cost advantages ($\sigma = 1$), bundle pricing has no effect on either consumers' or producers' welfare, when consumers' preferences are perfectly positively correlated.*

For $\sigma \neq 1$, however, the effect on welfare is not as obvious. First, recall from Lemma 4.9 that under the bundle pricing regime the incumbents will not alter their equilibrium quality as a response to a change in σ, while under separate pricing, both firms adjust their qualities downwards (upwards) if σ increases (decreases). Knowing that quality levels coincide at $\sigma = 1$, I can directly conclude from the proofs of Lemma 4.7 and 4.9 that the following inequalities hold for $\sigma > 1$:[3]

$$
\begin{aligned}
q_{A1}^{b*} > q_{A1}^{s*} \quad &\text{and} \quad q_{B1}^{b*} \ll q_{B2}^{s*} \quad \text{(high-quality levels)} \\
q_{A2}^{b*} < q_{A2}^{s*} \quad &\text{and} \quad q_{B2}^{b*} \gg q_{B1}^{s*} \quad \text{(low-quality levels)}
\end{aligned}
\tag{5.1}
$$

The intuition behind inequalities (5.1) is as follows: Under separate pricing an increase in σ will cause the entrant to lower the quality of its service type, such that marginal revenue equals marginal cost again. As a consequence, the incumbent's marginal revenue rises (Ronnen 1991) and due to the convexity of the cost function the incumbent will lower the quality of his service as well. Under bundle pricing, however, Lemma 4.9 revealed that the incumbents will not adjust their quality levels as a response to an increase in σ. Moreover, as firm 1 offers the high-quality service in market B now, despite having a cost disadvantage, the equilibrium quality q_{B1}^{b*} is considerably smaller than q_{B2}^{s*}. In fact, recall from (4.5) that $q_{B1}^{b*} = \frac{1}{\sigma}25.33$. Similarly, because q_{B2}^{b*} is fixed at the level that would have prevailed for $\sigma = 1$ under separate pricing, it is much larger than q_{B1}^{s*} which is directly affected by σ. Hence, under bundle pricing we can expect a sharp decline in quality of the high-quality service in market B as σ increases. Conversely, the low-quality service in market B will stay at a relatively high quality-level compared to separate pricing. On the contrary, in market A the relative quality differences are less pronounced, due to firm 1's incumbency. In summary, one can conclude that under bundle pricing aggregate qualities decline in the high-quality segment ($q_{A1}^{b} + q_{B1}^{b} < q_{A1}^{s} + q_{B2}^{s}$) for $\sigma > 1$, while aggregate qualities in the low quality segment rise ($q_{A2}^{b} + q_{B2}^{b} > q_{A2}^{s} + q_{B1}^{s}$). Call this the *quality effect*.

Furthermore, under separate pricing the overall disparity between equilibrium qualities increases (i.e. $\frac{\partial \mu}{\partial \sigma} < 0$), as the entrant is much more sensitive to changes in σ and therefore adjusts its quality level relatively more than the incumbent. This leads to higher quality deflated prices and, eventually, to an upwards shift of marginal consumers in each market. Under the bundle pricing regime, on the contrary, only the entrants adjust their qualities downwards. Therefore, competition softens on market A, but intensifies on market B. However, by Lemma 4.9 I could show that the overall level of competition remains constant as σ changes. Consequently, the

---

[3] All inequalities are reversed for $\sigma < 1$.

same consumers buy at the same quality deflated prices under bundling, whereas consumers under separate pricing have to pay a relatively higher price. Denote this as the *price effect*.

As will soon be seen, the quality effect and the price effect generally point in opposite directions. First, I show that the direction of the price effect is decisive for the assessment of producers' surplus.

Lemma 5.8 (Producers' Surplus Under Correlated Preferences). *Compared to separate pricing, producers' surplus is lower (higher) under bundling if $\sigma > 1$ ($\sigma < 1$).*

Proof. From Lemma 4.9 we know that the level of competition and the quality deflated prices remain constant under bundling and thus neither firm profits from an increase in σ. However, both firms suffer a loss because they have to bear increased marginal costs in their secondary market, such that overall producers' surplus is decreased under bundling. At the same time, under separate pricing an increase in σ reduces the profit of the low quality firm, but increases revenue of the high quality firm, because price competition is lessened. One can easily verify that the high quality firm's gain overcompensates the low-quality firm's loss, such that overall producers' surplus is increased. The lemma obtains since producers' surplus is identical under both pricing regimes when $\sigma = 1$. □

In the light of the two opposing effects, consumers' surplus could potentially go either way. On the one hand, the quality effect leaves consumers worse off under bundling, as firm 1's efficiency deficit in market B drives quality down in the important high-quality segment. On the other hand, by the price effect consumers enjoy relatively lower prices than under separate pricing when $\sigma > 1$.

Lemma 5.9 (Consumers' Surplus Under Correlated Preferences). *Compared to separate pricing, consumers' surplus is lower (higher) under bundling if $\sigma > 1$ ($\sigma < 1$).*

Proof. Under separate pricing, consumers' surplus of the high ($\overline{CS}^s$) and low quality buyers ($\underline{CS}^s$) are given by

$$\overline{CS}^s = 100 \int_{\tilde{\theta}^s}^{1} \left[\theta \left(q_{A1}^s + q_{B2}^s \right) - \left(p_{A1}^s + p_{B2}^s \right) \right] d\theta$$

$$\underline{CS}^s = 100 \int_{\hat{\theta}^s}^{\tilde{\theta}^s} \left[\theta \left(q_{A2}^s + q_{B1}^s \right) - \left(p_{A2}^s + p_{B1}^s \right) \right] d\theta$$

Similarly, under bundle pricing, consumers' surplus of the high $(\overline{CS}^b)$ and low quality buyers $(\underline{CS}^b)$ are

$$\overline{CS}^b = 100 \int_{\widehat{\theta}^b}^{1} \left[\theta \left(q_{A1}^b + q_{B1}^b \right) - (p_1^b) \right] \, d\theta$$

$$\underline{CS}^b = 100 \int_{\widehat{\theta}^b}^{\widetilde{\theta}^b} \left[\theta \left(q_{A2}^b + q_{B2}^b \right) - (p_2^b) \right] \, d\theta$$

First notice that for $\sigma > 1$, consumers with low θ are better off under bundle pricing as both the

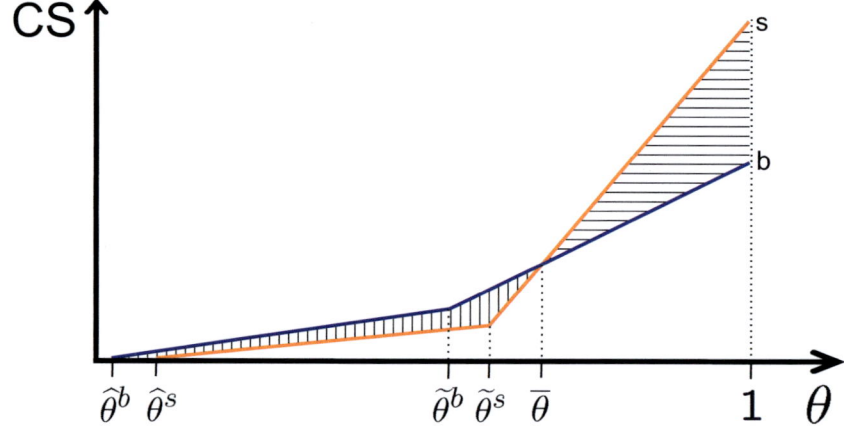

Figure 5.3: *Perfectly Positively Correlated Preferences: Comparison of Consumers' Surplus under Separate and Bundle Pricing for $\sigma > 1$*

quality and the price effect are positive for them. More formally, from equations (4.1),(4.2) and (4.3), as well as (4.4),(4.5), (4.6), (4.7) and inequalities (5.1), we know that $q_{A2}^b + q_{B2}^b > q_{A2}^s + q_{B1}^s$ and $p_2^b > p_{A2}^s + p_{B1}^s$ for $\sigma > 1$.[4] That is, in this parameter range of σ, aggregate qualities and prices are generally higher in the low-quality segment under bundle pricing. Moreover, we know that the marginal consumer who is indifferent between purchasing or not is shifted upwards under separate pricing. Taken together, I can immediately conclude that consumers' surplus must be higher under bundle pricing for $\sigma > 1$ (cf. Figure 5.3). Conversely, in the high-quality segment, it holds that $q_{A1}^b + q_{B1}^b < q_{A1}^s + q_{B2}^s$ and $p_1^b < p_{A1}^s + p_{B2}^s$ for $\sigma > 1$. Thus, due to the higher aggregate service quality available under separate pricing, consumers can derive higher surplus here compared to the bundle pricing regime. In particular, Figure 5.3 exemplifies that consumers whose willingness-to-pay for quality is above $\overline{\theta} = \frac{p_{A1}^s + p_{B2}^s - p_1^b}{q_{A1}^s + q_{B2}^s - (q_{A1}^b + q_{B1}^b)}$ are better

---

[4]Of course, all inequalities are exactly opposite for $\sigma < 1$.

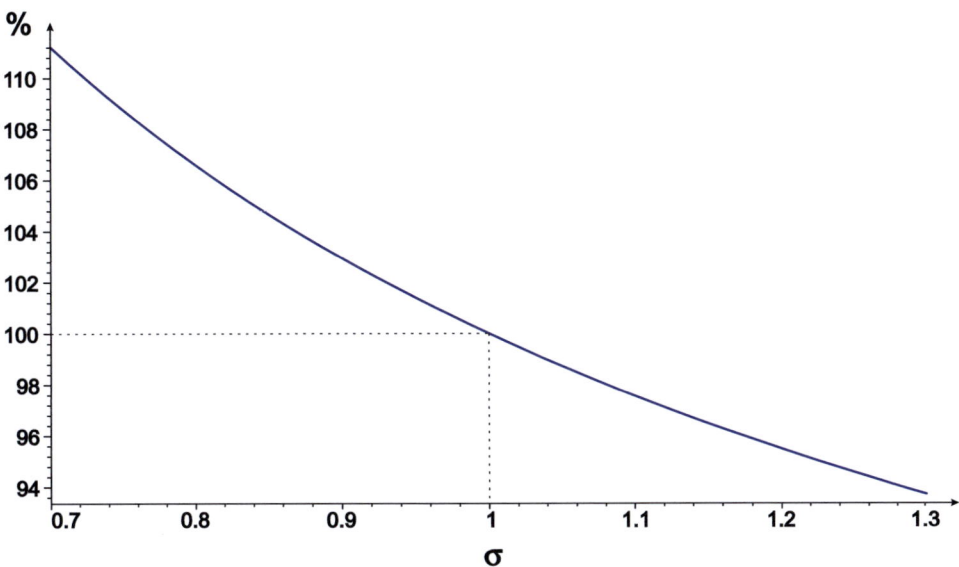

Figure 5.4: *Consumers' Surplus Under Bundle Pricing in Per Cent of Consumers' Surplus Under Separate Pricing When Consumers' Preferences are Perfectly Positively Correlated*

off under separate pricing, while the consumers below $\bar{\theta}$ are better off under the bundle pricing regime when $\sigma > 1$. Consequently, for consumers with high θ the negative quality effect offsets the positive price effect. To prove the lemma, it must be clarified whether the positive effect of bundling on low θ consumers is larger or smaller than the negative effect exerted upon the high θ consumers. To this extend, consumers' surplus under bundle pricing is expressed in per cent of consumers' surplus under the separate pricing regime in Figure 5.4. The figure reveals that the effect of bundling on the high quality segment outweighs the effect on the low quality segment and is therefore decisive for the overall net effect on consumers' welfare. Thus, consumers' surplus is lower (higher) under bundle pricing compared to separate pricing iff $\sigma > 1$. □

Finally, since the net effect of bundle pricing on both consumers' and producers' surplus points into the same direction, the following proposition follows trivially.

Proposition 5.10 (Welfare Under Correlated Preferences). *When preferences are perfectly positively correlated, total welfare is lower under bundle pricing compared to separate pricing if entrants have a cost disadvantage ($\sigma > 1$). Conversely, for $\sigma < 1$ total welfare is increased through bundle pricing.*

Chapter 6

Regulatory Implications, Empirical Evidence and Economic Prospects

In this chapter I will enrich the results of my analytical analysis with a brief reference to price regulation and empirical findings in the communications industry. Finally, I will comment on possible future scenarios in the light of the mutual forbearance theory.

6.1 Policy Implications for Price Regulation

One must be very cautious when deducing policy implications from the abstract mindset underlying game-theoretic models. However, the main insights of the present model are believed to be fairly robust and especially noteworthy in the context of *price regulation*. The German Telecommunications Law (TKG),[1] for example, defines the regulatory motives for price regulation in §27(1):

> *"The aim of price regulation is to prevent abusive exploitation, impediment, or discrimination of end users or competitors through pricing measures of undertakings with substantial market power."*

Thereby, contrary to general competition law (Article 82 EC Treaty), price regulation explicitly seeks to protect not only the consumers, but also the competitors of firms with market

---

[1]I refer to the TKG from June 22, 2004, last amended on February 18, 2007, which implements the latest EU Directives, including 2002/21 (cf. Section 1.2.3). The following translations of the TKG are my own and therefore not legally binding.

power.[2] With respect to consumers' welfare, Chapter 5 has revealed that bundle pricing is generally not harmful. However, the leverage results obtained in Chapters 3 and 4 strongly confirm that bundle pricing can be employed to diminish rivals' profits and are therefore highly relevant to price regulation, as pointed out by §28(1) TKG:

> "[...] An abusive conduct exists, if the [dominant] undertaking demands prices which [...] impair the competitive prospects of other undertakings on the communications market considerably, [...] unless factual justification for this conduct can be established."

Moreover, §28(2) TKG explicitly recognizes bundling as a means of abusive conduct:

> "An abuse according to para. 1 is presumed, if [...] an undertaking employs **factually unjustified bundling** of its products. To clarify whether this is the case, the Federal Network Agency has to check whether **efficient competitors** of the undertaking with significant market power are able to offer a comparable bundle at a similar price."

Unfortunately, the rules prescribed by §28 TKG are vague at best. For the law to be applicable, one must agree on a common understanding of the notion of the terms "factually unjustified" and "efficient competitor". Until today there exists no relevant previous rulings on the basis of §28, from which one could draw conclusions concerning the applicability of this legal norm (Monopolkommission 2005).

Holznagel, Hombergs, and Rosengarten (2004) comment on the criterion "factual unjustified" that it is notoriously imprecise, but can generally be approved if bundling is only possible because of a dominant market position. Mayen (2005) notes that one should consider previous jurisdiction in anti-trust cases. Furthermore, he argues that the allegation of an abusive conduct can only be maintained if bundling is shown to be "competitively relevant". According to a ruling of the German Federal Court of Justice (BGH), this is only the case if the bundle contains goods whose nature does not require to sell them together or whose joint sale is not customary within the industry.[3] Both cases do not hold in the present context: First, facilities-based

---

[2]More specifically, for the course of the TKG the approach to market definition is laid down in §10 TKG in combination with the framework directive Article 15(3) EC Treaty. Furthermore, "market power" is defined in §11 TKG.

[3]BGH, March 30, 2004. KZR 1/03.

communications firms certainly have neither a technical nor a factual justification for tying the provision of their secondary service to the purchase of their home service. DT, for example, could well offer an IPTV service without simultaneously demanding a voice telephony subscription. Likewise, cable companies would be able to offer Internet access or voice telephony without requiring a basic TV subscription.[4] Second, from an economic perspective Triple Play is customary within the communications industry. Both firms currently offer such bundles, and also the current analytical framework confirms that bundle pricing is in fact an equilibrium strategy for both firms.

However, despite bundling does not appear to be "competitively relevant" in this context, it has been shown that considerable market leverage can nevertheless be achieved. Therefore, the implications of the present model advise the regulator not to allow bundle pricing per se just because it is seen as a customary practice.

In an effort to clarify the notion of "efficient competitors" in the communications industry, the Federal Network Agency (BNetzA) itself has published its policy view on the matter (Bundesnetzagentur 2005). Therein, BNetzA denotes that its main task is the establishment of a regulatory framework which ensures (i) that efficient competitors must be provided access to all parts (here: services) comprising the bundle and (ii) that access is provided at prices which allow the provision of a competitive rival bundle. Furthermore, BNetzA points out that access to all essential parts of the bundle must not be warranted for *any* competitor, but merely for *efficient* ones. Of course, this immediately raises the question how the agency is to determine efficiency (Möschel and Haug 2003). To this extend, BNetzA announces that it will not judge the efficiency of specific undertakings, but rather evaluate the efficiency of business models at an abstract level. Thereby the term 'business model' is employed in reference to either (integrated) network operators, service operators or resellers (cf. Section 1.1.5). The agency further regards the current set of business models in the market as given, and thus declines to mandate firms to pursue a different business model in order to ensure the emulation of the dominant bundle. Rather, BNetzA argues that §28(2) TKG requires that efficient competitors are – in principle – able to offer a competitive bundle without having to bear inadequate additional economic risks.

With respect to the context of this paper, it is doubtful whether the view of BNetzA is able to achieve the regulatory aims of price regulation; even if the efficiency of firms and their business models could be reliably assessed: Within the present analytical framework both firms

---

[4]Some cable companies in the US, like Comcast, do not tie their broadband offers to their TV subscription, for instance.

are perfectly symmetric - in terms of their business model as well as with regard to efficiency. Furthermore, both firms are (in principle) able to offer the same bundles at identical prices, and, finally, both firms possess market power in their respective home markets. Consequently, from the agency's viewpoint, no regulatory intervention is necessary (nor legally allowed) because there exists an efficient competitor (here firm 2) which is able to emulate the bundle of the firm with substantial market power (here firm 1). In addition, firm 2 has substantial market power itself (albeit in a different market).

However, although ex ante each firm has equal economic prospects, the present game-theoretic reasoning has shown that bundling may nevertheless lead to considerable asymmetry in payoff and is therefore of relevance to price regulation. More precisely, bundling acts as a quality leverage device, which enables one firm to provide the more profitable high-quality services in both markets, whereas the competitor is left with providing a low-quality, i.e. less profitable, service quality in both markets. The impact of this quality leverage effect on firms' payoffs has been shown to be substantial. The example of Section 3.3.5 e.g. has revealed that one firm was able to more than double its profits under bundle pricing compared to separate pricing. At the same time, the profits of the competitor diminished to about three per cent of what it earned under separate pricing regime. It is important to recognize that firms' ex post asymmetry is *not* a result of differences in efficiency. Here service differentiation is rather a mutually best response (i.e. a Nash equilibrium) in the light of fierce price competition. Therefore, the quality leverage effect can be considered long-lasting from an economic perspective. Hence, BNetzA is advised to carefully reconsider its criteria concerning "efficient competitors" and "factually unjustified bundling" in general, and rather adopt an *effects-based approach* by judging on a case-by-case basis. Even more so, since the agency has already recognized that the threat of competition impediment is especially high in the communications industry (Bundesnetzagentur 2005, p.19).

In conclusion, the present model provides ample evidence that the currently highly debated *more economic approach* to jurisdiction should not only be applied to general competition law (Articles 81ff EC Treaty), but also to the sector-specific regulatory frameworks. With respect to the TKG, for example, the present economic analysis has revealed that the law's implicit and old-fashioned presumption of *intra-modal* competition,[5] which rests on the assumption that

---

[5]Recall that "intra-modal competition" refers to the competition between firms employing the *same* network technology (e.g. cable or DSL), whereas "inter-modal competition" describes the competition between firms employing *different* broadband delivery technologies (e.g. cable and DSL)

exactly *one* firm holds a dominant position in the relevant market, may not be contemporary anymore in the age of digital convergence. Indeed, the present paper points out that the rules of the game may be quite different under *inter-modal* competition where *two* firms hold some significant market power in different segments of the converged market. Although neither firm can be regarded to have an ex ante advantage in the joint market, competition can promote asymmetries in payoff and thereby hinder the economic prospects of one of the firms significantly. This situation is currently not properly accounted for in the law.

6.2 Empirical Evidence and Market Maturity

In strong support of the results of the present model, Maldoom et al. (2005, p.48) write:

> *"The European broadband consumer market has been characterised by two major trends: price reductions and increased differentiation in product offerings. Both are consistent with the maturing of broadband into a mass-market product.[...] Competition between DSL and cable operators for subscribers appears to be an important driver of price decreases and product differentiation."*

I argue that the same holds true for the Triple Play market in general, given market maturity. More specifically, the analytical results of the present model suggest, that product differentiation is a result of fierce price competition, which in turn stems from a lack of differentiation as firms switch from the separate pricing to the bundle pricing regime. Consequently, in an immature industry, where reciprocal entry has just taken place, each firm will provide a high-quality service in its home market, but only a low-quality service in its secondary market. As the market matures, firms begin to offer service bundles, possibly also to shield themselves from single service competitors. Moreover, in the short run, firms will not adjust their quality levels, resulting in scenario LH which is characterized by fierce price competition. In a mature industry, on the other side, firms realize that declining profits can only be countervailed through increased service differentiation. Quite possibly, at an interim state, both firms will fight for the quality leadership (scenario HH), yielding even lower profits. But eventually – and this is the hypothesis of the present paper – scenario HL will prevail, where firms coordinate on being either the low- or the high-quality provider for the entire Triple Play market.

Unfortunately, rigorous econometric analyses of this hypothesis are not available. In particular, previous related studies of the price developments in the communications market usually neglect changes in the rapidly changing quality of the services. An notable exception is Karamti (2007), who successfully employs the *hedonic method* to explain firms' pricing behavior in the French mobile telephony market between 1996 and 2002. The hedonic method is an empirical means of determining a price function which incorporates the (quality) characteristics of the goods sold in differentiated product markets. It was developed by Waugh (1928) and Court (1939) and later refined by Griliches (1961). The hedonic method is particularly promising in the context of the present paper, because it is able to derive the quality deflated price of the services and thus directly measures the level of price competition (cf. Section 4.3). In this vein, later scholars, beginning with Rosen (1974), related the observed hedonic prices with the equilibrium predictions of formal game theoretic models. More specifically, following Pakes (2003), these models - as well as mine - rely on three primitives:

- Utility functions, which are directly defined on the characteristics of the product (here quality) and not on the product per se. Different consumers are assumed to have different preferences for each characteristic and aggregate demand will depend on the distribution of these preferences.

- Firms' cost functions, which typically include characteristics of the good, as well as the scale of production and 'efficiency' as its arguments.

- An equilibrium assumption (here: Bertrand competition), which determines prices given demand and costs.

Here firms' bundles have two characteristics, constituted by the quality of either service. Let q_i be the vector of the relevant characteristics of bundle i, and p_i its price. Furthermore, consumers have heterogeneous preferences for each of the characteristics. Thus, let Θ denote the vector characterizing the distribution of preferences for each service type. Under a pure bundling regime, the demand for product i is then given by (cf. Section 3.3)

$$D_i(\cdot) = D_i(q_i, p_i; q_{-i}, p_{-i}; \Theta),$$

where subscript $-i$ denotes the competitors' variables. Since firms' marginal costs of quality are zero, prices depend only on the demand elasticity, i.e.

$$p_i = \frac{D_i(\cdot)}{|\partial D_i(\cdot)/\partial p|}.$$

The *hedonic function*, finally, is the expectation of price, conditional on the product characteristic, q_i:

$$h(q_i) \equiv E[p_i|q_i] = E\left(\left.\frac{D_i(\cdot)}{|\partial D_i(\cdot)/\partial p|}\right| q_i\right)$$

A thorough econometric analysis of mature and immature Triple Play markets employing the hedonic method eludes the scope of this paper and should be carried out elsewhere. Moreover, collection of quality related data is a tedious and non-trivial task, since service providers are usually very reluctant to making quality related data available. To provide at least some empirical evidence, I have collected some publicly observable data of the German Triple Play market from August 2006 until September 2007. Unequivocally, during this time period the German Triple Play market was in its infancy (cf. Section 1.3). Deutsche Telekom AG (DT), the German PSTN incumbent and former monopolist, started to offer a Triple Play package in October 2006. In the beginning, DT tied the Triple Play bundle to a subscription of its new VDSL access.[6] DT's package "Complete Basic" initially included 55 free TV channels, a voice telephony flatrate and unlimited Internet access with up to 25 Mbps bandwidth, selling at 80.84€ per month. Prior to DT, also several cable operators had Triple Play packages at offer already. The biggest incumbent in the German CATV market, Kabel Deutschland Group (KDG)[7], sold its "Professional" bundle comprising over 50 free digital TV channels, a voice telephony flatrate and unlimited 6 Mbps Internet access at 66.80€. Figure 6.1 shows the development of the bundle prices of DT and KDG over the last year. Inevitably, monthly prices have fallen during that period. In particular, in May 2007 DT renamed its "Complete Basic" package to "Entertain Comfort VDSL" and simultaneously lowered the price by 16% to currently 69.95€ in response to very reluctant Triple Play uptake. Likewise, KDG renamed its "Professional" bundle to "Deluxe" while downsizing price, but has also previously steadily reduced the effective monthly price for its Triple Play bundle by offering free initial months. The Deluxe package currently sells at 56.80€, i.e. almost 18% cheaper than the original "Professional" package. Although this price decline in itsself is notable, it does not report the full extend of the price competition. During the same time, firms have also constantly increased the quality characteristics of their services. DT, for example, added more than 15 channels to its TV ser-

---

[6]DT's reasons should be obvious in the context of this paper. However, at the time, DT argued that the high access speeds of VDSL were necessary to provide a video and TV service (Heise 2006). Surprisingly, today a comparable Triple Play offer is available over a ADSL2+ connection with 16 Mbps.

[7]Cf. Section 1.3 for an overview of the German CATV and PSTN market.

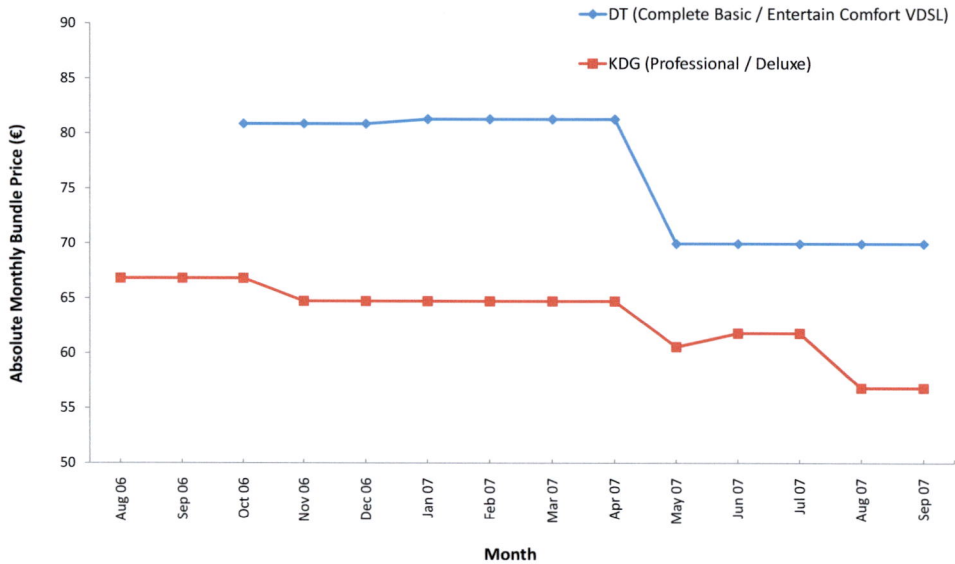

Figure 6.1: *Triple Play Price Trend in Germany from August 2006 - September 2007: Comparison of absolute monthly prices[†] for selected Triple Play bundles of network incumbents DT and KDG.*

[†] Prices include all monthly fees based on a two year subscription, but exclude one-time payments for set-up and hardware. *Source: Firms' website.*

vice; KDG even about 50. Furthermore, KDG's bundle now comes with a bandwidth of up to 25 Mbps, instead of the initial 6 Mbps. If one was to incorporate these quality changes to obtain the quality-deflated price, e.g. through the hedonic method, the decline in bundle prices would obviously be even more pronounced. In a naive approach, I have calculated the bandwidth-deflated prices for the above bundles to exemplify this point (Figure 6.2). Thereby changes in the remaining characteristics are neglected. Since the bandwidth guarantees for DT's bundle have not changed over time, here the bandwidth-deflated price still confirms a mere 16% price drop. KDG's bundle, however, went from a bandwidth-deflated price of $\frac{66.80€}{6\text{Mbps}} = 11.13€/\text{Mbps}$ to $\frac{56.80€}{25\text{Mbps}} = 2.27€/\text{Mbps}$, a decline of 490%. In the light of these figures, it is not surprising that Forrester Research has prophesied that DT's Triple Play offers are "financial suicide", given the enormous sunk costs (roughly 3 billion euros) associated with the necessary build of the infrastructure (Handelsblatt 2006). Likewise, cable companies are suffering from the financial burden of their HFC network upgrade, bestowing KDG a net loss of 26.8 million euros in the year 2006 (Heise 2007). However, with respect to more advanced Triple Play markets, such as the French

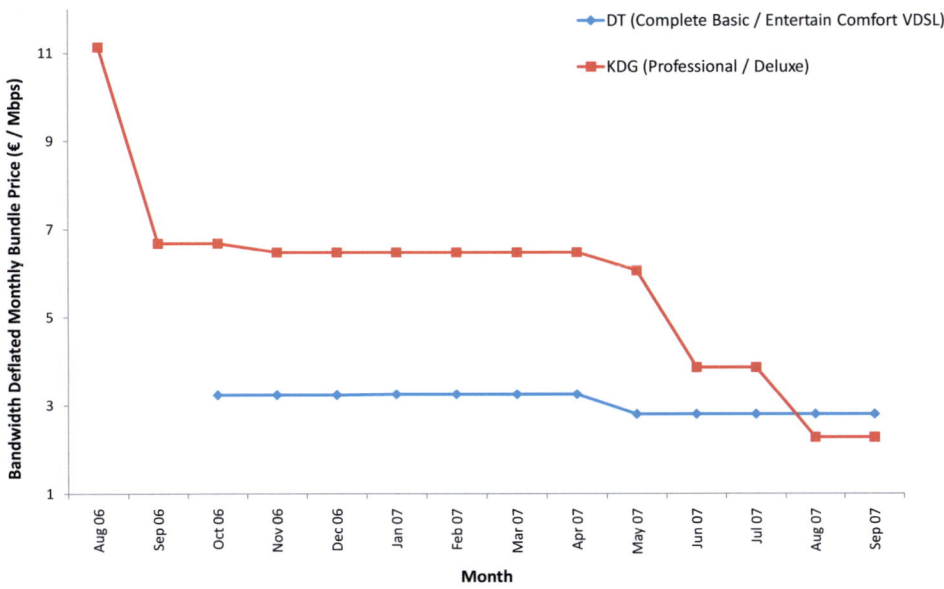

Figure 6.2: *Bandwidth Deflated Triple Play Price Trend in Germany from August 2006 - September 2007*

or Japanese markets, (quality-deflated) prices are still relatively high in Germany. In France, for example, absolute prices have manifested at a level of 45€ for some years now.[8] Nevertheless, also here quality has constantly increased during that time (Freyberg 2007, p.19ff): Today, market leader *Free*'s Triple Play package includes not only an unlimited 28 Mbps Internet access, but also over 200 TV channels and free voice telephony to all national and 70 international destinations. Recently the quality improvements to this bundle have become less fundamental though and Free's possibilities to improve value-generating product characteristics seem almost exhausted. Maybe these are the first signs that the quality-deflated price has reached a lower bound.

The present model assumes a mature industry being characterized by (i) constant quality-deflated prices (ii) and market satiation (i.e. fixed consumer mass). While the example of Free provides evidence that prices already start to level out in some countries, several studies (e.g. Booz Allen Hamilton 2007) suggest that the demand for Triple Play services is still growing. Of course, this latter effect counteracts the negative impact of diminishing profit margins and might fuel the battle for quality leadership (scenario LH or HH) for some time to come. In

---

[8]Based on a monthly bundle fee of 30€ and a basic subscription fee of 15€.

the end, it will be interesting to see if appropriate econometric studies can confirm the present analytical prophecy (scenario HL).

6.3 Mutual Forbearance: The Prisoners' Dilemma Revisited

My model considers a static framework where product differentiation is the firms' only possibility to relieve price competition. In a dynamic context, the IO literature proposes yet another means out of this dilemma. More precisely, Edwards (1955) formulates a hypothesis of *mutual forbearance* between multi-market firms; a form a tacit collusion which is thought to be facilitated through repeated interaction of the same firms in multiple product markets (*multiple-point competition*; cf. Karnani and Wernerfelt 1985). Edwards notes:[9]

> "A prospect of advantage from vigorous competition in one market may be weighed against the danger of retaliatory forays by the competitor in other markets. Each [...] competitor may adopt a live-and-let-live policy designed to stabilize the whole structure of the competitive relationship. Each may informally recognize the other's primacy of interest in markets important to the other, in the expectation that its own important interest will be similarly respected."

Thereby Edwards explicitly addresses the notion of reciprocal home market entry. He presumes that firms will refrain from price wars, because each firm fears a retaliatory counter-attack (cf. Watson 1982), should it act aggressively in the other's market territory. While being concerned with social interaction in general, also sociologist Simmel (1950, p.286ff) expressed a similar view. He argued that those rivals meeting in multiple domains will gain by allowing the other to be superordinate in some domains in exchange for similar treatment in other domains. In this vein, in a dynamic framework firms could manage to maintain high prices in scenario LH, while retaining quality leadership in their respective home market.

Porter (1980) offers two reasons of why the threat of a retaliatory attack might be extraordinarily credible under multiple-point competition. First, since the firms meet in multiple markets, the competitor can simultaneously retaliate in all markets, allowing for considerably severer punishments. Second, the competitor can choose to retaliate in those markets where its own potential losses are relatively small, leaving the defecting firm much worse off. A third argument

---

[9]As quoted by Scherer (1980, p.340).

in favor of the mutual forbearance hypothesis has been put forth by Boeker et al. (1997) and Jayachandran, Gimeno, and Varadarajan (1999), who argue that the high interconnectedness of the multi-market competitors will augment their knowledge about each other. The longer and the more often the rival firms meet, the more they learn about each other's past competitive behavior and may thus anticipate future actions more accurately. Such knowledge of the other's 'weak spots' may then help to sustain a credible commitment to tacit collusion.

It is also in the context of these arguments, that Karnani and Wernerfelt (1985) have motivated the *mutual foothold equilibrium* (cf. Section 2.2.1), a strategy which deliberately creates multiple points of competition to facilitate collusion. In this way, multi-market contact creates strategic exit barriers, because it leads firms to continue competing in those markets where they might perform poorly (Baum and Korn 1999). This view provides further evidence that scenario LH – where firms perform well in their home, but poorly in their secondary market – may well be maintained outside a static framework.

Although the above arguments are compelling at first glance, for a long time the mutual forbearance hypothesis has rested on weak formal grounds. Bernheim and Whinston (1990), for example, point out that Porter's argument contains a logical flaw: "Once a firm knows that it will be punished in every market, if it decides to cheat, it will do so in every market." Albeit multiple-point competition raises the severeness of the punishment, it is likely to equally raise the benefit of defection. In their seminal paper, Bernheim and Whinston consider an infinitely repeated game with two firms. In each period firms may choose their prices cooperatively or non-cooperatively, the latter being subsequently punished by infinite competitive pricing behavior of the other firm (*trigger-strategy*; cf. Friedman 1971). At first, Bernheim and Whinston establish an *irrelevance result*, which states that multi-market contact does not aid in sustaining collusive outcomes when *identical firms* with *identical constant-return-to-scale technologies* meet in *identical markets*. However, the authors also prove that if any of these three conditions is violated, in particular if firms' technology exhibits scale economies, repeated multiple-point competition pools the firms' incentive constraints governing the implicit agreements between them and thereby enables mutual forbearance. Furthermore, in a similar spirit Matsushima (2001) shows that the mutual forbearance hypothesis is theoretically also sustainable if firms can only imperfectly monitor their opponents.

In closing, there is ample formal analytical support that mutual forbearance is feasible in the present context. In addition, some empirical studies provide further evidence that multi-market contact facilitates tacit collusion in telecommunications (Parker and Röller 1997) and media (Waldfogel and Wulf 2005) markets. Finally, it should be annotated that the currently fierce price competition in the Triple Play market does not yet contradict the possibility of mutual forbearance. To the contrary, Gimeno and Woo (1996, p.326) argue from a more dynamic perspective that the initial "development of multi-market contacts spark episodes of intense rivalry". But as firms realize the implications of multi-market contact on competition, they are guided towards more collusive equilibria. Thus, in the future a combination of mutual forbearance and increased service differentiation seems to offer the facilities-based communications firms a plausible way out of their current dilemma.

Conclusion and Outlook

During the last two decades, bundling has become a hot topic for Industrial Organization economists, mainly as a result of legal actions against Microsoft (Crampes and Hollander 2007). In this spirit, the literature has thus far focused on asymmetric settings where one firm holds a monopoly for some type of service, while the competitors have only limited or no market power. In this paper, I consider a symmetric reciprocal duopoly setting, where both firms have some additional market power in their respective home market. This market structure has been constituted in the communications industry as a direct consequence of the digital convergence phenomenon, which led previously distinct integrated network operators to offer essentially the same kinds of services. Today, voice telephony, Internet and TV services are all available from either the telephone- or cable network incumbents, both of which frequently bundle these services to one so-called Triple Play package.

Moreover, previous literature has typically considered communications services as a homogeneous good. To the contrary, I argue that these services differ in various quality measures, such as bandwidth, content, or failure rates. For the firms, the provision of high-quality services is more costly than the provision of low-quality services. Conversely, consumers have a greater reservation price for higher service qualities. Therefore firms face a trade off between revenues and cost when selecting the optimal service quality.

While carefully recognizing the technological, legal and economic framework, I have investigated whether bundle pricing is indeed a profitable pricing strategy in this industry, if it can facilitate market power leverage and whether it emerges as an equilibrium strategy. To this extend, a three-stage game was considered, in which firms decide whether to offer their services in a bundle or separately in stage one, determine the quality of their services in stage two, and compete in prices in stage three. I can show that bundle pricing serves as a powerful leverage device. This is achieved through a vertical differentiation effect, which accrues as the firms wish to shield themselves from increased price competition in the market for bundles.

Absent bundling, each firm can exploit its limited market power and obtain quality leadership (associated with higher profits) in its home market. Under bundle pricing, however, one firm emerges as the high-quality, high-profit provider in *all* markets, whereas the competing firm has to settle for low qualities and profits. This quality leverage effect is said to be 'powerful' because it holds under some fairly general terms and for a number of worst-case assumptions. First, recall that market power is rather limited in the present framework because neither firm holds a monopoly position. Nevertheless, leverage is achieved under all feasible settings. Next, I have restricted the analysis to those settings for which interior price equilibria exist for all four possible scenarios of the bundle pricing regimes. Alternative settings tend to strengthen my results. Furthermore, I have assumed consumers' quality preferences to be uncorrelated across service types. This has been shown to be least appreciated by the quality leverage effect because demand is evenly spread out up to every corner of the market. Finally, the quality leverage effect is robust to variations in the cost structure, as long as the costs of quality improvement are convex and fall on fixed costs mainly. It neither relies on service complementarity nor on any other efficiency gains due to economies of scope or transaction costs. The effect even prevails under a unilateral mixed bundling regime.

Furthermore, the welfare effects of bundle pricing have been studied under various settings. Quite surprisingly, I found that both consumers' and producers' welfare generally rise, because each group assesses the impact of the *price effect* and the *bundling effect* differently: On the one hand, consumers enjoy lower average prices, while on the other hand, firms benefit from reduced service variety. However, the quality leverage effect of bundling crucially affects the distribution of firms' profits and should therefore be considered in the context of price regulation.

Hence, the present model may serve as a fruitful basis for future work on entry deterrence; a topic which has only been discussed briefly here. I have commented earlier that in my model - unlike many others - bundling has the potential to deter entry without requiring any prior commitment. Moreover, deterrence is achieved although consumers' preferences are uncorrelated, similar to Nalebuff (2004), and despite of the reciprocal duopoly structure in which each firm has limited market power.

Furthermore, future work should extend the present static model to a dynamic framework, allowing for a more direct assessment of entry deterrence as well as the mutual forbearance hypothesis. At the same time it may also be necessary to allow for ex-ante asymmetries, since Bernheim and Whinston (1990) have shown that the mutual forbearance is 'irrelevant' when firms and markets are symmetric. Also switching costs or network effects have the ability to turn small initial asymmetries into large advantages over time, and may thus facilitate entry deterrence.

In conclusion, it is annotated that the current framework is believed to be applicable for any digital goods industry characterized by high fixed costs and near zero marginal costs. The software industry, for example, exhibits many of the same economic peculiarities discussed in the light of the communications industry, such as high sunk costs, economies of scale and scope, network effects and compatibility or switching costs.

Appendix

A.1 Proof of Lemma 3.3

I consider each of the scenarios subsequently:

Scenario LH^{bb} : Figure 3.3 shows firms' demands in this scenario.[10] In particular, firms' revenue is given by

$$R_1^{bb}(LH) = 100 \left(\int_{L_A^{bb}}^{1} \widetilde{\theta}_B^{bb} \, d\theta_A - \int_{L_A^{bb}}^{\frac{p_1^{bb}(LH)}{q_H}} \widehat{\theta}_{B1}^{bb} \, d\theta_A \right) p_1^{bb}(LH)$$

$$R_2^{bb}(LH) = 100 \left(1 - \int_{0}^{L_A^{bb}} \widehat{\theta}_{B2}^{bb} \, d\theta_A - \int_{L_A^{bb}}^{1} \widetilde{\theta}^{bb} \, d\theta_A \right) p_1^{bb}(LH),$$

Solving these equations for optimal prices and setting $q_L = \mu \, q_H$, one finds the unique price equilibrium to be:

$$p_1^{bb}(LH) = p_2^{bb}(LH) = q_H \frac{\sqrt{(2-\mu) + 3\mu^3} - 1 - \mu}{1 - 3\mu} \qquad (A.1)$$

Notice that positive prices exist for all $\mu \in (0, 1)$. However, prices decrease when services become less differentiated, such that for $\mu = 1$, i.e. $q_H = q_L$, prices eventually drop to zero.

---

[10]Specifically, I assume $\frac{p_1^{bb}(LH)}{q_H} < \frac{p_2^{bb}(LH)}{q_L}$, because under the alternative assumption there exists no interior price equilibrium. Detailed proofs of this and following side notes are available from the author upon request.

Scenario HL^{bb}: Here the demand pattern looks as in Figure 3.4.[11] Firms' revenues are now

$$
R_1^{bb}(HL) = 100 \left(1 - \int_0^{\frac{p_1^{bb}(HL) - p_2^{bb}(HL)}{q_H - q_L}} \widetilde{\theta}_B^{bb} \, d\theta_A \right) p_1^{bb}(HL)
$$

$$
R_2^{bb}(HL) = 100 \left(\int_0^{\frac{p_1^{bb}(HL) - p_2^{bb}(HL)}{q_H - q_L}} \widetilde{\theta}_B^{bb} \, d\theta_A - \int_0^{\frac{p_2^{bb}(HL)}{q_L}} \widehat{\theta}_{B2}^{bb} \, d\theta_A \right) p_2^{bb}(HL) \quad ,
$$

and optimal prices are uniquely determined as:

$$
\begin{aligned}
p_1^{bb}(HL) &= q_H \frac{2 - 4u + 2u^2 - \alpha^2 u^2 - 9\alpha^2 + 18\alpha^2 u}{8u\alpha} \\
p_2^{bb}(HL) &= q_H \, \alpha \, \mu
\end{aligned}
\tag{A.2}
$$

where $\alpha(\mu) = \dfrac{\sqrt{6}\sqrt{(11u^2 - 54u + 27)(17u^2 - 18u + 9 - 8\sqrt{4u^4 - 6u^3 + 3u^2})}}{3(11u^2 - 54u + 27)}$ and $\mu = \frac{q_L}{q_H}$ again.

See that $p_1^b(HL) > p_2^b(HL)$. However, in order for $p_2^b(HL) > 0$ it must hold that $\alpha > 0$, which is fulfilled iff $\mu < \frac{27 - 12\sqrt{3}}{11} \approx 0.565035483$.

Scenarios HH^{bb} and LL^{bb}: Say both firms choose $q_X \in \{q_H, q_L\}$ in market B, then their revenue functions are (cf. Figure 3.5):[12]

$$
R_1^{bb}(XX) = 100 \left(1 - L_A^{bb} - \int_{L_A^{bb}}^{\frac{p_1^{bb}(XX)}{q_H}} \widehat{\theta}_{B1}^{bb} \, d\theta_A \right) p_1^{bb}(XX)
$$

$$
R_2^{bb}(XX) = 100 \left(L_A^{bb} - \int_0^{L_A} \widehat{\theta}_{B2}^{bb} \, d\theta_A \right) p_2^{bb}(XX),
$$

where optimal prices are given by:

$$
\begin{aligned}
p_1^{bb}(XX) &= q_H \Big[\frac{18\beta_X^2 \mu - 9\beta_X^2 \mu^2 + \beta_X^2}{2\mu(4\beta_X - 5\mu + 3\mu^2 + 2)} \\
&\quad - \mu_X \frac{14\beta_X \mu - 12\beta_X \mu^2 - 2\beta_X - 2 + 4\mu - 2\mu^2}{2\mu(4\beta_X - 5\mu + 3\mu^2 + 2)} \Big] \\
p_2^{bb}(XX) &= q_H \, \beta_X
\end{aligned}
\tag{A.3}
$$

where

$$
\mu_X = \begin{cases} 1 & \text{if} \quad q_X = q_H \\ \mu & \text{if} \quad q_X = q_L \end{cases}
$$

---

[11]The Figure assumes $\frac{p_1^{bb}(HL) - p_2^{bb}(HL)}{\Delta q} \leq 1$, which is the only setting for which an interior price equilibrium exists.

[12]The Figure assumes again that $\frac{p_1^{bb}(XX)}{q_H} < \frac{p_2^{bb}(XX)}{q_L}$, which is the only setting for which I obtain an interior price equilibrium.

and β_X is the positive real root of $(81\mu^3 - 162\mu^2 + 33\mu)\beta_X^4 + (16 + 4\mu + 324\mu^2 - 216\mu^3)\beta_X^3 + (108\mu^3 - 228\mu + 56)\beta_X^2 + (48\mu^3 - 208\mu^2 + 240\mu - 80)\beta_X - 20\mu^3 + 56\mu^2 - 52\mu + 16 = 0$ if $q_X = q_H$ or

$(81\mu^3 - 162\mu^2 + 33\mu)\beta_X^4 + (16 + 4\mu + 324\mu^2 - 216\mu^3)\beta_X^3 - (108\mu^3 - 144\mu^4 + 88\mu^2 + 12\mu)\beta_X^2 + (72\mu^2 - 24\mu^4 - 32\mu - 16\mu^3)\beta_X - 24\mu^5 + 68\mu^4 - 64\mu^3 + 20\mu^2 = 0$ if $q_X = q_L$.

In the LL^{bb} scenario I must assume that $\mu < \frac{1}{2-\sqrt{3}} \approx \frac{1}{3.73205}$ in order for $\frac{p_1^{bb}}{q_H} < \frac{p_2^{bb}}{q_L}$ to hold: A result, which I have forestalled in my assumptions. In the HH^{bb} scenario this equilibrium condition is less restricting and amounts to $\mu < \frac{10}{9} + \frac{17}{9\xi} - \frac{\xi}{9} \approx \frac{1}{2.30739}$, where $\xi = \sqrt[3]{269 + 27\sqrt{106}}$.   □

A.2   Proof of Lemma 3.4

To make the analysis tractable, I approximate the revenue functions linearly. This is possible because generally all revenue functions have the form of $R_i = q_H g_i(\mu)$, where $\frac{\partial g_i(\mu)}{\partial \mu}$ is monotone in μ. In the small range of $\mu \in (0, \frac{1}{4}]$ numerical comparisons show that these linear approximations are very close to the original functions (see e.g. Figure A.1 for such a comparison). More specifically, I will use the approximation

$$g_i(\mu) \approx g_i(0) - 4\left(g_i(0) - g_i(\tfrac{1}{4})\right)\mu,$$

where $g_i(0) = \lim_{\mu \to 0} g_i(\mu)$.

Given this approximation scheme and the precise revenue functions as stated in the proof of Lemma 3.3, I obtain the following values for the bb-subgame:

$$
\begin{aligned}
R_1^{bb}(HH) &= q_H\left(36.879 - 4\left(36.879 - 29.879\right)\mu\right) &= q_H\left(36.879 - 28\mu\right) \\
R_2^{bb}(HH) &= q_H\left(6.705 - 4\left(6.705 - 6.320\right)\mu\right) &= q_H\left(6.705 - 1.54\mu\right) \\
R_1^{bb}(HL) &= q_H\left(54.410 - 4\left(54.410 - 47.145\right)\mu\right) &= q_H\left(54.410 - 29.06\mu\right) \\
R_2^{bb}(HL) &= q_H\left(0 - 4\left(0 - 2.155\right)\mu\right) &= q_H\,8.62\,\mu \\
R_i^{bb}(LH) &= q_H\left(17.158 - 4\left(17.158 - 16.199\right)\mu\right) &= q_H\left(17.158 - 3.836\mu\right) \\
R_1^{bb}(LL) &= q_H\left(25 - 4\left(25 - 24.624\right)\mu\right) &= q_H\left(25 - 1.504\mu\right) \\
R_2^{bb}(LL) &= q_H\left(0 - 4\left(0 - 3.634\right)\mu\right) &= q_H\,14.536\,\mu
\end{aligned}
$$

□

A.3 Amendment to Proof of Lemma 3.5

Figure A.1 shows the goodness of fit of the linear approximations for the feasibility function $\overline{f}(\mu)$ and the threshold functions $\overline{r}_i^{bb}$ by comparing them with the exact functions in the interval $\mu \in (0, \frac{1}{4}]$.

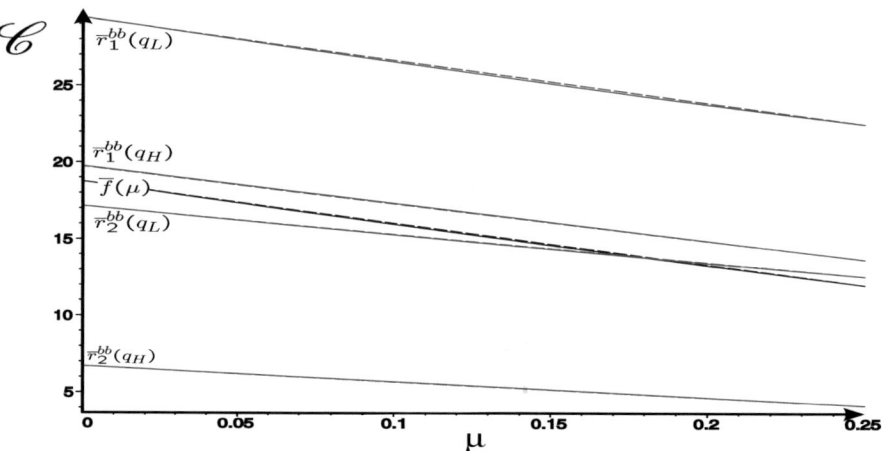

Figure A.1: *Comparison of Exact Functions (solid lines) and Linear Approximations (dashed lines)*

A.4 Proof of Lemma 3.9

I consider each of the scenarios subsequently again:

Scenario LH^{bs} : Recall the demand pattern of Figure 3.6(a). Set $q_{B1} = q_L$ and $q_{B2} = q_H$. Demand is then given by:

$$D^{bs}_{(1_H 1_L)}(LH) = 100[\int_{L_A^{bs}}^{\frac{p_1^{bs} - p_{A2}^{bs} - p_{B2}^{bs}}{q_H - q_L}} (\widetilde{\theta}_B^{bs+++} - \widetilde{\theta}_B^{bs+}) \, d\theta_A +$$

$$\int_{\frac{p_1^{bs} - p_{A2}^{bs} - p_{B2}^{bs}}{q_H - q_L}}^{\frac{p_1^{bs} - p_{A2}^{bs}}{q_H - q_L}} (1 - \widetilde{\theta}_B^{bs+++}) \, d\theta_A + \int_{\frac{p_1^{bs} - p_{A2}^{bs}}{q_H - q_L}}^{1} 1 \, d\theta_A]$$

$$D^{bs}_{\emptyset 2_H}(LH) = 100 \int_{0}^{\frac{p_{A2}^{bs}}{q_L}} (1 - \frac{p_{B2}^{bs}}{q_H}) \, d\theta_A$$

$$D^{bs}_{2_L\emptyset}(LH) \quad = \quad 100[\int_{\frac{p^{bs}_{A2}}{q_L}}^{\frac{L^{bs}_A}{q_H}} \frac{p^{bs}_{B2}}{q_H} \, d\theta_A + \int_{L^{bs}_A}^{\frac{p^{bs}_1 - p^{bs}_{A2} - p^{bs}_{B2}}{q_H - q_L}} \tilde{\theta}^{bs+}_B \, d\theta_A]$$

$$D^{bs}_{2_L 2_H}(LH) \quad = \quad 100[\int_{\frac{p^{bs}_{A2}}{q_L}}^{L^{bs}_A} (1 - \frac{p^{bs}_{B2}}{q_H}) \, d\theta_A + \int_{L^{bs}_A}^{\frac{p^{bs}_1 - p^{bs}_{A2} - p^{bs}_{B2}}{q_H - q_L}} (1 - \tilde{\theta}^{bs+++}_B) \, d\theta_A]$$

Firms' revenue is

$$R^{bs}_1(LH) \quad = \quad D^{bs}_{(1_H 1_L)}(LH) \, p^{bs}_1(LH)$$

$$R^{bs}_2(LH) \quad = \quad \left(D^{bs}_{2_L\emptyset}(LH) + D^{bs}_{2_L 2_H}(LH) \right) p^{bs}_{A2}(LH) +$$
$$\left(D^{bs}_{\emptyset 2_H}(LH) + D^{bs}_{2_L 2_H}(LH) \right) p^{bs}_{B2}(LH).$$

Solving for optimal prices yields:

$$p^{bs}_1(LH) \quad = \quad q_H \frac{\phi^2(3 - \mu - 2) + 4(1 - \mu)(\phi + 1)}{8 - 2\mu}$$

$$p^{bs}_{A2}(LH) \quad = \quad q_H \, \mu \frac{5\phi^2 - 6\phi + 2(1 - \mu)}{8 - 2\mu} \tag{A.4}$$

$$p^{bs}_{B2}(LH) \quad = \quad q_H \, \phi,$$

where ϕ is the smallest positive real root of $(9\mu + 4)\phi^3 - (3\mu^2 - 2 + 8\mu)\mu^2 - (6\mu^2 - 26\mu + 20)\phi + 4\mu^2 - 8\mu + 4 = 0$. The revenue functions are monotone in μ and thus I can apply the linear approximation scheme used in the proof of Lemma 3.4 to obtain $R^{bs}_1(LH) \approx q_H(35.090 - 27\mu)$ and $R^{bs}_2(LH) \approx q_H(5.883 - 1.692\mu)$.

Scenario HL^{bs} :   From the demand pattern depicted in Figure 3.6(b) and by setting $q_{B1} = q_L$ and $q_{B2} = q_H$, I obtain:

$$D^{bs}_{(1_H 1_H)}(HL) \quad = \quad 100[\int_0^{\frac{p^{bs}_{A2}}{q_L}} (1 - \tilde{\theta}^{bs++}_B) \, d\theta_A + \int_{\frac{p^{bs}_{A2}}{q_L}}^{L^{bs}_A} (1 - \tilde{\theta}^{bs+++}_B) \, d\theta_A +$$
$$\int_{L^{bs}_A}^{\frac{p^{bs}_1 - p^{bs}_{A2}}{q_H - q_L}} (1 - \tilde{\theta}^{bs+}_B) \, d\theta_A + \int_{\frac{p^{bs}_1 - p^{bs}_{A2}}{q_H - q_L}}^1 1 \, d\theta_A]$$

$$D^{bs}_{\emptyset 2_L}(HL) \quad = \quad 100 \int_0^{\frac{p^{bs}_{A2}}{q_L}} (\tilde{\theta}^{bs++}_B - \frac{p^{bs}_{B2}}{q_L}) \, d\theta_A$$

$$D^{bs}_{2_L\emptyset}(HL) \quad = \quad 100[\int_{\frac{p^{bs}_{A2}}{q_L}}^{L^{bs}_A} \frac{p^{bs}_{B2}}{q_L} \, d\theta_A + \int_{L^{bs}_A}^{\frac{p^{bs}_1 - p^{bs}_{A2}}{q_H - q_L}} \tilde{\theta}^{bs+}_B \, d\theta_A]$$

$$D^{bs}_{2_L 2_L}(HL) \quad = \quad 100 \int_{\frac{p^{bs}_{A2}}{q_L}}^{L^{bs}_A} (\tilde{\theta}^{bs+++}_B - \frac{p^{bs}_{B2}}{q_L}) \, d\theta_A$$

Firms' revenue is calculated as

$$
\begin{aligned}
R_1^{bs}(HL) &= D_{(1_H 1_H)}^{bs}(HL)\, p_1^{bs}(HL) \\
R_2^{bs}(HL) &= \left(D_{2_L\emptyset}^{bs}(HL) + D_{2_L 2_L}^{bs}(HL)\right) p_{A2}^{bs}(HL) + \\
&\quad \left(D_{\emptyset 2_L}^{bs}(HL) + D_{2_L 2_L}^{bs}(HL)\right) p_{B2}^{bs}(HL).
\end{aligned}
$$

Solving for optimal prices yields

$$
\begin{aligned}
p_1^{bs}(HL) &= q_H\, \frac{\varphi^2(9+25\mu-2\mu^2)+2(1+\mu^2)-4\mu}{4\varphi(\mu+3)} \\
p_{A2}^{bs}(HL) = p_{B2}^{bs}(LH) &= q_H\,\varphi\mu,
\end{aligned}
\tag{A.5}
$$

where φ is the smallest positive real root of $(36\mu^3 - 192\mu^2 - 339\mu - 81)\varphi^4 - (40\mu^3 - 12\mu^2 + 32\mu - 60)\varphi^2 + 4\mu^3 - 12\mu^2 + 12\mu - 4 = 0$. The numerical linear approximation yields $R_1^{bs}(HL) \approx 54.409 - 31.364\mu$ and $R_2^{bs}(HL) \approx 6.652\mu$.

Scenarios HH^{bs} and LL^{bs}: Consider Figure 3.6(c) and let $q_{B1} = q_{B2} = q_X, q_X \in \{q_H, q_L\}$. Then

$$
D_{(1_H 1_X)}^{bs}(XX) = 100\left[\int_{\frac{p_1^{bs}-p_{A2}^{bs}-p_{B2}^{bs}}{q_H-q_L}}^{\frac{p_1^{bs}-p_{B2}^{bs}}{q_H-q_L}} (1 - \widetilde{\theta}_B^{bs+})\, d\theta_A + \int_{\frac{p_1^{bs}-p_{B2}^{bs}}{q_H-q_L}}^{1} 1\, d\theta_A \right]
$$

$$
D_{\emptyset 2_X}^{bs}(XX) = 100 \int_{0}^{\frac{p_{A2}^{bs}}{q_L}} \left(1 - \frac{p_{B2}^{bs}}{q_X}\right) d\theta_A
$$

$$
D_{2_L\emptyset}^{bs}(XX) = 100\left[\int_{\frac{p_{A2}^{bs}}{q_L}}^{L_A^{bs}} \frac{p_{B2}^{bs}}{q_X}\, d\theta_A + \int_{L_A^{bs}}^{\frac{p_1^{bs}-p_{A2}^{bs}}{q_H-q_L}} \widetilde{\theta}_B^{bs+}\, d\theta_A \right]
$$

$$
D_{2_L 2_X}^{bs}(XX) = 100 \int_{\frac{p_{A2}^{bs}}{q_L}}^{L_A^{bs}} \left(1 - \frac{p_{B2}^{bs}}{q_X}\right) d\theta_A
$$

with revenues of

$$
\begin{aligned}
R_1^{bs}(XX) &= D_{(1_H 1_X)}^{bs}(XX)\, p_1^{bs}(XX) \\
R_2^{bs}(XX) &= \left(D_{2_L\emptyset}^{bs}(XX) + D_{2_L 2_X}^{bs}(XX)\right) p_{A2}^{bs}(XX) + \\
&\quad \left(D_{\emptyset 2_X}^{bs}(XX) + D_{2_L 2_X}^{bs}(XX)\right) p_{B2}^{bs}(XX).
\end{aligned}
$$

Solving for optimal prices yields

$$
\begin{aligned}
p_1^{bs}(XX) &= q_H\, \frac{\rho^2(3\mu-2)+4\mu_X(1-\mu)(\rho+1)}{\mu_X(8-2\mu)} \\
p_{A2}^{bs}(XX) &= q_H\, \mu\frac{5\rho^2 - \mu_X(6\rho+2(1-\mu))}{8-2\mu} \\
p_{B2}^{bs}(XX) &= q_H\, \rho,
\end{aligned}
\tag{A.6}
$$

where ρ is the smallest positive real root of $(9\mu + 4)\rho^3 + \mu_X(14 - 23\mu)\rho^2 + \psi_X\rho + \mu_X^2(4 - \mu^2 - 8\mu + 4) = 0$, with $\psi_H = 26\mu - 6\mu^2 - 20$ and $\psi_L = 6\mu^3 + 2\mu^2 - 8\mu$. Here revenues can be well approximated by $R_1^{bs}(HH) \approx 36.9 - 30.556\mu$, $R_2^{bs}(HH) \approx 6.705 - 3.276\mu$, $R_1^{bs}(LL) \approx 25 - 0.952\mu$ and $R_2^{bs}(LL) \approx 13.468\mu$. □

A.5 Proof of Lemma 3.12

Since scenario LH^{sb} is analogous to scenario LH^{bs}, I must only consider scenarios HL^{sb} and XX^{sb} here. In this subgame consumers have the choice of five different service portfolios again: They may buy firm 2's bundle, firm 1's services separately (either one or both) or refrain from purchasing any service:

Consumers indifferent between buying firm 2's bundle and firm 1's A-service satisfy

$$\widetilde{\theta}_B^{sb+} = \frac{p_2^{sb} - p_{A1}^{sb}}{q_{B2}} + \theta_A \frac{q_H - q_L}{q_{B2}}$$

Consumers indifferent between buying firm 2's bundle and firm 1's B-service only are located at

$$\widetilde{\theta}_B^{sb++} = \frac{p_{B1}^{sb} - p_2^{sb}}{q_{B1} - q_{B2}} + \theta_A \frac{q_L}{q_{B1} - q_{B2}}$$

Consumers indifferent between buying firm 2's bundle and each of firm 1's services separately lie along

$$\widetilde{\theta}_B^{sb+++} = \frac{p_{A1}^{sb} + p_{B1}^{sb} - p_2^{sb}}{q_{B1} - q_{B2}} - \theta_A \frac{q_H - q_L}{q_{B1} - q_{B2}}$$

The locus of consumers indifferent between buying firm 2's bundle and either firm 1's A-service or both services of firm 1, i.e. where $\widetilde{\theta}_B^{sb+} = \widetilde{\theta}_B^{sb+++}$ is given by $L^{sb} = (L_A^{sb}, L_B^{sb})$, where

$$L_A^{sb} = \frac{q_{B1}\left(p_{A1}^{sb} - p_2^{sb}\right) + q_{B2}p_{B1}^{sb}}{\left(q_H - q_L\right) q_{B1}} \quad , \quad L_B^{sb} = \frac{p_{B1}^{bs}}{q_{B1}}.$$

Scenario HL^{sb} : Consider Figure A.2, which depicts the demand pattern in scenario HL^{sb}. Set $q_{B1} = q_H$ and $q_{B2} = q_L$. Demand is then given by:

$$D_{\emptyset 1_H}^{sb}(HL) = 100 \int_0^{\frac{p_{A1}^{sb}}{q_H}} (1 - \widetilde{\theta}_B^{sb++}) \, d\theta_A$$

$$D_{1_H 1_H}^{sb}(HL) = 100[\int_{\frac{p_{A1}^{sb}}{q_H}}^{L_A^{sb}} (1 - \widetilde{\theta}_B^{sb+++}) \, d\theta_A + \int_{L_A^{sb}}^1 (1 - L_B^{sb}) \, d\theta_A]$$

$$D^{sb}_{1_H\emptyset}(HL) \quad = \quad 100[\int_{\frac{p^{sb}_{A1}-p^{sb}_2}{q_H-q_L}}^{L^{sb}_A} \widetilde{\theta}^{sb+}_B \, d\theta_A + \int_{L^{sb}_A}^{1} L^{sb}_B \, d\theta_A]$$

$$D^{sb}_{(2_L2_L)}(HL) \quad = \quad 100- \quad D^{sb}_{\emptyset 1_H}(HL) - D^{sb}_{1_H1_H}(HL)-$$

$$D^{sb}_{1_H\emptyset}(HL) - \int_{0}^{\frac{p^{sb}_2}{q_L}} \widehat{\theta}^{sb}_{B2} \, d\theta_A$$

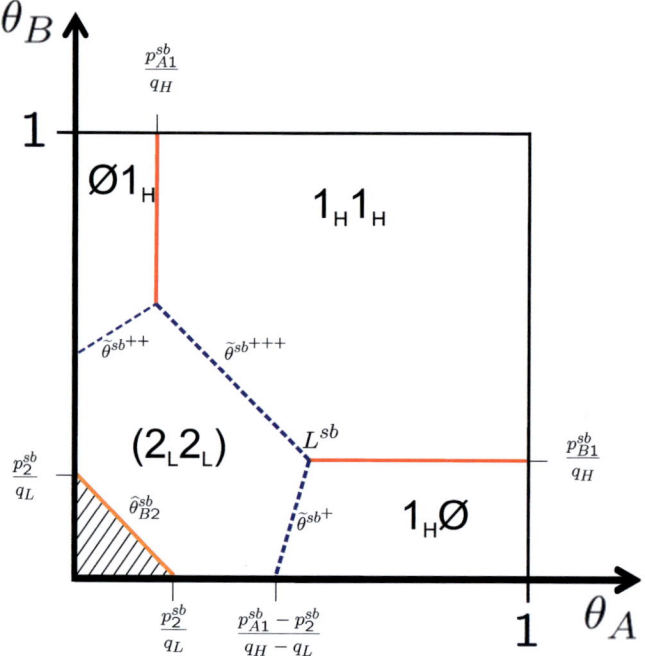

Figure A.2: *Bundle Pricing Subgame: Scenario HL^{sb}*

Firms' revenue is

$$R^{sb}_1(HL) \quad = \quad \left(D^{sb}_{1_H\emptyset}(HL) + D^{sb}_{1_H1_H}(HL)\right) p^{sb}_{A1}(HL) +$$
$$\left(D^{sb}_{\emptyset 1_H}(HL) + D^{sb}_{1_H1_H}(HL)\right) p^{sb}_{B1}(HL)$$

$$R^{sb}_2(HL) \quad = \quad D^{sb}_{(2_L2_L)}(HL) \, p^{sb}_2(HL).$$

The expressions representing the optimal prices are very lengthy and therefore omitted here, but most certainly available upon request. The revenue functions are monotone in μ, however, and thus I can apply the linear approximation scheme used in the proof of Lemma 3.4 again to obtain $R^{sb}_1(HL) \approx q_H(50.722 - 27.428\mu)$ and $R^{sb}_2(HL) \approx q_H(6.092\mu)$.

Scenarios HH^{sb} and LL^{sb}: Finally, see Figure A.3 for the demand pattern in scenario XX^{sb}, where $q_{B1} = q_{B2} = q_X$. Hence I find:

$$D^{sb}_{\emptyset 1_X}(XX) \quad = \quad 100 \int_0^{\frac{p_2^{sb}-p_{B1}^{sb}}{q_L}} (1 - L_B^{sb})\, d\theta_A$$

$$D^{sb}_{1_H\emptyset}(XX) \quad = \quad 100[\int_{\frac{p_{A1}^{sb}}{q_H}}^{L_A^{sb}} \widetilde{\theta}_B^{sb+}\, d\theta_A + \int_{L_A^{sb}}^1 L_B^{sb}\, d\theta_A]$$

$$D^{sb}_{1_H1_X}(XX) \quad = \quad 100 \int_{L_A^{sb}}^1 (1 - L_B^{sb})\, d\theta_A$$

$$D^{sb}_{(2_L2_L)}(HL) \quad = \quad 100[\int_{\frac{p_2^{sb}-p_{B1}^{sb}}{q_L}}^{\frac{p_{A1}^{sb}}{q_H}} (1 - \widehat{\theta}_{B2}^{sb})\, d\theta_A + \int_{\frac{p_{A1}^{sb}}{q_H}}^{L_A^{sb}} (1 - \widetilde{\theta}_B^{sb+})\, d\theta_A]$$

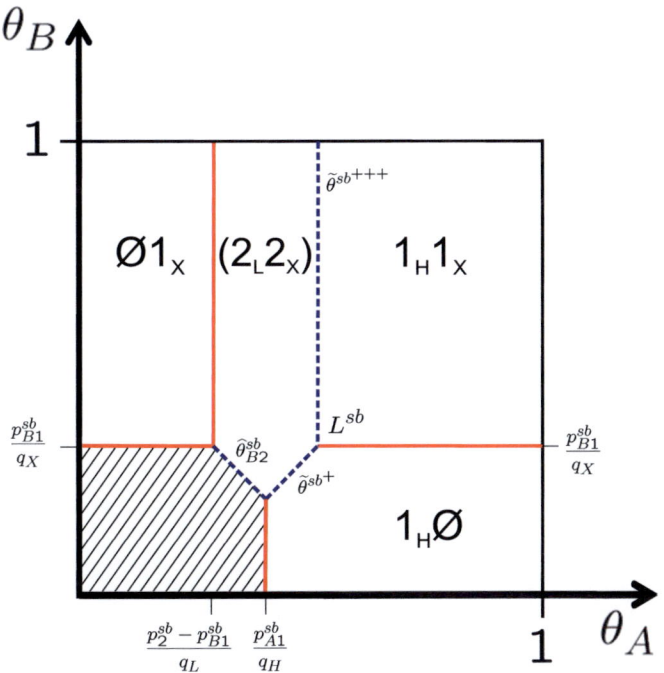

Figure A.3: *Bundle Pricing Subgame: Scenario XX^{sb}*

Firms' revenue is

$$R_1^{sb}(XX) \quad = \quad \left(D^{sb}_{1_H\emptyset}(XX) + D^{sb}_{1_H1_X}(XX)\right) p_{A1}^{sb}(XX) +$$
$$\left(D^{sb}_{\emptyset 1_X}(XX) + D^{sb}_{1_H1_X}(XX)\right) p_{B1}^{sb}(XX)$$
$$R_2^{sb}(XX) \quad = \quad D^{sb}_{(2_L2_X)}(XX)\, p_2^{sb}(XX).$$

Again, the optimal prices are very lengthy and therefore omitted. Likewise, the revenue functions are monotone in μ, and I apply the linear approximation scheme such that $R_1^{sb}(HH) \approx q_H(25 - 11.32\mu)$, $R_2^{sb}(HH) \approx q_H(8\mu)$, $R_1^{sb}(LL) \approx q_H(25 - 13.58\mu)$ and $R_2^{sb}(LL) \approx q_H(7.26\mu)$. $\qquad\square$

A.6 Proof of Lemmas 4.2 and 4.3

Scenario LH^{uu}: Consider Figure 4.1 and see that demand for each service portfolio can be written as:

$$D_{(1_H 1_L)}^{uu}(LH) = 100[\int_{L_A^{uu}}^{\frac{p_{A1}^{uu}}{q_H}} (\widetilde{\theta}_B^{uu^{+++}} - \widehat{\theta}_{B1}^{uu})\, d\theta_A +$$

$$\int_{\frac{p_{A1}^{uu}}{q_H}}^{\frac{p_{A1}^{uu}+p_{B2}^{uu}-p_2^{uu}}{q_H - q_L}} (\widetilde{\theta}_B^{uu^{+++}} - \frac{p_1^{uu}-p_{A1}^{uu}}{q_L})\, d\theta_A +$$

$$\int_{\frac{p_{A1}^{uu}+p_{B2}^{uu}-p_2^{uu}}{q_H - q_L}}^{1} (\frac{p_{A1}^{uu}+p_{B2}^{uu}-p_1^{uu}}{q_H - q_L} - \frac{p_1^{uu}-p_{A1}^{uu}}{q_L})\, d\theta_A]$$

$$D_{(2_L 2_H)}^{uu}(LH) = 100[\int_{\frac{p_2^{uu}-p_{B2}^{uu}}{q_L}}^{L_A^{uu}} (1 - \widehat{\theta}_{B2}^{uu})\, d\theta_A + \int_{L_A^{uu}}^{\frac{p_{A1}^{uu}+p_{B2}^{uu}-p_2^{uu}}{q_H - q_L}} (1 - \widetilde{\theta}_B^{uu^{+++}})\, d\theta_A]$$

$$D_{1_H\emptyset}^{uu}(LH) = 100 \int_{\frac{p_{A1}^{uu}}{q_H}}^{1} \frac{p_1^{uu}-p_{A1}^{uu}}{q_L}\, d\theta_A$$

$$D_{\emptyset 2_H}^{uu}(LH) = 100 \int_{0}^{\frac{p_2^{uu}-p_{B2}^{uu}}{q_L}} (1 - \frac{p_{B2}^{uu}}{q_H})\, d\theta_A$$

$$D_{1_H 2_H}^{uu}(LH) = 100 \int_{\frac{p_{A1}^{uu}+p_{B2}^{uu}-p_2^{uu}}{q_H - q_L}}^{1} (1 - \frac{p_{A1}^{uu}+p_{B2}^{uu}-p_1^{uu}}{q_H - q_L})\, d\theta_A$$

Consequently, firms' revenues amount to

$$R_1^{uu}(LH) = D_{(1_H 1_L)}^{uu}(LH)\, p_1^{uu} + \left(D_{1_H\emptyset}^{uu}(LH) + D_{1_H 2_H}^{uu}(LH)\right) p_{A1}^{uu}$$

$$R_2^{uu}(LH) = D_{(2_L 2_H)}^{uu}(LH)\, p_2^{uu} + \left(D_{\emptyset 2_H}^{uu}(LH) + D_{1_H 2_H}^{uu}(LH)\right) p_{B2}^{uu}$$

Setting $q_L = \mu\, q_H$ and solving for optimal prices yields:

$$p_1^{uu}(LH) = p_2^{uu}(LH) = q_H\, \epsilon \tag{A.7}$$

$$p_{A1}^{uu}(LH) = p_{B2}^{uu}(LH) = q_H \frac{\epsilon^2(3(1-\mu)+2\mu^2) + \epsilon(2(\mu^2-1) - \mu^3 + \mu)}{\epsilon(3(\mu^3+1) - \mu^2 - \mu) - 2(\mu^3 - \mu^2 - \mu + 2)} +$$

$$q_H \frac{\mu^4 - \mu^3 - \mu^2 + \mu}{\epsilon(3(\mu^3+1) - \mu^2 - \mu) - 2(\mu^3 - \mu^2 - \mu + 2)}, \tag{A.8}$$

where ϵ is the unique real root of $(21\,\mu^3 - 22\,\mu^2 + 21\,\mu)\,\epsilon^4 - (18\,\mu^4 + 30\,\mu^3 - 6\,\mu^2 + 18\,,\mu + 36)\epsilon^3 + (-9\,\mu^5 + 10\,\mu^4 + 50\,\mu^3 - 28\,\mu^2 + 7\,\mu + 66)\,\epsilon^2 + (28\,\mu^5 - 40 + 52\,\mu^2 - 28\,\mu^3 - 12\,\mu^4)\epsilon + 3\,\mu^7 - 2\,\mu^6 - 7\,\mu^5 + 12\,\mu^4 + 5\,\mu^3 - 18\,\mu^2 - \mu + 8 = 0$ for which the Hessian is negative semidefinite. To ensure the existence of the equilibrium, the denominator of the right hand side of (A.8) must be nonzero. This is warranted for all $\mu < 0.4068533092$.

Scenario HL^{uu}: In scenario HL firms specialize on either the high- or low-quality segment again. Thus, consumers have the option of buying a high- or low-quality bundle, i.e. (1_H1_H) or (2_L2_L), a high-quality service in market A or a low-quality service in market B individually, i.e. $1_H\emptyset$ or $\emptyset2_L$, or to assemble an individual service portfolio, i.e. 1_H2_L. If all of these services were offered, the demand structure would look as in Figure 4.2(a).

However, it turns out that it is in fact not optimal for firm 2, i.e. the designated low-quality firm, to offer its low-quality home product individually because thereby it would cannibalize the price of its bundle too much. Of course, if firm 2 refrains from offering its home service individually (or sets the price p_{B2}^{uu} arbitrarily high), consumers have two options less because they can neither buy $\emptyset2_L$ nor assemble a package of 1_H2_L. Thereby, the demand structure can be simplified to the one depicted by Figure 4.2(b).

Hence, firms' demand can be written as:

$$D_{(1_H1_H)}^{uu}(HL) = 100[\int_0^{P_A^{uu}} (1 - \widetilde{\theta}_B^{uu+++})\, d\theta_A + \int_{P_A^{uu}}^1 (1 - \tfrac{p_1^{uu} - p_{A1}^{uu}}{q_H})\, d\theta_A]$$

$$D_{1_H\emptyset}^{uu}(HL) = 100[\int_{\frac{p_{A1}^{uu} - p_2^{uu}}{q_H - q_L}}^{P_A^{uu}} \widetilde{\theta}_B^{uu++}\, d\theta_A + \int_{P_A^{uu}}^1 \tfrac{p_1^{uu} - p_{A1}^{uu}}{q_H}\, d\theta_A]$$

$$D_{(2_L2_L)}^{uu}(HL) = 100[\int_0^{\frac{p_2^{uu}}{q_L}} (\widehat{\theta}_B^{uu+++} - \widehat{\theta}_{B2}^{uu})\, d\theta_A + \int_{\frac{p_2^{uu}}{q_L}}^{\frac{p_{A1}^{uu} - p_2^{uu}}{q_H - q_L}} \widetilde{\theta}_B^{uu+++}\, d\theta_A +$$
$$\int_{\frac{p_{A1}^{uu} - p_2^{uu}}{q_H - q_L}}^{P_A^{uu}} (\widehat{\theta}_B^{uu+++} - \widetilde{\theta}_B^{uu++})\, d\theta_A]$$

From the corresponding revenue functions

$$R_1^{uu}(HL) = D_{(1_H1_H)}^{uu}(HL)\, p_1^{uu} + D_{1_H\emptyset}^{uu}(HL)\, p_{A1}^{uu}$$
$$R_2^{uu}(HL) = D_{(2_L2_L)}^{uu}(HL)\, p_2^{uu}$$

one can compute the optimal prices as:

$$p_{A1}^{uu*}(HL) = \varphi_u \, \mu \tag{A.9}$$

$$p_1^{uu*}(HL) = q_H \frac{\varphi_u^2(27\mu^3 - 147\mu^2 - 219\mu - 81) - \varphi_u(48\mu^3 - 144\mu^2 + 96\mu)}{\varphi_u(27\mu^3 - 102\mu^2 + 81\mu) - 12\mu^3 - 76\mu^2 + 196\mu - 108} +$$

$$q_H \frac{76\mu^3 - 106\mu^2 + 184\mu - 54}{\varphi_u(27\mu^3 - 102\mu^2 + 81\mu) - 12\mu^3 - 76\mu^2 + 196\mu - 108} \tag{A.10}$$

$$p_2^{uu*}(HL) = q_H \frac{\varphi_u^2(27\mu^3 - 198\mu^2 + 243\mu) - \varphi_u(72\mu^3 - 600\mu^2 + 1176\mu - 648)}{4(\varphi_u(27\mu^3 - 102\mu^2 + 81\mu) - 12\mu^3 - 76\mu^2 + 196\mu - 108)} +$$

$$q_H \frac{180\mu^4 - 847\mu^3 + 1640\mu^2 - 1378\mu + 432}{4(\varphi_u(27\mu^3 - 102\mu^2 + 81\mu) - 12\mu^3 - 76\mu^2 + 196\mu - 108)} \tag{A.11}$$

where $\varphi_u(\mu)$ is the unique positive real root of $(2673\,\mu^5 - 13491\,\mu^4 + 19683\,\mu^3 - 6561\,\mu^2)\varphi_u^4 + 2736\,\mu^5 - 39360\,\mu^4 + 120864\,\mu^3 - 119232\,\mu^2 + 34992\,\mu\varphi_u^3 + (21528\,\mu^6 - 106164\,\mu^2 - 46656 - 117020\,\mu^3 - 87572\,\mu^5 + 154656\,\mu + 183820\,\mu^4 - 2592\,\mu^7)\varphi_u^2 + (2304\,\mu^7 - 7360\,\mu^6 - 23328\,\mu^5 + 226560\,\mu^4 - 563648\,\mu^3 + 626112\,\mu^2 - 322848\,\mu + 62208)\varphi_u + 3088\,\mu^7 - 30848\,\mu^6 + 145284\,\mu^5 - 355564\,\mu^4 + 477884\,\mu^3 - 355236\,\mu^2 + 136128\,\mu - 20736 = 0$ at which the Hessian is negative semidefinite. Obviously, it must hold that $\varphi_u(\mu) > 0$, which translates into $\mu < 0.471442316$.

Scenarios HH^{uu} and LL^{uu}: First, see that when firms choose to offer the same service quality $q_X \in \{q_H, q_L\}$ in market B, consumers have no desire to assemble their own service portfolio: Buying the respective home services individually would give a consumer a high-quality service in market A and a service of quality q_X in market B. The very same service portfolio is offered through firm 1's bundle, however, at a presumably lower price. Thus, only four demand regions are feasible (cf. Figure 4.3). Demands are calculated as follows:

$$D_{(1_H 1_X)}^{uu}(XX) = 100[\int_{L_A^{uu}}^{\frac{p_{A1}^{uu}}{q_H}} (1 - \widehat{\theta}_{B1}^{uu}) \, d\theta_A + \int_{\frac{p_{A1}^{uu}}{q_H}}^{1} (1 - \frac{p_1^{uu} - p_{A1}^{uu}}{q_X}) \, d\theta_A]$$

$$D_{(2_L 2_X)}^{uu}(XX) = 100 \int_{\frac{p_2^{uu} - p_{B2}^{uu}}{q_L}}^{L_A^{uu}} (1 - \widehat{\theta}_{B2}^{uu}) \, d\theta_A$$

$$D_{1_H \emptyset}^{uu}(XX) = 100 \int_{\frac{p_{A1}^{uu}}{q_H}}^{1} \frac{p_1^{uu} - p_{A1}^{uu}}{q_X} \, d\theta_A$$

$$D_{\emptyset 2_X}^{uu}(XX) = 100 \int_{0}^{\frac{p_2^{uu} - p_{B2}^{uu}}{q_L}} (1 - \frac{p_{B2}^{uu}}{q_X}) d\theta_A$$

Revenues amount to:

$$R_1^{uu}(XX) = D_{(1_H 1_X)}^{uu}(XX)\, p_1^{uu} + D_{1_H \emptyset}^{uu}(XX)\, p_{A1}^{uu}$$
$$R_2^{uu}(XX) = D_{(2_L 2_X)}^{uu}(XX)\, p_2^{uu} + D_{\emptyset 2_X}^{uu}(XX)\, p_{B2}^{uu}$$

Computing the optimal prices yields

$$p_{A1}^{uu*}(XX) = p_1^{uu*}(XX) \tag{A.12}$$

$$p_{B2}^{uu*}(XX) = p_2^{uu*}(XX). \tag{A.13}$$

Consequently, no consumer will want to purchase any of the services sold separately, because he could also buy the firm's bundle at no extra cost. Thus, de facto firms refrain from offering their home services individually and I obtain the same results and prices as under pure bundle pricing (Section 3.3.3). $\square$

References

Adams, William James, and Janet L. Yellen. Aug., 1976. "Commodity Bundling and the Burden of Monopoly." *The Quarterly Journal of Economics* 90 (3): 475–498.

Anderson, Simon P., and Luc Leruth. 1993. "Why Firms May Prefer Not To Price Discriminate Via Mixed Bundling." *International Journal of Industrial Organization* 11 (1): 49 – 61 (1993/3).

Anderson, S.P., and R.D. Fischer. 1989. "Multi-Market Oligopoly with Production Before Sales." *The Journal of Industrial Economics* 38 (2): 167–182.

Andrews, P.W.S. 1949. *Manufacturing Business*. MacMillan.

Aoki, Reiko, and Thomas J. Prusa. 1996. "Sequential versus simultaneous choice with endogenous quality." *International Journal of Industrial Organization* 15 (1): 103–121 (February).

Areeda, P. 1990. "Essential Facility: An Ephitet in Need of Limiting Principles." *Antitrust Law Journal*, pp. 841–853.

Arthur, W.B. 1989. "Competing Technologies, Increasing Returns, and Lock-In by Historical Events." *The Economic Journal* 99 (394): 116–131.

Bain, Joe Staten. 1956. *Barriers to New Competition: Their Character and Consequences in Manufacturing Industries*. Cambridge, MA: Harvard University Press.

Bakos, Y., and E. Brynjolfsson. 1999. "Bundling Information Goods: Pricing, Profits, and Efficiency." *Management Sciences* 45:1613–1630.

———. 2000. "Bundling and Competition on the Internet: Aggregation Strategies for Information Goods." *Marketing Science* 19 (1): 63–82.

Baldwin, Thomas F., D. Stevens McVoy, and Charles Steinfield. 1996. *Convergence: Integrating Media, Information and Communication*. Sage Publications.

Bauer, Johannes M. 2007. Bundling, Differentiation, Alliances and Mergers: Convergence Strategies in U.S. Communication Markets. Munich Personal RePec Archive. MPRA Paper No. 2515, posted 03. April 2007.

Baum, Joel A. C., and Helaine J. Korn. 1999. "Dynamics of Dyadic Competitive Interaction." *Strategic Management Journal* 20 (3): 251–278.

Bernheim, B. Douglas, and Michael D. Whinston. 1990. "Multimarket Contact and Collusive Behavior." *RAND Journal of Economics* 21 (1): 1–26.

Boeker, Warren, Jerry Goodstein, John Stephan, and Johann Peter Murmann. 1997. "Competition in a Multimarket Environment: The Case of Market Exit." *Organization Science* 8 (2): 126–142.

Boom, Anette. Mar., 1995. "Asymmetric International Minimum Quality Standards and Vertical Differentiation." *The Journal of Industrial Economics* 43 (1): 101–119.

Booz Allen Hamilton, ˙ 2007, March 13. Enormes Wachstumspotenzial, aber kein Selbstläufer. Press Release: available at http://www.boozallen.de/presse/pressemitteilungen/pressemitteilung-detail/30333174, last accessed on Sept 29, 2007.

Bowman, Jr.W.S. 1957. "Tying Arrangements and the Leverage Problem." *Yale Law Journal* 67:19–36.

Braeutigam, Ronald R., Andrew F. Daughety, and Mark A. Turnquist. 1984. "A Firm Specific Analysis of Economies of Density in the U.S. Railroad Industry." *The Journal of Industrial Economics* 33 (1): 3–20 (sep).

Brander, James A., and Jonathan Eaton. 1984. "Product Line Rivalry." *The American Economic Review* 74 (3): 323–334.

Brander, James A., and Paul Krugman. 1983. "A Reciprocal Dumping Model of International Trade." *Journal of International Economics* 15:313–321.

Brennan, Timothy J. 2005, Oct. "Is Competition the Entry Barrier? Consumer and Total Welfare Benefits of Bundling." Working Paper, University of Maryland.

Brunell, Richard M. 2005. "Broadband." In *Network Access, Regulation And Antitrust*, edited by Diana L Moss, 151–177. Routledge.

Brunner, E. 1961. "A Note on Potential Competition." *Journal of Industrial Economics* 9:248–250.

Bulow, Jeremy I., John D. Geanakoplos, and Paul D. Klemperer. 1985. "Multimarket Oligopoly: Strategic Substitutes and Complements." *Journal of Political Economy* 93:488–511.

Bundesnetzagentur. 2005, Aug. Hinweise zu sachlich ungerechtfertigter Bündelung i.S.d. §28 Abs. 2 Nr. 3 TKG.

———. 2006. Jahresbericht 2005. available online at http://www.bundesnetzagentur.de/media/archive/5278.pdf.

———. 2007. "Entscheidungen der Präsidentenkammer der Bundesnetzagentur für Elektrizität, Gas, Telekommunikation, Post und Eisenbahn vom 19. Juni 2007 über die Anordnung und die Wahl des Vergabeverfahrens zur Vergabe von Fequenzen in den Bereichen 1,8 Ghz, 2 Ghz und 2,6 Ghz für den digitalen zellularen Mobilfunk." *Amtsblatt der Bundesnetzagentur für Elektrizität, Gas, Telekommunikation, Post und Eisenbahn* 14:3115 – 3147.

Cairns, Robert D., and D. Mahabir. 1988. "Contestability: A Revisionist View." *Economica* 55 (May = No. 218): 269–276.

Calem, Paul Seth. 1988. "Entry and entry deterrence in penetrable markets." *Economica* 55 (May = No. 218): 171–183.

Carbajo, Jose, David de Meza, and Daniel J. Seidmann. Mar., 1990. "A Strategic Motivation for Commodity Bundling." *The Journal of Industrial Economics* 38 (3): 283–298.

Carlton, D.W, and M. Waldmann. 2002. "The Strategic Use of Tying to Preserve and Create Market Power in Evolving Industries." *RAND Journal of Economics* 33:194–220.

Cawley, Richard A. 1997, Feb. '1998 And All That - Asymmetric Regulation Between Telecoms and Cable TV Operators'. European Commission Report. DG XIII.A.1.

Chae, Suchan. 1992. "Bundling subscription TV channels : A case of natural bundling." *International Journal of Industrial Organization* 10 (2): 213 – 230 (1992/6).

Champsaur, Paul, and Jean-Charles Rochet. May, 1989. "Multiproduct Duopolists." *Econometrica* 57 (3): 533–557.

Chen, Yongmin. Jan., 1997. "Equilibrium Product Bundling." *The Journal of Business* 70 (1): 85–103.

Choi, Chong Ju, and Hyun Song Shin. Jun., 1992. "A Comment on a Model of Vertical Product Differentiation." *The Journal of Industrial Economics* 40 (2): 229–231.

Choi, J.P. 2003. "Bundling new products with old to signal quality, with application to the sequencing of new products." *International Journal of Industrial Organization* 21:1179–1200.

———. 2004. "Tying and Innovation: A Dynamic Analysis of Tying Arrangements." *The Economic Journal* 114:83–101.

Choi, J.P., and C. Stefanadis. 2001. "Tying, Investment, and the Dynamic Leverage Theory." *The RAND Journal of Economics* 32 (1): 52–71.

COM, European Commission. 1987. Green Paper on the Development of the Common Market for Telecommunications Services and Equipment. COM(87)290.

———. 1992. 1992 Review of the Situation in the Telecommunications Services Sector. SEC(92)1048final.

———. 1993. Communication on the Consultation on the Review of the Situation in the Telecommunications Services Sector. COM(93)159final.

———. 1994. Green Paper on the Liberalisation of Telecommunications Infrastructure and Cable Television Networks. COM(94)682.

———. 1995. The Consultation on the Green Paper on the Liberalisation of Telecommunications Infrastructure and Cable Television Networks. COM(95)158final.

———. 1997. Green Paper on the Convergence of the Telecommunications, Media and Information Technology Sectors, and the Implications for Regulation. COM(97)623.

———. 1999. The Convergence of the Telecommunications, Media and Information Technology Sectors, and the Implications for Regulation. Results of the Public Consultation on the Green Paper [COM (97) 623]. COM(99)108final.

———. 2005. Commission expects most broadcasting in the EU to be digital by 2010. IP/05/595.

Constantatos, Christos, and Stylianos Perrakis. 1997. "Vertical differentiation: Entry and market coverage with multiproduct firms." *International Journal of Industrial Organization* 16 (1): 81–103 (November).

Cournot, Augustin A. 1838. *Recherches sur les principes mathématiques de la théorie des richesses*. Paris: L. Hachette. English translation: "Research into the Mathematical Principles of the Theory of Wealth, (N. Bacon, transl), McMillan,New York, 1929.

Court, Andrew. 1939. "Hedonic Price Indexes with Automotive Examples." In *The Dynamics of Automobile Demand*, 99–117. General Motors Corporation.

Crampes, Claude, and Abraham Hollander. 2007, June. Triple Play Time. Communications and Strategies. MPRA Paper No.3552, posted 13. June 2007.

Crandall, R.W., J.G. Sidak, and H.J. Singer. 2002. "The Empirical Case Against Asymmetric Regulation of Broadband Internet Access." *Berkeley Technology Law Journal* 17 (3): 953–987.

Damjanovic, Dragana. 2002. *Regulierung der Kommunikationsmärkte unter Konvergenzbedingungen*. Wien: Springer.

de Bijl, Paul, and Martin Peitz. 2002. *Regulation and Entry into Telecommunication Markets*. Cambridge University Press.

de Fraja, G. 1996. "Product Line Competition in Vertically Differentiated Markets." *International Journal of Industrial Organization* 14(3):389–414.

Diallo, Thierno. 2006. "Bundling in Vertically Differentiated Communication Markets." Université du Québec à Chicoutimi.

Digitalfernsehen.de. 2007. Die Erben des TV-Kabels der Telekom. accessed on 06/30/07.

Director, Aaron, and Edward Levi. 1956. "Law and the Future: Trade Regulation." *Northwestern University Law Review* 51:281–296.

Distaso, W., P. Lupi, and F.M. Manenti. 2006. "Platform competition and broadband uptake: Theory and empirical evidence from the European union." *Information Economics and Policy* 18 (1): 87–106.

Donnenfeld, Shabtai, and Shlomo Weber. Spring, 1995. "Limit Qualities and Entry Deterrence." *The RAND Journal of Economics* 26 (1): 113–130.

Durlauf, S.N. 1993. "Nonergodic Economic Growth." *The Review of Economic Studies* 60 (2): 349–366.

Eaton, B. Curtis, and Richard G. Lipsey. 1989. "Product Differentation." Edited by R. Schmalensee and R.D. Willig, *Handbook of Industrial Organization*, Volume 1. North Holland, 723–763.

Economides, N., G. Lopomo, and G. Woroch. 1996. "Strategic Commitments and the Principle of Reciprocity in Interconnection Pricing." Stern School of Business Working Paper EC-96-13, New York University.

Economides, Nicholas. 1989. "Desirability of Compatibility in the Absence of Network Externalities." *The American Economic Review* 79 (5): 1165–1181 (December).

———. 1993, November 1993. "Mixed Bundling in Duopoly." Stern School of Business, New York University.

Economides, Nicholas, and William Lehr. 1995. "The Quality of Complex Systems and Industry Structure." Edited by William Lehr, *Quality and Reliability of Telecommunications Infrastructure*. Lawrence Erlbaum, Hillsdale.

Edwards, Corbin D. 1955. "Conglomerate Bigness as a Source of Power." *Business Concentration and Price Policy*. Princton, NJ: Princton University Press, 331–352.

Einhorn, M.A. 1992. "Mix and Match Compatibility with Vertical Product Dimensions." *The RAND Journal of Economics* 23 (4): 535–547.

Farrell, J., and G. Saloner. 1985. "Standardization, Compatibility, and Innovation." *The RAND Journal of Economics* 16 (1): 70–83.

Feijoo, C., J.L. Gomez-Barroso, S. Ramos, and D. Rojo. 2006. "An Analysis of Fixed-Mobile Communications Convergence: Development, Social Benefits and Markets." *Information and Communication Technologies, 2006. ICTTA '06. 2nd*, Volume 1. 925–930.

Fransman, M. 2007. "Evolution of the Telecommunications Industry into the Internet Age." *The International Handbook on Telecommunications Economics*. Edward Elgar Publishing.

Freyberg, Axel. 2007. "Triple-Play-Entwicklung in Deutschland und weltweit." Edited by Arnold Picot, Andreas Bereczky, and Axel Freyberg, *Triple Play*. Springer.

Friedman, J.W. 1971. "A Non-cooperative Equilibrium for Supergames." *The Review of Economic Studies* 38 (1): 1–12.

Gabszewicz, J., and J.F. Thisse. 1979. "Price Competition, Quality, and Income Disparities." *Journal of Economic Theory* 20:340–359.

Gimeno, Javier, and Carolyn Y. Woo. 1996. "Hypercompetition in a Multimarket Environment: The Role of Strategic Similarity and Multimarket Contact in Competitive De-Escalation." *Organization Science* 7 (3): 322–341.

Greenstein, Shane. 1999. "Industrial Convergence." Edited by Richard Dorf, *The Technology Management Handbook*. CRC Press.

Greenstein, Shane, and Tarun Khanna. 1997. "What Does Industry Convergence Mean." *Competing in the Age of Digital Convergence*, pp. 201–226.

Griliches, Zvi. 1961. "Hedonic Price Indexes for Automobiles: An Econometric Analysis of Quality Change." In *The Price Statistics of the Federal Government*, 173–196. New York: National Bureau of Economic Research.

Haber, L.J., and D.T. Levy. 1988. "Decision Making in the Multiproduct Firm: Adaptability and Firm Organization." *Managerial and Decision Economics* 9 (4): 331–338.

Handelsblatt. 2006, June, 22. Forrester prohezeit der Telekom "finanziellen Selbstmord". Handelblatt No. 118, p. 14.

Haucap, Justus, U. Heimeshoff, and A. Uhde. 2006. "Credible Threats as an Instrument of Regulation for Network Industries." Edited by P. Welfens and M. Weske, *Digital Economic Dynamics: Innovations, Networks and Regulations*. Berlin: Springer, 161–192.

Hausman, J.A., J.G. Sidak, and H.J. Singer. 2001. "Cable Modems and DSL: Broadband Internet Access for Residential Customers." *The American Economic Review* 91 (2): 302–307.

Heise. 2006, August, 31. VDSL bei der Telekom nur mit Triple Play. heise online news report, available at http://www.heise.de/newsticker/meldung/77547, last accessed on Sept. 29, 2007.

———. 2007, February, 28. Kabel Deutschland schreibt rote Zahlen. heise online news report, available at http://www.heise.de/newsticker/meldung/85981/, last accessed on Sept. 29, 2007.

Holznagel, Bernd, Anne Hombergs, and Volker Rosengarten. 2004. "Die Zulässigkeit von Optionstarifen der T-Com nach dem neuen TKG." *Kommunikation und Recht* 11:505–510.

Jayachandran, Satish, Javier Gimeno, and P. Rajan Varadarajan. 1999. "The Theory of Multimarket Competition: A Synthesis and Implications for Marketing Strategy." *Journal of Marketing* 63:49–66.

Johnson, Justin P., and David P. Myatt. 2003. "Multiproduct quality competition: fighting brands and product line pruning." *The American Economic Review* 93 (3): 748–774.

Judd, Keneth L. 1985. "Credible Spatial Preemption." *Rand Journal of Economics* 16 (2): 153–166.

Kabel Baden Wuerttemberg AG. 2006. Stellungnahme zur Anhörung der Bundesnetzagentur zur Indentifizierung 'neuer Märkte'. Amtsblatt der Bundesnetzagentur. Nr. 04/2006.

Kabel Deutschland GmbH. 2006. Stellungnahme zur Anhörung der Bundesnetzagentur zur Indentifizierung 'neuer Märkte'. Amtsblatt der Bundesnetzagentur. Nr. 04/2006.

Kabelverband, Deutscher. 2006, Sept. 5th. Kabelbetreiber: Triple-Play-Wettbewerb ausbauen. Press Release, available at www.kabelverband.de.

———. 2007, April 11th. Kabelnetzbetreiber verdreifachen Zahl der Breitband-Internetanschlüsse. Press Release, available at www.kabelverband.de.

Karamti, Chiraz. 2007, March. Hedonic Price Indexes For Mobile Telephony Services and Firms' Pricing-Quality Behaviors in France. Working Paper. Presented at the 34th EARIE Conference, Valencia, Spain.

Karnani, Aneel, and Birger Wernerfelt. 1985. "Multiple Point Competition." *Strategic Management Journal* 6 (1): 87–96.

Katz, M.L., and C. Shapiro. 1985. "Network Externalities, Competition, and Compatibility." *The American Economic Review* 75 (3): 424–440.

Keeler, Theodore E. 1974. "Railroad Costs, Returns to Scale, and Excess Capacity." *The Review of Economics and Statistics* 56 (2): 201–208 (may).

Klemperer, Paul. 1992. "Equilibrium Product Lines: Competing Head-To-Head May Be Less Competitive." *The American Economic Review* 82 (4): 740–755.

———. 1995. "Competition when consumers have switching costs: an overview with applications to industrial organization, macroeconomics, and international trade." *The Review of Economic Studies* 62 (4 = No. 213): 515–539.

Klemperer, Paul, and A. Jorge Padilla. 1997. "Do firms' product lines include too many varieties?" *Rand Corporation: The Rand journal of economics* 28 (3): 472–488.

Koenig, Christian, Sascha Loetz, and Andreas Neumann. 2004. *Telekommunikationsrecht.* Verlag Recht und Wirtschaft.

Kopalle, P.K., A. Krishna, and J.L. Assuncao. 1999. "The Role of Market Expansion on Equilibrium Bundling Strategies." *Managerial and Decision Economics* 20:365–377.

Krämer, Jan. 2007a. "Bundling as a Quality Leverage Device in Oligopoly: The Case of Digital Convergence." Edited by Erkaan Erdil and Hakan Yetkiner, *Proceedings of the 2nd*

International Conference on Technology and Economic Development, 25-26 May. Izmir, Turkey. ISBN:978-975-8789-13-9.

————. 2007b. "Digital Convergence, Pricing Strategies and Firms' Profits in the Telecommunication and Entertainment Media Industry." Edited by Heikki Hämmäinen, Dimitris Varoutas, and Ilari Welling, *Proceedings of the 6th Conference on Telecommunication Techno-Economics (CTTE), June 14-15.* Helsinki, Finland: IEEE. ISBN: 1-4244-1233-1.

Kreps, David M., and Robert Wilson. 1982. "Reputation and Imperfect Information." *Journal of Economic Theory* 27:253–279.

Krämer, Jan, Siegfried Berninghaus, and Christof Weinhardt. 2006. "Competing on Many Fronts: Entry Networks in an Economy of Multi-Product Firms." Edited by Christof Weinhardt Thomas Dreier, Rudi Studer, *Information Management and Market Engineering.* Universitätsverlag Karlsruhe, 139–151.

Krugman, Paul. 1980. "Scale Economies, Product Differentiation, and the Pattern of Trade." *The American Economic Review* 70 (5): 950–959.

Kuhn, M. 2007. "Minimum quality standards and market dominance in vertically differentiated duopoly." *International Journal of Industrial Organization* 25 (2): 275–290.

Laffont, Jean-Jacques, Patrick Rey, and Jean Tirole. 1997. "Competition between telecommunications operators." *European Economic Review* 41 (3-5): 701–711 (April).

————. 1998a. "Network Competition: II. Price Discrimination." *The RAND Journal of Economics* 29 (1): 38–56.

————. 1998b. "Network Competition: I. Overview and Nondiscriminatory Pricing." *The RAND Journal of Economics* 29 (1): 1–37.

Laffont, Jean-Jacques, and Jean Tirole. 2000. *Competition in Telecommunications.* Edited by Hans-Werner Sinn. MIT Press.

Lal, Rajiv, and Carmen Matutes. 1989. "Price Competition in Multimarket Duopolies." *Rand Journal of Economics* 20:516–537.

Larouche, Pierre. 2000. *Competition Law and Regulations in European Telecommunications.* Hart Publishing.

Latzer, M. 1997. *Mediamatik: Die Konvergenz von Telekommunikation, Computer und Rundfunk.* Westdeutscher Verlag.

Lehmann-Grube, Ulrich. Summer, 1997. "Strategic Choice of Quality When Quality is Costly: The Persistence of the High-Quality Advantage." *The RAND Journal of Economics* 28 (2): 372–384.

Lommerud, Kjell Erik, and Lars Sorgard. 2003. "Entry in telecommunication: customer loyalty, price sensitivity and access prices." *Information Economics and Policy* 15 (1): 55 – 72 (2003/3).

Machuca, Carmen Mas, Oyvind Moe, Joerg Eberspaecher, Monika Jaeger, and Andreas Gladisch. 2007. "Service cost modeling and cost comparative study." *Proceedings of the 6th Conference on Telecommunication Techno-Economics, 14-15 June, Helsinki, Finland.*

Maldoom, Dan, Richard A D Marsden, J Gregory Sidak, and Hal J Singer. 2005. *Broadband in Europe: How Brussels Can Wire the Information Society.* Springer.

Marcus, J. Scott, and Peter Stamm. 2006, Nov. "Kabelinternet in Deutschland." Technical Report, wik Consult. Policy Paper für den deutschen Kabelverband.

Martin, Stephen. 1999. "Strategic and welfare implications of bundling." *Economics Letters* 62 (3): 371 – 376 (1999/3/1).

Matsushima, Hitoshi. 2001. "Multimarket Contact, Imperfect Monitoring, And Implicit Collusion." *Journal of Economic Theory* 98 (1): 158–178.

Matutes, Carmen, and Pierre Regibeau. 1988. ""Mix and Match": Product Compatibility without Network Externalities." *The RAND Journal of Economics* 19 (2): 221–234.

———. 1992. "Compatibility and Bundling of Complementary Goods in a Duopoly." *The Journal of IndustrialEconomics* 40:37–54.

Mayen, Thomas. 2005. "Marktregulierung nach dem novellierten TKG: Ausgewählte Rechtsfragen der Zugangs- und Entgeltregulierung." *Computer und Recht* 1:21–30.

McAfee, R. Preston, John McMillan, and Michael D. Whinston. May, 1989. "Multiproduct Monopoly, Commodity Bundling, and Correlation of Values." *The Quarterly Journal of Economics* 104 (2): 371–383.

Milgrom, Paul, and John Roberts. 1982. "Predation, Reputation and Entry Deterrence." *Journal of Economic Theory* 27:280–312.

Mitchell, B.M., and I. Vogelsang. 1991. *Telecommunications Pricing: theory and practice.* Cambridge University Press.

Monopolkommission. 2005. Wettbewerbsentwicklung bei der Telekommunikation 2005: Dynamik unter neuen Rahmenbedingungen. Sondergutachten Nr. 43.

Moorthy, K.S. 1988. "Product and Price Competition in a Duopoly." *Marketing Science* 7:141–168.

Motta, Massimo. Jun., 1993. "Endogenous Quality Choice: Price vs. Quantity Competition." *The Journal of Industrial Economics* 41 (2): 113–131.

Möschel, Wernhard, and Jochen Haug. 2003. "Der Referentenentwurf zur Novellierung des TKG aus wettbewerbsrechtlicher Sicht." *Multimedia und Recht* 8:505–508.

Mussa, Michael, and Sherwin Rosen. 1978. "Monopoly And Product Quality." *Journal of Economic Theory* 18 (2): 301–317 (August).

Nalebuff, Barry J. 2003, Feb. Bundling, Tying, and Portfolio Effects. Department of Trade and Industry economics paper.

———. 2004. "Bundling as an Entry Barrier." *The Quarterly Journal of Economics* 119 (1): 159–187 (February).

Neumann, Karl-Heinz. 1999. "Marktzutrittsschranken und Markteintrittsstrategien im deutschen Telekommunikationsmarkt." Edited by Peter Oberender, *Die Dynamik der Telekommunikationsmärkte als Herausforderung an die Wettbewerbspolitik*, Volume 266 of *Schriften des Vereins für Socialpolitik*. Duncker & Humblot, Berlin, 73–88.

Nora, Simon, and Alain Minc. 1980. *The Computerization of Society: A Report to the President of France.* MIT Press. Translation of: 'L'Informatisation de la société'. Paris : La Documentation Francaise, 1978.

OECD. 2006. Policy Considerations for Audio-Visual Conent Distribution in a Multiplatform Environment. DSTI/ICCP/TISP(2006)3/FINAL.

———. 2007a. Internet Traffic Priorisation: An Overview. DSTI/ICCP/TISP(2006)4/FINAL.

———. 2007b. OECD Broadband Statistics to December 2006. www.oecd.org/sti/ict/broadband. accessed 06/30/2007.

———. 2007c. OECD Communications Outlook 2007. www.oecd.org.

Oi, W.Y. 1971. "A Disneyland Dilemma: Two-Part Tariffs for a Mickey Mouse Monopoly." *The Quarterly Journal of Economics* 85 (1): 77–96.

O'Reilly, Charles, and Jennifer Chatman. 1986. "Organizational commitment and psychological attachment: The effect of compliance, identification, and internalization on prosocial behavior." *Journal of Applied Psychology* 71:492–499.

Ortiz Jr., Sixto. 2006. "Phone Companies get into the TV Business." *Computer*, Oct., 14–17.

Pakes, Ariel. 2003. "A Reconsideration of Hedonic Price Indexes with an Application to PC's." *The American Economic Review* 93 (5): 1578–1596.

Panzar, John C., and Robert D. Willig. 1981. "Economies of Scope." *The American Economic Review* 71 (2): 268–272.

Papandrea, F., N. Stoeckl, and A. Daly. 2003. "Bundling in the Australian Telecommunications Industry." *The Australian Economic Review* 36 (1): 41–54.

Parker, Philip M., and Lars-Hendrik Röller. 1997. "Collusive conduct in duopolies: multimarket contact and cross-ownership in the mobile telephone industry." *Rand Corporation: The Rand journal of economics* 28 (2): 304–322.

Peitz, Martin. 1995. "Utility maximization in models of discrete choice." *Economic Letters* 49:91–94.

———. 2006. "Bundling may blockade entry." *International Journal of Industrial Organization* In Press:–.

Pennings, Johannes M., and Phanish Puranam. 2001, 20-23. Sept. "Market Convergence & Firm Strategy: New Directions for Theory and Research." *The Future of Innovation Studies*. Eindhoven University of Technology, the Netherlands. Conference.

Pernet, Sophie. 2007, June. Bundles and Range Strategies: The Case of Telecom Operators. Communications and Strategies. MPRA Paper No.3550, posted 13. June 2007.

Picot, Arnold, Andreas Bereczky, and Axel Freyberg, eds. 2007. *Triple Play*. Münchner Kreis: Springer.

Pinto, B. 1986. "Repeated Games and the 'reciprocal dumping' model of trade." *Journal of International Ecoomics* 20:357–66.

Pool, Ithiel de Sola. 1983. *Technologies of freedom*. Belknap Press Cambridge, Mass.

Porter, Michael E. 1980. *Strategic Interaction : Some Lessons From Industry Histories For Theory And Antitrust Policy*. Division of Research, Graduate School of Business Administration, Harvard University.

Posner, R.A. 1976. *Antitrust Law: An Economic Perspective*. University of Chicago Press.

Rappoport, P., D.J. Kridel, L.D. Taylor, J.H. Alleman, and K.T. Duffy-Deno. 2002. "Residential Demand for Access to the Internet." *The International Handbook of Telecommunications Economics*, vol. 2.

Reisinger, Markus. 2006, 04.08.2006. "Product Bundling and the Correlation of Valuations in Duopoly." University of Munich.

Röller, L.H., and L. Waverman. 2001. "Telecommunications Infrastructure and Economic Growth: A Simultaneous Approach." *American Economic Review* 91 (4): 909–923.

Ronnen, Uri. Winter, 1991. "Minimum Quality Standards, Fixed Costs, and Competition." *The RAND Journal of Economics* 22 (4): 490–504.

Rosen, Sherwin. 1974. "Hedonic Prices and Implicit Markets: Product Differentiation and Pure Competition." *The Journal of Political Economy* 82 (1): 34–55.

Salinger, M.A. 1995. "A Graphic Analysis of Bundling." *Journalof Business* 68:85–98.

Scherer, Frederic M. 1979. "The Welfare Economics of Product Variety: An Application to the Ready-To-Eat Breakfast Cereals Industry." *The Journal of Industrial Economics* 28, no. 2.

———. 1980. *Industrial Market Structure and Economic Performance*. 2. Chicago: Rand McNally.

Schmalensee, Richard. 1978. "Entry Deterrence in the Ready-to-eat Breakfast Cereal Industry." *The Bell Journal of Economics* 9 (2): 305–327.

———. 1982. "Commodity Bundling by a Single-Product Monopolist." *Journal of Law and Economics* 25:67–71.

———. 1984. "Gaussian Demand and Commodity Bundling." *Journal of Business* 57:211–230.

Schultheiß, Kerstin. 2004. "Europäische Telekommunikationsstandardisierung." Ph.D. diss., Universität Hamburg.

Säcker, Franz Jürgen, ed. 2006. *Berliner Kommentar zum Telekommunikationsgesetz*. Kommunikation und Recht. Frankfurt a.M.: Recht und Wirtschaft.

Seidmann, Daniel J. Nov., 1991. "Bundling as a Facilitating Device: A Reinterpretation of Leverage Theory." *Economica* 58 (232): 491–499.

Selten, Reinhardt. 1975. "Reexamination of the Perfectness Concept for Equilibrium Points in Extensive Games." *International Journal of Game Theory* 4:141–201.

Shaked, Avner, and John Sutton. 1982. "Relaxing Price Competition Through Product Differentiation." *The Review of Economic Studies* 49 (1): 3–13.

———. 1983. "Natural Oligopolies." *Econometrica* 51:1469–1483.

———. 1984. "Natural Oligopolies and International Trade." Edited by Henryk Kierzkowski, *Monopolistic Competition and International Trade*. Oxford University Press, 34–50.

———. 1990. "Multiproduct firms and market structure." *Rand Corporation: The Rand journal of economics* 21 (1): 45–62.

Shy, Oz. 2000. Digital Convergence, Competition, and Antitrust Law. mimeo, Department of Economics, University of Haifa, Israel.

———. 2001. *The Economics of Network Industries*. Cambridge University Press.

Simmel, Georg. 1950. *The Sociology of Georg Simmel*. New York: Free Press.

Sonnenschein, Hugo. 1968. "The Dual of Duopoly Is Complementary Monopoly: or, Two of Cournot's Theories Are One." *The Journal of Political Economy* 76 (2): 316–318 (March).

Spector, David. 2007. "Bundling, Tying, and Collusion." *International Journal of Industrial Organization* 25:575–581.

Srinivasan, Kannan. 1991. "Multiple Market Entry, Cost Signaling and Entry Deterrence." *Management Science* 37 (12): 1539–1555.

Stallings, William. 2007. *Data and Computer Communications*. Prentice Hall.

Stigler, George J. 1963. "United States vs. Loew's Inc.: A Note on Block Booking." *Supreme Court Review* 152:152–157.

Stole, Lars A. 2003, Dec. Price Discrimination and Imperfect Competition. Survey prepared for the Handbook of Industrial Organization. mimeo: University of Chicago, GSB, USA.

Sutton, John. 1991. *Sunk Costs And Market Structure*. MIT Press Cambridge, Mass.

———. 1998. *Technology and Market Structure: Theory and History*. The MIT Press Cambridge, Mass.

Teece, David J. 1980. "Economies of scope and the scope of the enterprise." *Journal of Economic Behavior and Organization* 1 (3): 223–247.

————. 1982. "Towards an Economic Theory of the Multiproduct Firm." *Journal of Economic Behavior and Organization* 3:39–63.

Thatcher, M. 2001. "The Commission and national governments as partners: EC regulatory expansion in telecommunications 1979–2000." *Journal of European Public Policy* 8 (4): 558–584.

Tirole, Jean. 1988. *The Theory of Industial Organization.* MIT Press.

van Wegberg, Marc. 1995. "Capacity As A Commitment Instrument In Multi-Market Competition." Chapter 12 of *Market Evolution*, edited by Arjen van Witteloostuijn, 197–228. Kluwer.

van Wegberg, Marc, and Arjen van Witteloostuijn. 1991. "Multimarket Competition: Entry Strategies and Entry Deterrence When the Entrant Has a Home Market." Chapter 6 of *Microeconomic Conribution to Strategic Management*, edited by J. Thépot and R.-A. Thiétart, Volume 16 of *Advanced Series in Management*, 93–119. Elsevier Science.

————. 1992. "Credible Entry Threats into Contestable Markets: A Symmetric Multi-Market Model of Contestability." *Economica* 59 (236): 437–452.

Vaubourg, Anne-Gael. 2006. "Differentiation and discrimination in a duopoly with two bundles." *International Journal of Industrial Organization* 24 (4): 753 – 762 (2006/7).

Venables, A.J. 1990. "International Capacity Choice and National Market Games." *Journal of International Economics* 29:23–42.

Verbrugge, S., S. Pasqualini, F.-J. Westphal, M. Jager, A. Iselt, A. Kirstadter, R. Chahine, D. Colle, M. Pickavet, and P. Demeester. 2005. "Modeling Operational Expenditures For Telecom Operators." *Optical Network Design and Modeling, 2005. Conference on.* 455–466.

Veugelers, R. 1995. "Strategic Incentives for Multinational Operations." *Managerial and Decision Economics* 16 (1): 47–57.

Vogelsang, Ingo. 2003. "The German Telecommunications Reform - Where did it come from, Where is it, and Where is it Going ?" *Perspektiven der Wirtschaftspolitik* 4 (3): 313–340.

Waldfogel, Joel, and Julie Wulf. 2005. "Measuring the Effect of Multimarket Contact on Competition: Evidence from Radio Broadcast Ownership Deregulation." Working Paper, University of Pennsylvania.

Wang, R., and Q. Wen. 1998. "Strategic Invasion in Markets with Switching Costs." *Journal of Economics & Management Strategy* 7 (4): 521–549.

Warf, Barney. 2003. "Mergers and acquisitions in the telecommunications industry." *Growth and change* 34 (3): 321–344.

Watson, Craig M. 1982. "Countercompetition abroad to protect home markets." *Harvard Business Review* 65 (1): 40–42.

Waugh, F. 1928. "Quality Factors Influencing Vegetable Prices." *Journal of Farm Economics* 10:185–196.

Waverman, Leonard, and Esen Sirel. 1997. "European Telecommunications Markets on the Verge of Full Liberalization." *Journal of Economic Perspectives* 11 (4): 113–126.

Weinhardt, Chistof, Carsten Holtmann, and Dirk Neumann. 2003. "Market Engineering." *Wirtschaftsinformatik* 45 (6): 635–640.

Welfens, Paul J.J. 2006. Die Zukunft des Telekommunikationsmarktes - Volkswirtschaftliche Aspekte digitaler Wirtschaftsdynamik. Stabsabteilung der Friedrich-Ebert-Stiftung, www.fes.de. Gutachten im Auftrag der Friedrich Ebert Stiftung.

Whinston, Michael D. Sep., 1990. "Tying, Foreclosure, and Exclusion." *The American Economic Review* 80 (4): 837–859.

Williamson, O.E. 1979. "Transaction-Cost Economics: The Governance of Contractual Relations." *Journal of Law and Economics* 22 (2): 233–261.

Wolinsky, Asher. 1986. "The nature of competition and the scope of firms." *The journal of industrial economics* 34 (3): 247–259.

Yip, George S. 1982. "Gateways to entry." *Harvard Business Review* September-October 1982:85–92.

Yoffie, David B., ed. 1997. *Competing in the Age of Digital Convergence.* Harvard Business School Press.

List of Figures

List of Symbols

p	Price
q	Quality level
μ, ν	Proportion of (equilibrium) quality levels
$\mathscr{C}$	Prevalence of costs
R	Revenue
Π	Profit
θ	Consumers' willingness-to-pay for quality
$\widetilde{\theta}$	Consumer indifferent between two services or service bundles
$\widehat{\theta}$	Consumer indifferent to purchasing a service (bundle)
BR	Best Quality Response Function
$\overline{r}$	Best Quality Response Threshold Function
$\overline{f}$	Feasibility Constraint Function
σ	Cost efficiency parameter
CS	Consumers' Surplus
PS	Producers' Surplus
W	Total Welfare
bb	Bundle vs. Bundle Pricing Regime
bs	Bundle vs. Separate Pricing Regime
sb	Separate vs. Bundle Pricing Regime
ss	Separate vs. Separate Pricing Regime
uu	Unilateral Mixed Bundle vs. Unil. Mixed Bundle Pricing Regime

List of Abbreviations